# WHO'S RUNNING THE ASYLUM?

## INSIDE THE INSANE WORLD OF SPORTS TODAY

By
**Wilt Chamberlain**

# WHO'S RUNNING THE ASYLUM?

## INSIDE THE INSANE WORLD OF SPORTS TODAY

© 1997, WILT CHAMBERLAIN

PUBLISHED BY:
PROMOTION PUBLISHING
3368F GOVERNOR DRIVE
SUITE 144
SAN DIEGO, CA 92122

**(800) 231-1776**

**ISBN 1-57901-005-9**

Building photo courtesy of Ernest W. Hahn II and John Sanders.

**I**F YOU ARE TIRED OF PUTTING UP
WITH LESS FROM PEOPLE WHO
CLAIM THAT THEY'RE THE BEST
AND YOU WANT TO STRAIGHTEN
OUT THIS MESS...
THIS IS THE BOOK FOR YOU!

# TABLE OF CONTENTS

# INTRODUCTION

## PROFESSIONAL SPORTS
### A SINKING SHIP AND A SAD STATE OF AFFAIRS

The inmates *are* running the asylum. If you don't think so, read the papers. Then, if you still have doubts, watch television—commercials and all. Or ask your kids who their heroes are—and why.

Professional sports in this country are in trouble. Deep trouble. The games that are our national pastimes seem to be caught in a downward spiral. Now, that's not good, but what's even worse is that the negative trend in sports affects all of us.

Sports may not be your particular cup of tea, but you *will* have to admit they do have a significant influence on our lives. Since the world has become so small, with jet planes, TV and all, it seems as though the actions of just a few people can affect everyone. Think about it: when Michael Jordan came back to play in the National Basketball Association, the *stock market* jumped! There may not have been a direct cause and effect relationship here, but when an entity as pervasive as sports goes awry, the residual effects can make us all cry.

I believe that sports are a metaphor for life. They often seem to represent what is going on in our country as a whole. So, who should be surprised that the changes we've seen in sports (and in too many of our athletes as well) appear to mirror what's happening in present day society. Pro sports and society seem to be on parallel paths—*downward*. That is why we should all be concerned, and why we need to head sports in a more positive direction.

I love all kinds of sports, and they have occupied a large part of my life. If you feel about them as I do, we both have to wonder what has brought about so many negative changes, and why these changes have been allowed to become so overwhelming. The problems are so obvious that I would have thought the powers that be would have remedied most of them by now, but an amazing number of fans, coaches, athletes and announcers don't even seem to realize that there *are* any. Or, even if they are aware of the situation, they don't have a clue as to how big the problems are or how negative their effects can be.

You may ask, "How is this possible, when a deaf and dumb, blind jackass can see and hear most of them?" Good question! That's what I am going to address in this book.

In most cases, books are written either to inform or to entertain. Most are clearly either fiction or non-fiction, but occasionally they fall somewhere in between. They can look like one thing, while really being the other. There are words that entice us to believe them because they are so cleverly presented, or maybe they say something we want to believe anyway. Some of what we read, though it could be true, might also be an illusion we'd like to think of as the truth.

What you will read in these pages, you may regard with skepticism—or you may choose to take every word at face value. It's up to you. But what you can be absolutely sure of finding herein is my point of view—unvarnished, bluntly stated, and in many cases, unflattering.

This book is the result of my doing a lot of sitting and thinking. It consists, more or less, of my random thoughts and the expression of my beliefs about a number of issues.

I am not going to hyperbolize the facts. (That's the only big word I know!) I will use clear and concise language and, aside from *that* word, everything will be easy to understand. I intend to tell the truth as I see it, and to dispel a few illusions. Sure, the content will be opinionated (what did you expect?). But I hope the opinions I express will be taken as constructive in nature.

It seems to me that in order to be constructive, you first have to pinpoint what needs attention. What I tell you about in these pages should do exactly that. The factual information I present, coupled with some statements of my own personal beliefs, will (I hope) change your view of what is going on in sports today, and inspire you to join me and my friends in applying the brakes to the downward direction of our great sports institutions. Writing this volume would be pointless if I can't make you understand that your help is needed.

Think back to Hitler's rise to power. Many people of that time ignored him and his ideology, hoping that he would just fade away. Was it wishful thinking or were they just too lazy or timid to get involved? This may not be the greatest possible comparison to the situation in sports today, but it seems to me to be a good example of the consequences of not getting involved. By not acting, do we actually contribute to how things turn out?

So let's get started. Put on your thinking caps, ladies and gentlemen. I know you will find in these pages much that will interest you. What's more, I have a plan that could turn things around for you and every other sports fan in America. For the moment, however, the inmates are in control. And, in case you are in doubt, here are some things to think about.

I find John Lucas' position in sports downright confusing. Is he the coach and general manager of the 76ers, or is he the caretaker for the drug addicts of the sports world? (I have a feeling he won't be either very much longer.) It is nice that he cares so much for people who are involved in drugs.

Lucas himself had a drug problem, so it is understandable why he has such compassion for players who are so afflicted. But in the meantime his team suffers because he is worrying about helping guys that are not straight, and are not going to be straight until they get the kind of treatment they need—proper treatment which is far, far away from the game. Maybe Lucas should be at his clinic healing those who need help, and leave basketball coaching and managing in the NBA to people who want to do that full time.


You may never have heard of the Jon Koncak award. Though there may be some similarities if you look deep enough, it should definitely *not* be confused with the Heisman Trophy. It's a tongue-in-cheek award that the media in some areas give in the Game of the Week, or even at the Game of the Month, to the player whose on-court production comes closest to zero.

Why Jon Koncak? Why did they pick this guy to name the award for? As far as I can make out, if you take what he's earned over the past several years, and weigh this against his contribution to the teams he's played for (basically the Atlanta Hawks), he probably deserves the money the least of any player around.

4

A few years ago Koncak became a free agent and (if you can believe this) teams actually fought for the right to his services. Undoubtedly, these teams saw something in him that most of us who have watched him play can't begin to fathom.

His stats go like this: four points a game and three rebounds, or maybe three points and two rebounds, with a blocked shot every third or fourth game for good measure. Yet they have been willing to pay over $2 million a year for his services. (This does help me see more clearly why other jocks in basketball feel they have the right to demand such incredible contracts.) Hence, when sportswriters want to indicate a player's notable lack of contribution in a given game, they use the JK award. The player coming closest to getting all zeros is your winner!

I don't have a problem with this award being given. It's meaning is clear, and in many situations it can be extremely descriptive (and often well deserved). But I was taken aback when I discovered that Koncak had been chosen captain of his Atlanta Hawks team in the 1994-95 season before he was traded. "Why," I asked myself, "Jon Koncak as captain?" I could see maybe Magic, Bird or Sir Charles Barkley in that position. They are the backbones of their teams, and their presence always makes their teammates perform at a higher level and helps everybody look better.

Then it hit me like a ton of bricks. *Jon Koncak also makes his teammates look better!* When he plays (and he must play if he is the captain) his teammates' stats will always shine in comparison to his, so they can't help but look good no matter how badly they may be playing. I believe they made him captain because they knew that no one could make them look any better than he did, if only by virtue of what he was *not* doing.

5

Unlike Magic Johnson or Larry Bird, men who helped make their teammates *play* better by what they were able to do on the court, Koncak, through lack of performance and what he was unable to do, made his teammates *look* better—not *do* better. They all looked good next to him. While he was doing nothing, they all appeared, in contrast, like they were worth a million dollars! But maybe that's as good a reason as any to be picked as captain. Koncak *has* made an undeniable contribution to the morale of his team. Even if they didn't do anything out there, their morale remained intact!

Of course, this revelation started me wondering where *I* fit in, since I had been captain at one time or another for every team I played for: the Los Angeles Lakers, the Philadelphia 76ers, and the Philadelphia/San Francisco Warriors. I was proud of being chosen captain because that honor usually comes from respect and from what your teammates think of you as a contributor to the team effort. But had I made the other players look better because I was playing so badly or because I was the backbone of the team? I guess I'll leave that decision to you.

Perhaps we should not be too surprised to learn that Atlanta is doing much better since their ex-captain was traded, even though they now must survive on their own merit and not on how good Koncak made them look.

Who better could exemplify the Koncak Award than the man himself? His last line for the last game of the year was zero for one from the field, zero for zero foul attempts, zero for zero for offensive and defensive rebounds, zero assists, zero blocked shots, and zero anything else, unless you want to count his getting one foul—a negative accomplishment. He achieved this brilliant record in a little over eight minutes of play—about as close as you can possibly get to having a perfect game under the Koncak system!

They didn't have the Koncak award when I was playing, or "Sixth Man" awards or "Comeback Player" awards, or others like that. But the Koncak Award may be quite significant in today's world: It mirrors all that is wrong with professional sports and the dismal level of play we have suffered with for too long. The sad thing here, and what we all should fear, is the direction that the recipients of the JK Award are headed—downward toward zero, not upward toward 100.

## WILTISM

**THERE IS ONLY ONE WAY TO PLAY,**

**AND THAT IS TO GIVE YOUR ALL EVERY DAY.**

# ONE

## THE INMATES ARE RUNNING THE ASYLUM

We often hear professional athletes referred to as "selfish prima donnas," or even "overpaid, thankless so-and-so's who don't give a damn about the teams they play for or the fans who support them.

*Oops, I just made my first mistake in this book.* They do care about something else. Above all, they care about being used in a manner that will showcase them to their best advantage, even if this can be accomplished only to the detriment of the rest of the team.

### JUST KIDS!

Many athletes—more than we may imagine—are, in my opinion, just kids with childlike mentalities. When Jamal Mashburn was a rookie with the Dallas Mavericks, within a week or so of joining the team, he let it be known that he was an unhappy camper and that things must change—*or else*. Trying to learn the ins and outs of pro basketball should be enough to keep a rookie (or anyone else) busy and out of trouble—but not Jamal. This, he thought, was the proper time to show a little muscle by voicing his disapproval of the coach's system. The way I see it, that's like trying to fly before learning to crawl; but with the millions he's paid, maybe he should be in control of it all.

## THE ASYLUM

Every man, no matter what his profession, has the right to try to obtain the most he can in exchange for his services. *But wait a minute here, Wiltie.* (Yes, I do talk to myself when things are just too hard for me to believe.) How about Derrick Coleman of the New Jersey Nets? He could not possibly have turned down 70 million dollars, could he? *Yes, Wiltie he did just that.* Wow! To turn down 70 million dollars, just for playing a few silly games of basketball.

Coleman has earned a unique claim to fame, and can say he did something that no other person in their right mind ever did. And yet I'd bet that if this guy were to walk down the street in any major city in America, (forget the rest of the world), he would not be recognized by a single soul. (I take it back: there is a slim chance that a member of his family or some extreme basketball devotee might, just by coincidence, be in the city that day and recognize him.)

I can't believe it. I just told my second lie. In all honesty, I cannot say that Coleman has been the only player to turn down that kind of money for playing basketball. There was that brash rookie of the Milwaukee Bucks, "Big Dog." (Or is it "Big Hog?" I'm not really sure.) In any case, a couple of years ago, Big Dog—or Big Hog—asked for the tidy sum of $100 million (that's right, $100 million), leading me to believe that he probably turned down a great deal more money than Coleman did. You are thinking that his credentials must have qualified him for such a lofty request, and that, like Bill Russell, Bill Walton, and Kareem, he had won many NCAA crowns. Perhaps, you're thinking, like Ervin Johnson and Larry Bird, he was considered a franchise foundation. *I don't think so, Wiltie.* Believe it or not, he hadn't played a single game in the pros. His college team did get to the NCAA tournament, but they lost in the second round. Big deal, Big Dog!

I don't mind a guy looking for all he can get, but let's be somewhat sensible. What was going through Big Dog's mind? Why would he ask for that kind of salary, apparently doing the impossible by turning down other sizable monetary offers? I'll tell you why. Big Dog and Coleman are just kids playing childish games. You know how kids play games. Kids will say, "I'll bet you two billion dollars I can jump over that water puddle and you can't." And another kid replies, "Okay, I'll take that bet, but remember you already owe me five billion for not being able to hold your breath under water for five hours."

It's simple. They have no sense of the real value of money. What kid does?

*I know I'm putting players under a great deal of stress by implying that they might take somewhat less.*

*From my present point of view, this seems to be the right time, though I don't know if I'd have done the same in my prime.*

If you think I am jealous of today's players because they are making too much money, don't give it a thought. I have accumulated a great deal of wealth on my own. As a matter of fact, I have money buried all around the world. Lucky me! There's only one problem: I can't remember where I buried it.

## WILTISM

### THEY'RE REACHING THE BOTTOM
### WHEN MONEY HAS GOT 'EM.

A coach's career path is rarely a smooth one. The lovable Magic appeared not so lovable after he got the coach of his first pro team fired. Then, not long ago it was reported that the Lakers, almost to a man, demanded the dismissal of Riley. (I wrote that bit years ago, but no one believed me at the time.) In a similar case, the New York Knicks came to a near standstill and refused to perform for Don Nelson, who had just been fired from the Golden State Warriors because of a run-in with a rookie named Chris Webber. There have, in fact, been any number of incidents involving players who managed to get coaches dismissed.

When records slip, or if big games are not won, the coach is the first to go—unless he wields a mighty big stick. That is why many coaches try to get the additional role of general manager—or for that matter, any other position that will give them the power to pick and choose their teams. Many have tried, but few have achieved this goal.

The only thing that seems to appease fans and owners alike is a win—preferably the big one. But is this realistic? Let's crunch some numbers. There are 29 teams in the NBA. If each team took its turn in winning the championship, it would take 28 years before a team could get a second win. And if a team should happen to miss their turn the first time around, 56 years would have to pass before they would next have a championship team—assuming they won on their next turn. And, if they missed two turns around, they probably would not live long enough to see a winner in their city. That is just the way the numbers would work out.

I suggest that fans stop being so demanding. All that the fans, coaches or owners have a right to expect from a team is that each player will put forth a 100% effort. The owners' job is to put on the court the very best team they can afford. The coaches' responsibility is to play the team members as they deserve to be played and to create the best team possible with the players they are given to work with. And the players, for their part, must give whatever talents they have 100% of the time.

## RESPONSIBLE ATHLETES

Consider the always-polite and ever-so-correct Grant Hill of the Detroit Pistons. In each of his first two years in the league, Hill was voted to the All-Star team, *and* with the most votes ever earned by any player. *"Can you believe this one, Wiltie?"* He received more votes than the more talented Barkley, Hakeem, Robinson, or a host of others. So why was Hill accorded such an honor? The answer is quite simple. Hill is a nice guy, so the question of talent went out the window. He was rewarded for being the type of person that people think jocks *should* be.

Personally, I enjoy Hill's game and respect his up-bringing. I know his father, and I can see that the elder Hill had a strong influence on him, but that vote sucks. It likewise sucks that Rodman didn't make the 1996 All-Star team after helping the Bulls to their amazing win-loss record before the All-Star game. I guess you're picked because of your smile, and no one cares about your guile. Can you believe that the voters thought Hill more valuable and a better All-Star than Michael Jordan? Can you conceive of Hill getting more votes than the great one? I don't think so.

Jerry Rice of the San Francisco 49ers is a football player for whom I have the greatest respect. Jerry knows what work is all about, both on and off the field. His days of laboring in hot, sunny Mississippi helped instill in him the work ethic that has served him so well in the NFL. Too bad more of his colleagues in football and other sports haven't picked up the same kind of character trait, but unfortunately, most of them have never held a job in the "real" work world.

I have not been a favorite of many of the big guys who have come into the league during the past 10 to 20 years. These players—Manute Bol and others like him, appear to have been brought into the league simply because of their imposing height. They can stand under the basket, arms up not even moving, while dumb players shoot the ball right into their arms. But because these big guys have no mobility and lack much of anything else in the way of athletic ability, smart guys simply take the ball to the basket and dunk it right over them.

For some reason beyond my understanding, there have been some coaches who seem to like this type of player. One of these coaches (and a guy who has disappointed me occasionally) is Don Nelson, who coached at San Francisco and New York. Don was fired from his last two teams, and I've always thought that one of the contributing causes for these dismissals might have been that he chose to employ unusual players in weird ways. One such choice was his use of Manute Bol to shoot three-pointers. Wow! To think that Nelson allowed this player to grace his team more than once, and even let him shoot three-point shots, just because he was able to throw one or two in from outside.

Everyone gasped—even laughed—as they watched Manute's unorthodox attempts, thinking it was a big joke. The man had no basic basketball talent at all, but he was able, as I said, to stand there, hold his hands up, and block a shot. The downside of all this was that he was occupying a spot on the team that could have been filled by someone who was more capable and who would have given the fans a better game. On the whole, I have not been happy with the way some seven-footers have been used on our courts of late.

Another kind of seven-footer, Gheorghe Muresan, has created an altogether different picture on the court. Gheorghe was voted this year as the "most improved player." Not only is he the most improved, he is one of the very best of those who are playing the center position. No one hustles or gives any more of himself than Gheorghe Muresan. In addition to hustle, he has talent, a very nice shooting touch, and along with a good hook shot, an array of shots in the pivot position. He goes after blocked shots and rebounds as best he can, and does a very commendable job. His size and talent, together with a very soft touch, make him a major threat on the basketball court.

Muresan is often called for fouls—many of them, I believe, because he is a novice player. Referees seem to like calling fouls on the newer and weaker guys who have no clout—fouls they wouldn't dare call on the more polished, popular big-name players, like Shaq for one. If Muresan were given the same respect as Shaq, as far as fouls are concerned, I believe he would be as good as Shaquille O'Neal. Yes, that is correct. Even though he doesn't have Shaq's athletic ability, in many ways and in a variety of areas, he possesses *more* talent than Shaq. If I had to choose, I would take Gheorghe Muresan.

Something is very, very wrong with sports when Mahmoud Abdul-Rauf is handed only a one-day suspension for not standing up for the playing of the national anthem. He wasn't suspended at all, as it turned out. The league conceded that if he would agree to stand up for the anthem in the future, all would be forgiven. Many fans and members of the media not only condoned his action, they accepted his reason for it. They felt that Abdul-Rauf had a perfect right to say and do as he did.

I would like to sit down and have a little talk with those in the media who considered Abdul-Rauf's conduct acceptable. I am curious what *their* feelings about their country might be. I am an American, and I believe that each of us must stand up for our country. Adbul-Rauf did so in the end, probably after his Muslim brothers pointed out that he was not doing their religion any favors by getting that kind of attention. His brothers, without a doubt, laid down the law, probably telling him to stop making all of them look so stupid, and pressuring him to back down and acknowledge his respect for the flag and the nation. There must be a better way for him to express his beliefs and how he feels about this country, but my main concern here is not with his actions, but with the response to them— especially on the part of the media, who more or less soft-pedaled the entire affair.

When Shaq breaks down backboards in commercials one after one, he is rewarded for doing things that should not be done.

*"Wiltie, how do you feel about baskets being torn down? Could you tear down baskets?"* Quite honestly, in all my years of playing, from junior high through high school, college, and the pros, I never tore down a basket.

And in the thousands of games I played with the Trotters, I didn't find basket destruction a necessary or desirable part of dunking a ball, even though I dunked the ball hard, and the rims in those days were a lot weaker than they are now. Baskets today are made in such a way as not to break easily, but these young men (or should we say, "kids?") are tearing them down because they jump and dunk, then grab the rim, swinging on it like gymnasts on a piece of apparatus. Baskets are made to shoot into, not to swing on. No purpose is served by hanging on the rim unless you are trying to protect yourself, and that situation seldom occurs.

Most of the commercial advertisements that Shaq made early in his career seemed to focus on his power to destroy. Unfortunately, his destructive bent was concentrated on demolishing equipment rather than teams; he didn't even make it to the playoffs in his first couple of years. It's too bad that a player is rewarded for tearing baskets down instead of building his team up. Shattering backboards has nothing to do with the game of basketball; it is just another way of demonstrating a false kind of power and venting it in the wrong way.

Destructive talent is a strange reason for hiring anyone unless, of course, you're building a search and destroy team. And corporations like Reebok or Nike do not help at all when they reward players handsomely for doing commercials that feature this kind of stupidity.

The practice of tearing down baskets should be corrected. Think of the image presented to the young ones who love to mimic. Who is going to change the minds of kids who grow up thinking that this is the kind of thing they must do to be successful? And who is going to fix the rims and backboards that are being broken in school yards all over the country?

## IRRESPONSIBLE ATHLETES

Overindulgence has become a way of life for too many of us. We spend too much time on what we wear, and too little time with how much we care. We give too much attention to feeding our bodies and not enough to nourishing our souls. The NBA is no exception to all of this, and is suddenly full of overweight players—guys who apparently care nothing about their appearance or how much better they would be able to help their team if they only were to lose some weight.

In sports, especially in basketball, everyone has learned to lie about everything. They lie about how tall a player is; they lie about how much he weighs; and they lie about how much they are willing to pay. Basketball would be better served by the truth, but the NBA is undoubtedly too embarrassed to admit the truth about some of its players' weight relative to their height. I do know that, for about ten years in a row, I was listed at 275 pounds, although I never weighed 275 on any day during that entire period. I weighed 310 to 315 pounds, more or less, but *never* 275. I was listed as being seven-foot-one, and occasionally as seven-foot-two, but I never reached either of those altitudes. I am exactly seven feet plus one-sixteenth of an inch.

Taking a page out of the John Madden book, I have created my "All-Fat Team." Bear in mind, fans, that I am not talking about a Sumo wrestling team or a group of linemen from a football team; this is (supposed to be) a basketball team.

Let me introduce my All-Fat Team: Carl Herrera is one of my forwards, and Kevin Duckworth is the other. My choice for center is the new guy from the Boston Celtics, Thomas Hamilton. The next two play the forward position, too, even though they are centers: Brian Williams, the young man from Los Angeles who plays with the

18

Clippers, and Anthony "Pig" Miller from the Los Angeles Lakers. (Pig is such a great—and appropriate—name, I'm tempted to apply it to the whole team: "The Piggys.")

Coming off the bench, I have 295- to 300-pound Stanley Roberts, formerly of the Clippers. Although Stanley weighs slightly more now, he has been fluctuating between 330 and 300 pounds for the last 2 to 3 years. He gets suspended for being too heavy, and he never loses much weight—but they still pay him big money for his big size. Another of my bench warmers would be Victor Alexander. He is six-foot-nine and weighs in at about 290 pounds, though they say he weighs only 265. As bench warmers, these guys are perfect. Just the two of them will fill the whole bench. No point in trying for more depth—there is no room for anyone else.

The "Big O" once stood for the great Oscar Robertson, but now the term refers to the great *big* Oliver Miller, the first member of my All-Fat Team. He was impressively large in '95-'96, and was formally listed as weighing about 290 pounds. I guarantee, however, that it has been many a month since he was *that* slender. A better guess would be that he now weighs in at closer to 330 or 340 pounds.

My advice is to maintain a healthy skepticism when you hear figures such as Oliver Miller's 290-pound weight. Remember that he was released by a couple of teams because he couldn't (or wouldn't) get down to a weight that their scales would even register. Or it might have been that they didn't want to buy a scale big enough to accommodate him. Oliver may, in fact, have eaten his way out of another job (or out of the league altogether) as I no longer see him on the Raptors roster.

Miller is a wonderful player, to be sure, but when you are overweight, you can play wonderfully for only a very short while. Weight eventually takes its toll. The bigger you are, the bigger the toll that must be paid, and the more it will cost a team in the long run. You may hear it said, "For a fat guy, he is really playing well." Well, he is doing all right for a fat player, but if he were to drop down to his ideal playing weight, he could do a whole lot better.

Funny how we are apt to hear announcers make remarks such as, "There's that big Oliver Miller," but we never hear them refer to "that *fat* Oliver Miller." They'll call a player "tall" or even "skinny," but heaven forbid they should ever call him "fat!"

The next member of our All-Fat Team is Kevin Duckworth. The name almost tells it all. When you want the world's best pâtè, you first find a duck (actually, they use geese), you nail the bird's feet to a board, then stuff him with food until his liver becomes enlarged and diseased. After the liver has been chopped up and a few goodies tossed in, the mixture can be sold for incredible prices. Well, the Duck is receiving an incredible amount of money for playing; ignoring his real worth, his fans (not I) pay to watch him play. Duckworth is another guy whose quoted numbers are questionable. You'll see him listed at about 290 pounds, although he must actually weigh closer to 330, and probably has not been under 300 pounds since I was in knee pants.

My next selection is Brian Williams, presently playing for the Los Angeles Clippers. Williams, who is listed now at 295 pounds, got in trouble with the Washington Bullets because he would not conform to their weight regulations, and after two or three years of trying in vain to get him below 330 pounds, the Bullets finally let him go. Williams came into the league weighing about 230 pounds, but he put on 100 pounds within a year or two and has done very little about it since. He is very talented, but not willing to lose weight. Too bad!

There is a guy with the Lakers whose name says it all: he is referred to as "Pig." That's right, Pig Miller. Need

I say more? There is no mystery as to why his teammates chose that nickname, but Pig takes it in stride, just as the other big guys do. They appear to accept their rotundness with a light heart, though their heart is probably the only part of them that *could* be described as "light."

The fourth member of my All-Fat team is Victor Alexander of the Golden State Warriors. He is listed at six-foot-ten and 265 pounds, but actually tips the scales at a minimum of 290. The fifth guy on the starting team is ex-Clipper Stanley Roberts who is listed at 290 pounds but who weighs in at well over 300. How much over 300 pounds? I'm not sure, but believe me, if Stanley doesn't weigh between 340 and 350 pounds, he doesn't weigh an ounce.

As a matter of curiosity, I would like to ask my friend, the general manager of the Los Angeles Clippers, this question, "Why hire two players, Stanley Roberts and Brian Williams, each of whom is 50 to 100 pounds overweight, and put them on a team that is already suffering with a heavy load of other problems? Did you think that their weight was going to provide the team with balance or ballast? Sure, they have a certain amount of talent, but that talent is only going to be good out there on the court for a very short time before they run out of breath. Why would you hire players like those, knowing that in the long run they cannot and will not be a bona fide help to the team? I would really like to hear your answers to these questions, Elgin."

*FLASH!*—Duckworth was just signed by the Clippers as a free agent. *Talk to me, Elg:* Not *another* fat guy! Tell me you and the management aren't so cheap that you're trying to get the equivalent of two players for one salary. Are you doubling your pleasure and doubling your fun, getting two guys rolled up into one?

Coming off my "Blubber Bench" is a guy who out-weighs them all. Thomas Hamilton plays for the Boston Celtics, and we are told that he weighs 360 pounds. Now, if you go along with my little rule of thumb that these guys are listed at 20 to 50 pounds less than their actual weight and an inch or two taller, *you* tell *me* how large Hamilton really is. I heard one of the announcers for the Boston Celtics comment, "If Thomas Hamilton weighs 360 pounds, I weigh 300—and I weigh only 240!" His guess, and mine, is that Hamilton's actual weight is at least 400 pounds instead of 360. Whew!

Every time Thomas runs up and down the floor, the Boston announcer, sounding worried, usually says something like, "At the rate they are playing this game, I am a little bit fearful that, carrying this kind of weight, Thomas may have some kind of seizure or a heart attack." Think about it: here is an athlete who is playing on a professional team, yet the announcers are afraid that he is too heavy to keep up the pace for even two or three minutes, and express concern that he is going to end up hurting himself. Remember Thomas Hamilton's name. I don't know whether he will be around next year, but he is definitely present this year—all 400 pounds of him.

Another All-Fat player coming off the bench is Wayman Tisdale of the Phoenix Suns. A big game player who broke many of my college records, he came into the league listed at 230 pounds. Now, at a listed 270 pounds (actual weight probably closer to 290), he has become a sub for the Suns.

Here's another plus for my All-Fat Team. When the time comes, Waymon Tisdale will be my choice to sing the national anthem. Then he can play. He will go double-double duty: as a singer and a player. (Granted he's a great musician, but he must be spending a lot of time playing with knives and forks, as well.)

When team owners and general managers put these guys out on the floor, expecting us to pay to watch them play, it occurs to me that their mistake is geographical. They are simply in the wrong area. Ship them to Japan, let them put on another 100 pounds or so, and they will be ready to take on the local Sumo pros. My All-Fat Team members are not yet Sumo wrestlers, but they could easily qualify.

Another bit of good news. What with all the overweight types who are crowding the NBA rosters, we no longer need to look for a fat lady to sing signifying that the game is over. We can just grab a trio of overweight Clippers.


I am not trying to legislate against fat men, or tall men, or short men, or men of any particular size or shape. The only requirement for any professional team should be ability—being good enough to get the job done. Some of these fat guys can do the job, but only for a very short while. *All* of them could lose more weight if they tried hard enough. J. R. Reed provides a refreshing contrast to the rest of the fatsos. He came in last year weighing 270 or 280, and, by dint of diligent effort, he's now down to 230 or 235. Reed is living proof that you *can* slim down if you want to. The rest of the fat guys should use him as their pin-up.

A general principle in sports is: "The less you weigh, the better your chance to stay," though baseball may be an exception to the rule. Every now and then you see a baseball player who weighs a ton, but he's not expected to get out there and run, as long as he can hit the ball a ton, can jog around the bases, and has an arm like a gun. In basketball it's different. You have to use your body continuously, so the less you weigh, the better chance your chance to stay. Weight—rather, the *lack* of it—is the key to being able to sustain any type of athletic endeavor. Once again, boys and girls: *The less you weigh, the better your chance to stay.*

The real harm of being fat in sports may not be easy to see, because the drawbacks are obscured by all that size. Being grossly overweight leads to nothing but bad outcomes. If a fat man scores 20 points in a game, had he been leaner, he probably should have (and could have) scored 40. Injuries are much more frequent among overly heavy players, and endurance is always a big problem. People will always make statements such as, "You know, for a guy his size, he really is mobile." But what if he were the size he should be? How much more mobile might he be?

I am often asked why the Bulls have so consistently been better than the rest. My answer is that, mentally and physically, their team members have fit the pattern of the ideal prototype basketball player. (The only fat thing on the Bulls' team that gets any play is their logo.) That being said, I'd like to ask the other general managers and owners why they don't use the great World Championship Chicago Bulls as a model for their own teams. They could do a lot worse!

Perhaps you have noticed, as I have, that the worst teams seem always to end up with the big, fat guys. This reminds me of the old chicken-and-the-egg question: which came first?

## BACK TO THE ASYLUM

The fame they have acquired through media attention has made life tougher for athletes today. Well known players have little privacy, fans are into the celebrity syndrome, and the whole world seems to be autograph crazy. Today's star athletes are subject to considerable harassment, enough that I can actually work up a bit of sympathy for them.

Sports fans, let me give you a clue as to what to do when you come across one of your heroes. You might think that it's cool just to say, "Hello," and wait for a response of some kind. But if the guy doesn't respond as you expect he should, do you feel as if you've been cheated? Is he suddenly no longer your hero? Well, consider this: a simple "hello" doesn't constitute harassment, but if our hero is walking from one end of the beach to the other or is in some other well-populated spot, he may pass several hundred people every few minutes. If each of these people were to get a response to their greeting, this poor guy might have to go through this routine a thousand times a day.

A simple greeting, multiplied by several hundred, becomes harassment, and a relaxing walk on the beach becomes a hassle. It's very human to think, "Gee, he could at least have said 'hello,'" but it isn't *your* hello that's the problem. It's the other 999.

Then there is the matter of autographs. For the benefit of you fans who think that autograph signing is a piece of cake, and expect that each request for a sports figure's signature should be met with a cheerful smile, check out these figures.

Assume that autograph-signing occupies, on average, one and a half hours per day (a figure that is not, believe it or not, an exaggeration). I would then have spent ten hours each week signing my name, forty-five hours a month, five hundred thirty hours each year, and a total of twenty-three thousand, eight hundred fifty hours during my 45 years as a sports figure. That amounts to more than *two and one-half years* of my life, friends!

Unless you've been there, you haven't a clue how much this time would cost you. *Would you do it?*

There was always supposed to be an illegal zone defense in pro basketball. It was on the books when I was playing, but was seldom called by the officials. In actual practice, I was often surrounded well before the ball got there.

Today they are more strict about what constitutes an illegal zone defense. But looking at it from *any* angle, the whole concept is ridiculous, and no way to play the game of basketball. A team should be allowed to come up with all sorts of skillful ways to keep the opponent from scoring without being told by the referees that they can't stand here and they can't stand there because at this particular time those specific parts of the floor are illegal.

The rule, itself, is convoluted, but putting it as simply as possible, when you are on defense you must guard one certain player. Only the player with the ball can be double-teamed—not the player you *think* is going to get the ball—and if you guard a specific part of the floor, that is called an "illegal zone defense." You cannot help out your teammates sooner rather than later because doing so is also an illegal defense. Teaming up on a player who does not have the ball is also a no-no, even though everyone in the world knows the ball is going to that guy eventually. Even though you might want to prevent the ball from going to him, you can't do it.

Illegal zone defense is a stupid rule and should be changed so that wonderfully talented athletes can play the game as they see fit instead of being limited by rules that don't make any sense. College basketball has the right idea: play zone, play man-to-man—however and whatever your team can do best. As offensively strong as today's pros are, they are good enough to handle *any* defense. But the powers that be want to give the stars more scoring opportunities; hence the ridiculous rules.

Here is a question that I can answer: How is it that Patrick Ewing, as a professional, has been such a splendid offensive player, when in college he averaged barely 12 points a game? It's crazy! During his college career, did he not have a touch? Did he not know how to shoot a jump shot? Why, as a pro, did he suddenly become so offensively prolific? I'll tell you why. When Ewing was in college, John Thompson, his coach (and a friend of mine) wanted him to mimic Bill Russell, who had been one of John's teammates. Ewing could have picked a worse role model: Russell had led the Celtics to eleven world championships. But John failed to consider, or perhaps didn't realize, that Ewing had talents that Russell never possessed. I'm referring here to Ewing's exceptional offensive touch.

Many good college coaches, for some very good reasons, suppress their players, keeping them from doing things that, if given the opportunity, they could do very well. Sometimes college coaches do this for the betterment of their team's overall performance, even though they realize that certain individual players may suffer. They may, in other cases, believe they are acting in the best interests of the player. Whatever the reason, the end result can be the stunting or concealing of a real talent.

Michael Jordan provides a classic example. Jordan played for Dean Smith when North Carolina won a national championship, but you sure wouldn't have recognized him as the Michael Jordan we know today. Differences in coaching philosophy and in the way the coach played the team were responsible for the difference, I'm sure. Team concept is very important to coaches; therefore, the individual greatness of MJ had to wait until a later day. (In

27

contrast, Larry Bird at Indiana and Magic Johnson at Michigan State were allowed to do their thing in college, and have kept it going all through their pro years.)

In order for a basketball team to become great, the players, at least the mainstays, have to stay together for at least three to five years. But how can teams stay together nowadays with the free agency situation as it is? Free agency (started by Curt Flood) is supposed to be good for players, but unfortunately it is bad for teams. Free agency puts players squarely into a position where their self interest can directly oppose the best interests of their team. Every free agent is looking to better himself, and will go wherever he can get the most money. That, more often than not, means going to another team. You can't blame him for acting in his own best interest, but what happens to the three-to-five-year togetherness period that I said was so important? His team is going to suffer.

There is another reason why the faces on so many teams change every year. An athlete's reason for wanting to go somewhere else often involves their desire to be on a championship caliber team. They want to get a championship under their belt before leaving the NBA. That's what we heard from Barkley when he left Philadelphia, and what Clyde Drexler said when he left Portland for the Rockets.

## Wiltism

ONE THING YOU MUST UNDERSTAND: FREE AGENCY DOES NOTHING FOR THE FANS. IT'S ALL ABOUT MONEY AND THAT'S NO CRIME. I ONLY WISH THEY'D ADMIT IT, JUST ONE TIME.

Beside having to deal with the challenges presented by free agency, teams have to cope with incidents like this one. Rod Strickland just stopped coming to practice one day, saying, "I will not put a shoe on for Portland for the rest of my basketball career." Now, this man is being paid by a professional team. That, for most of us, would be quite an honor. Quite aside from the honor involved, he also signed a contract under which he is getting enormous amounts of money. Yet, in spite of the honor and in spite of his duty under the contract, he felt compelled to say, "Hey, I'm through. You are going to get me out of here and, if you don't, I just won't play any more."

Anyway you cut it, this is a breach of his contract and, though they *could* sue him every which way, they don't. They don't because *he* is Strickland and *they* are chicken. Both the owners and the NBA are faint-hearted—the NBA, because it doesn't want to upset the applecart, and the team, because they don't want a cloud on their image.

In all the years I have been watching this new generation of basketball players, I have never seen any of them sacrifice anything or perform a truly unselfish act. Today's athletes, Mashburn and others like him, complain about systems they don't like but are forced to play. The guys in New York claimed that, under their new system, they were not getting the ball enough or getting enough shots per game. They were so annoyed, in fact, that they mutinied against the coach–the same Don Nelson they applauded so enthusiastically when he replaced Pat Riley.

Demanding players like these are childishly cutting off their noses to spite their faces. Most of them need someone in their lives to give them discipline and a reason for being—someone like Bobby Knight of Indiana University or John Chaney of Temple University. Under that kind of coach, if they didn't respond to discipline, they would be told bluntly to ". . . get your ass out of here."

How can we help young athletes (or "older kids," as they sometimes seem) make the transition into adulthood prepared to withstand the trials and tribulations that come with being a pro? How do we enable them with the ability to deal with the riches soon to be bestowed upon them? The wisest of men would agree that this question has no single answer, but I am certain that we all would concede that next to experience (which can be a very hard teacher), the most potent way of acquiring wisdom is through the example of people we admire.

This principle is as true for young basketball players as it is for the rest of us. The number of professionals who have become icons in our lives is extremely small, yet these people have a tremendous impact. We watch how they handle themselves as human beings and, when we feel a strong connection to them—in some way even identifying with them—the effect of their every deed is magnified many times over.

There may be as many as 3,000 professionals in the four major sports (basketball, football, baseball, and hockey) plus a few minor sports such as tennis, soccer, etc. Of these 3,000 or so professional athletes, there are perhaps fifty who receive enormous media coverage and whose names are constantly before us.

Think about it: only fifty pros, but they affect upwards of 250 million people in our country alone. Is it realistic—or even healthy—for young people to look to such a small group of athletes as their models of behavior and barometers of success? If not, how do we tell the tens of thousands of kids who dream of being like these fifty superstars that they should not necessarily try to emulate them?

Here is a story that illustrates what I am talking about—a tale that involves Wilt, himself. I am a night person. I frequently do not sleep well, so I sometimes go out at late hours. At about 4:00 a.m. on the night in question, I was in front of the VIP Lounge of a popular night club in South Beach, Miami (where I live during part of the year) talking with the manager. He said to me, pointing, "Looks like a basketball team coming in here." I looked, and sure enough, it *was* a basketball team—the Chicago Bulls. They had played the previous evening in Atlanta, and were scheduled to play that night in Miami against the Heat.

Pippen walked by me on his way to the VIP Lounge, threw his hand out to say a quick hello, and kept on going. Five or six other Bulls followed him into the lounge and I watched them drinking Absolut and cranberry juice until about a 4:45 a.m., when I left to go home. I found out later on that they had left the lounge about 5:15 a.m. for their hotel which was almost an hour's drive away.

Now, the Heat were a hapless team, so, to a certain degree, I could understand why they thought that they could be out carousing at 4:15 or 4:30 in the morning. But I had to wonder, as the people who saw them out there that morning must have wondered, "Are these guys really playing tonight? Are they going directly from the VIP Lounge to practice, or what? What is really going on here?" To make a long story short, the Bulls did play that night against the Miami Heat, who beat them by about 30 points.

I have to admit that at least the Bulls were together as a team. There wasn't just one individual involved; over half the team was there that night. Staying out late apparently violates none of the rules for the Bulls who are breaking all sorts of basketball records. Seems they can play very well no matter what time they go to bed. As for setting a good example, I'm not so sure.

31

To be caught out at 6:00 in the morning on the day we were playing (or not playing, for that matter) would have been unheard of when I was playing. I can't recall this kind of carrying on ever happening—so many members of the same team hanging out till dawn, carousing in 0., and showing so little sensitivity concerning their public image. It is obvious that today's pros play the game differently both on and off the court. These guys just march to a different drummer than we did in my day.

I thought I had seen it all, but watching Rodman swap kisses with one of the better-known transvestites at a Miami Club called "Bash" shocked even me. Understand that I am not knocking Rodman's choice of women, men, or any combination thereof. What bothers me is that if this type of carefree (careless?) behavior is an example of what we now choose to condone in our heroes, what can we expect next? It's scary!

These new heroes don't hesitate to show us their real side (which may actually be the only side they have, and quite shallow). Does their in-your-face behavior mean that they sincerely want to show us their true selves, or just that they don't give a rip about how we see things? All that can be said for sure is that they are up front about it.

I wondered if the people of Miami, where everyone knew about this transvestite and what a low-life Rodman was dealing with, were not somewhat shocked at his deportment. It seemed, however, that whether Rodman knew what he/she was all about didn't seem to matter one way or the other.

I don't care what anyone says, there is a right way and a wrong way to carry out your public life. Privacy should be engaged a little more often. I am not questioning Rodman's right, only the wrongness of bringing it all into sight. The world sure has changed!

Continuing our saga of the unbelievable bullshit that is going on in the NBA today, Shawn Kemp was suspended in the last game of the season for getting into a fight—a fight that could do nothing but hurt his team, as the team he was playing against was not going to the playoffs. His fit of temper resulted in his being ousted for one game of the playoffs. At least the NBA didn't back away from making his consequences effective during the post-season—and that's more than can be said for baseball's action in the Alomar incident.

Since Kemp is the main player on the Supersonics, you would think that his teammates might have been upset about his suspension, but something strange was revealed here. A reporter asked one of Kemp's teammates what not having Shawn on the floor for the very first game would cost the team. Surprisingly, the player answered, "I think we will be better off without him." The reporter, for the moment at a loss for words, muttered, "What?" The player went on to explain, "Yeah, I think we'll do as well, or better, without Kemp."

We are becoming accustomed to hearing cohorts talk about each other, vocalizing negative feelings publicly. In fact, this kind of expression seems to be very much in vogue today. Even though Kemp's teammate may actually have meant what he said, I believe that his feelings would better have been kept in-house. As it turned out, however, he was a prophet after all. The Supersonics, without Kemp, won their first game by about 25 points. In the very next game, against the same team, in the same arena, but with Kemp back, the Sonics lost. (Kemp had nine turnovers.)

The point here is that professional athletes feel very strongly about each other, and the enemy is not always the team they are playing against. In today's sports, your foe could be your coach, the owner, or even your teammate. It is hard, sometimes, to know for sure.

## PLAYERS IN THE ASYLUM

One of the reasons for the downhill momentum of professional sports is that, unfortunately, the asylum is being run by the inmates. The truth of this statement has never been seen more clearly, at least for professional basketball, than during March and April of 1996. In a single two-week period, three major stars, via the media, made downright amazing announcements about their future careers. I am talking about Michael Jordan, Magic Johnson and Karl Malone. Each has been with the same team since coming into the NBA, and all will be free agents next year, so the question on everyone's mind was, "Where are they going to be next year?"

Rumors had already begun to spread about the possibility that Jordan might be on his way to New York City. My point here, however, is not where Jordan was to be playing. The important thing is what Jordan had to say about where he was going, and how he said it.

Michael made a statement to the Chicago press that if his coach, Phil Jackson, and teammate Scottie Pippen were not kept in Chicago, he would not be there, either. If that is not putting a knife to the throat of management, I don't know *what* it is.

Jordan is a man who is well respected by all, and whose fans have stood behind him through thick and thin, lose or win. But now that he is winning, Jordan feels that he can flatly state that his decision to remain with his current team is contingent on the right people being there (or the wrong people leaving). He could have said, "Look, I have been very happy in Chicago, and things have gone well for me here; so if a deal can be worked out, this is where I'd like to be next year." But no; his statement is, "This is where I will be—but *only* if you keep the coach *and* if you keep Pippen."

Moving a little farther west, we find Karl Malone of the Utah Jazz giving the same kind of ultimatum: he would no longer be around unless the coach of his team, Jerry Sloan, was kept. Malone added that he might just retire, but, in any case, he would not be playing in Utah. Malone's reason for making this statement was a rumor that, because Sloan has not been able to win the big games, management is somewhat tentative about keeping him on. Now, Karl has not won the big games, either; but he said that if Jerry is fired because the team did not do what they were expected to do, he would also leave. So, Malone, too, has put a knife to his management's throat.

Then behold Magic Johnson who, though he has many times retired and unretired, threatened during the last three weeks or so of the 1995-96 season that he would not come back next year because he did not like certain developments that had taken place involving the Lakers' team. Cedric Ceballos, for example, got into trouble, and then Nick Van Exel got into trouble, prompting Magic to go to the press claiming that he had never before seen such occurrences on any team that he had been a part of. He added that the resulting dissension had affected his mental state and his feelings about professional basketball. Therefore, Magic didn't know whether he was going to come back next year.

When the season was over for the Lakers, Magic was asked by the media for his current thoughts about leaving. "Magic," they said, you have just lost three games in a row. Are you going to come back next year?" (Remember that Magic was terrible throughout the entire playoff series.) He replied, "I don't really know. I think I'd like to come back next year, but only if they are willing to change my role." Give him credit, folks. He didn't say he would come back if they fired someone or didn't fire someone. He went straight for the jugular, saying, "I'll come back if you play it the way I want it played." *Play it again, Sam—or in this case, play it again, Magic—the way I want it played. Only then will I be back.*

When three people of the stature of Johnson, Jordan and Malone lay down similar demands to management, we have to give the situation some attention. Remember, these are basketball's role models, and all of them are well loved. They are not the Colemans', the Andersons', or the others who don't have as large a following.

These three stars have earned their right to make certain demands, but the things they are demanding are not the things they have earned the right to control. Basketball is a team game, not an individual game. They have not earned the right to decide who should be where, how and why. Those decisions are management's job; players are paid to *play.* But playing alone, is apparently no longer enough for these three stars; the playing must now be done *their way.*

Just in case you think I am just a man who enjoys blowing his horn (and his top) for no good reason, I suggest you take a look backward in time and remember that dignified Hall of Famer and one-time coach of the Denver Nuggets, Dan Issel. Dan, if you recall, just up and retired in the middle of the season. His only explanation was that coaching was no longer fun. Unlike yours truly, he was not (and is not) the type to blow his horn or call names. He didn't spout off in public about players who have lost all real concern for the game of basketball or for their own teams—players who desire more of everything for themselves, but who are willing to give up very little in return.

Other coaches have retired for similar reasons, among them K.C. Jones, who had been a member of many world championship teams (my Laker team for one) and coached a world champion team. Many great coaches, failing to get any backup from team owners, have simply decided to retire rather than take more of what their players were dishing out. This is not hearsay, but actual fact, and tells us that there is an undercurrent out there that merits attention.

Too many players today have no dignity and no respect for those who deserve it. Translation: "No class." Sure, they have plenty of money, but money never did buy class.

## WILTISM

**PLAYERS CAN MAKE A LOT OF MONEY, AND GAIN IMMENSE SUCCESS, BUT WITHOUT INTEGRITY AND PRIDE, THEY'LL NEVER PASS LIFE'S TEST.**

When I watch Bill Wennington and Luc Longley of Chicago, or Will Perdue, an ex-Chicago player who is now playing with the Spurs, I see clearly that, even though these guys appear to have less innate athletic ability than some of the bigger talents, the small things they do on a regular basis are the big reasons that their teams win. I wonder why some of the so-called "more talented" big men of the league do not follow these guys' lead. Is it possible that we have placed too much emphasis on "raw talent?" If we look at what they contribute to their teams, I think that the Longleys' and the Perdues' might be considered just as "talented" as some of the players we hear a great deal more about.

Our benchmark for measuring talent needs to be reevaluated. Does a great hook shot qualify a player for "talented" status? If so, what do you call the ability to get loose balls? I call it a form of talent. Why is the guy who makes the hook shot any more important to a team than the one who dives on the floor for balls, picks up all the loose crap, and does the other things no one else wants to do. How would society get along if we had only doctors and lawyers, and no garbage collectors?

We often hear announcers tell their listeners that "this guy does the little things." I wondered while listening to the New York Knicks game against Chicago, why the new announcer, Danny Ainge, commented on Mason's and Ewing's exceptional talent, though Chicago player Luc Longley and some of the other guys were really doing a better job on offense and on the boards. Ainge was a wonderfully talented athlete in his own right as well as a hard worker who did both the little things and big things equally well. He should realize that talent comes in many different forms, and that Longley and Perdue, with their particular variety of talent, are just as valuable as Mason and Ewing are with theirs.

I have observed, although I may not be polite in pointing it out, that some guys have a tendency to choke—even great golfers like Greg Norman. In crucial situations, when basketball players find themselves facing better teams or better players, their game may very suddenly go down the drain. Basketball players, in particular, seem to be subject to this affliction. They may do extremely well against the lowly teams in the league, but against the big boys, the three-point shots don't go in, and the other maneuvers that worked so well against the no-threat teams don't work anymore—just when they are needed the most! And, once again, we hear nothing of value from the media.

From commentators we get statements such as, "I wonder what happened to the stroke such-and-such a player had a couple of games ago when he was playing against whoever. Now that they are playing against Chicago, he can't seem to find that stroke at all." And in interviews after the game, players will whine, "I don't know what happened; I just couldn't hit the basket today." Why don't they simply say, straight out, "You know, it's different when you play against the best. Hitting those shots against a really good team is a lot harder than when you're playing guys who are less than top-of-the-line."

What is the ingredient of personality or character that causes certain key players to lose their quality of excellence in the playoffs (especially toward the end when it is needed most) in spite of having acquitted themselves well all season? For some reason, certain individuals seem able to handle crisis situations better than others who tend to choke or to get nervous at crucial moments.

Some people call those athletes who fade in the high-pressure crunches, "chokers." Others look on them merely as players who are not willing to make the big plays—players who prefer, instead, to remain obscure in history by passing the ball off, letting someone else become either the hero who shoots the winning basket or the "goat" who fails to score when the chips are down.

How do you explain the inability of David Robinson to do in the big games the very things that came natural to him during the regular season? Or how do you explain Dennis Scott of the Orlando Magic? He can throw in more three-pointers than anyone else in the world, but against Chicago, he cannot make either a simple or critical basket. Sometimes he cannot even get free to attempt one. As I watch him in a big game, for the umpteenth time he seems unable to make an open three-point shot. No one is guarding him. He is out there shooting all by himself— and he still cannot make one. Remember, this guy is the number one three-point shooter during the regular season!

Please understand that I am not discounting the Bulls' tenacious defense. I have seen Stockton, the world's greatest passer, unable to complete an extremely simple pass during the waning moments of a very important game. And I've watched a big bruiser like Malone, with just seconds to go, allow someone—without even contesting him—to come down the middle and make an easy lay-up or dunk.

In contrast to Robinson, Scott, Stockton, Malone, and others, there are players like Reggie Miller of Indiana and Michael Jordan. These are guys who would die to have the ball at a crucial moment, and who would go through walls or do whatever else it takes to make that last important play. They fight for this chance, even knowing that if they miss or slip up, they could end up as the "goat." Players like these are willing to grab such opportunities because of their supreme confidence in themselves.

Larry Bird, Magic Johnson, Jerry West, and Elgin Baylor all had this quality. Many players have it, but my concern is with the ones who do *not*. Don't they see the picture clearly? Are they aware that they have just passed the ball off to someone else rather than taking a shot that they could very easily have taken? Do they see themselves as tightening up under pressure, or as being unlike the player they normally are? I am not sure they fully recognize what is going on and I doubt whether anyone else ever tells them. Instead of looking at themselves and the situation squarely, they, along with many of their friends and teammates, probably find endless other reasons for losing the game.

No one is impervious to fear. Although some of us seem to think we are, and some of us pretend we are not affected by it, everyone, at one time or another, is willing to give in to their fears, preferring to do nothing rather than risk the pain that might result from failing to do exactly the right thing. Referees are told when they make a call to make it quickly and firmly, and to sound as if they know precisely what they are talking about (even if they don't). Authoritative words and actions increase believability, but only if done immediately and without hesitation. This advice might well be taken by athletes who are frequently caught in do-or-die situations. Times such as these are not for thinking about what to do. These are times for relying on reflex action, doing what is natural, and letting the chips fall where they may. Nike is right: "JUST DO IT!"

No one appears to be at fault, but someone must be to blame when, after three quarters, the Orlando Magic has accumulated a total of nineteen rebounds to the Chicago Bulls' forty-nine. A thirty-rebound deficit might not raise eyebrows if it had been accumulated over a total of four or five games; but being down by thirty after only three quarters of one game can lead to only one conclusion: this team is not even *thinking* about rebounding.

You may recall seeing one of Shaq's commercials in which he says something to the effect that, ". . . many people think I have too many things on my mind, but all I'm really thinking about is that I have these ten fingers," (and he holds them up for us to see) "but no rings." He then goes on to claim that he loves jewelry.

I say to Shaq,

Bullshit. Your commercial really should have said, 'The most important thing on my mind is that championship ring.' We all know that you must care about the things that are grossing you millions of dollars; so why didn't you just say so without the bull? A little honesty can go a long way, Shaq. Don't let them write bullshit lines like that for you to say on TV; you are

41

above all that BS. Just use those ten fingers to get some rebounds—then you'll be on the righteous road to jewelry.

And I would go on to say to him,

Basketball should be the number one topic on your mind, because without basketball, the other wonderful things in your life would not have happened. Forget about ripping down baskets, and just rip down some rebounds.

I am often asked my opinion of the quality of today's players, and I reply that, without a doubt, they are great. They have an abundance of athletic ability—perhaps even more than any of the guys of my era. I am afraid, however, that for most of them, discipline is sadly lacking. And without discipline and a measure of common sense to go along with great athletic ability, a person can soon come to resemble a runaway train.

Shawn Kemp of Seattle presents a perfect example of what I am talking about. Shawn seems to be the embodiment of everything a basketball player could hope to be. He has a superb body, he is capable of jumping to the moon (figuratively speaking), he can run like a gazelle, and he possesses a will that allows him to perform feats that are downright unbelievable. Unfortunately, he does not know how to channel these superb assets. No coach has taken the time to teach him the importance of self control and how to use it.

Kemp was not a college player, so he missed acquiring the discipline that is learned, demanded in fact, if you play for schools such as Indiana, Kansas or North Carolina. Unfortunately, there is just no substitute for the kind of instruction and experience that is gained in college play, and without it, a young player is apt to get into hot water with some of the basics. Shawn seems always to be in foul trouble and finds himself on the bench when he should be on the floor—a direct result of lack of discipline and poor use of common sense.

Kemp perfectly demonstrates the importance of young athletes' decisions about entering college, and the need for carefully weighing all the pros and cons. Kids should remember that going to college is worth a lot more than just gaining two or three years of playing experience. It is all about growing up. The background acquired during this important period can make a big difference later on in life, and young athletes should be made aware of all they may be giving up if they bypass a college opportunity. That big contract may be tempting; but *all that glitters is not gold.*

There are a great many things I do not understand well, but one of the things I understand *least* is the learning process of athletes, especially the current batch. These players have been able, somehow, to avoid picking up anything of value from their own mistakes or from the mistakes of others. They observe first-hand all that happens, yet they fall into the same traps time after time— with drugs and in other areas of misbehavior. The last three or four weeks of the '95-'96 season provide an horrendously typical example.

Rodman's action in butting the official's head brought everyone to the unavoidable conclusion that players were becoming far too focused upon themselves and far too little concerned about anyone or anything else, including their teams, the officials, or almost anyone. One might assume at this point that other players, having observed the consternation caused by the Rodman incident, might have picked up a bit of wisdom that would lead them to try to avoid similar mishaps. But this was not to be.

Shortly after the Rodman fiasco, we saw Nick Van Exel of the Lakers push an official into a table, and watched Magic bump an official. (The above incidents, I am pleased to report, resulted in fines and suspensions.) Next we observed Jordan verbally pound an official in a way you wouldn't believe—and without any consequence, not even a technical foul. And following that, for some unfathomable reason, there were fights by the bucketful—fight after fight after fight.

I don't know what this series of events was all about. Tension? Stress? They needed a rest? I can guarantee, however, that further incidents would not have occurred if, at any time, the powers that be had said, "That's it, guys: one more altercation or similar incident and you'll find yourself missing one of the playoff games, and maybe even the entire playoffs."

The teams and the NBA must put a collective foot down. As long as meaningless little penalties are the only consequences to befall offending players, nothing will change. The recent penalties handed to Rodman and Magic actually turned out to be rewards for their respective teams: while the two sinners had a chance to rest, their teammates, who otherwise would not have had a chance to play, got some valuable time on the court—a plus for everyone concerned. Is there any incentive here for players to go forth and sin no more? *I think not, Wiltie.*

The baby wonder, Shawn Kemp, using no sense at all, often drives from almost the half-court line and, on his way, runs right over Rodman who is merely standing under the basket. This is ridiculous! Should we be surprised that offensive fouls are called against Kemp? Kemp shows us power of body, but certainly not of brains.

The mentality of some players is so unbelievably bad that it is difficult to comprehend how they could have become professionals. Why hasn't a coach taken someone like young Kemp aside and said, "Listen, kid, this is basketball you are playing, not bowling. Rodman saw you coming, and just stood there. You didn't try to go around him, you tried to run right through him!" Now, is Rodman provoking this kind of action? Or have professional restraint and discipline gone down the drain, and too much money driven these guys insane?

In a different scene, I recall watching Hubie Davis from the New York Knicks being repeatedly knocked on his ass by Michael Jordan. Hubie, never saying anything, would just get up and resume play. (Of course, the referees were not about to call anything in favor of Hubie). I hope that it is enough for Davis just to know that one day he will be able to tell his grandchildren how MJ knocked him on his butt in all those games. Maybe he'll even be able to boast, "See, I still have the bruises on my backside to prove it!" Unfortunately, for confirmation of the story, he'll probably have to get MJ to autograph the site. What a joke!

What salary do you think players would really be willing to play for? One million dollars? A half-million dollars? One hundred thousand dollars? Or maybe even fifty thousand? If we were to shift back into a world of reality where players were paid what they deserved, I guarantee that the amount they would play for would shock you!

Suppose the owners were to say something like this: "Guess what! From now on we are going to treat you guys just like we would treat anyone else in the workaday world. You have a good job and you are making good money, but from now on, if you want to play, $75,000 per year (not per game), is what you are going to be paid—and that is *all* you are going to be paid." If this were to happen, I guarantee that those guys, almost to a man, would be playing for the offered amount. The ones who have already made their millions might go on to retire, but everyone else would be playing, whether for $75,000 or $100,000. (That's what many are doing now in the CBA and other leagues—and for a lot less.)

Do you seriously think that today's pros wouldn't rather be playing basketball for that kind of money than teaching school for $40,000 or $50,000 a year? They would definitely rather be out there playing basketball, or any other sport for that matter. Take my word for it!

A lot of people think that the accumulation of statistical numbers really doesn't mean very much, but that idea is a bunch of hogwash. If you don't think that numbers mean a lot, why do you think people are concerned about how many hits a baseball player gets? Why do they always want to know his batting average, how many home runs he had this year or last week, or how many points he scored?

The greatness of Jordan is reflected in how many points he gets. He could be the best at whatever else, but if he weren't scoring points, he would not be getting that much attention. The numbers bring him the attention, not his rings. Jordan got all that attention long before the rings came along.

The three or four extra points Jordan gets in technical fouls make enough difference to elevate him above the masses of other players in scoring. If he weren't to shoot those technical fouls, and consequently got three or four fewer points each game, Malone would probably be the highest scorer in the league—and that would make a big difference to a lot of people.

Sonny Hill, a friend of mine of Philadelphia fame, said to me as I left Philadelphia to come to California and play for the Lakers, "Hey Big Fella, get back to your scoring! Your scoring is your statement in sports. No one does it better than you, and scoring is how you should be—and will be—remembered. Don't give that up to others." But I didn't listen. I thought there were other things that I should be doing to benefit my team, and I allowed myself to give up the quest for points. Whatever else I did, I put scoring second, third, or fourth behind the other facets of my game.

I sometimes wish that I hadn't set my priorities in this way because most people do relate to, and remember you for those numbers—especially the fans who know about points, stats, home runs, and such. Even today when I walk the streets, the first (and sometimes the only) comment I hear is, "Oh, yeah; he's the guy who scored 100 points." No one cares that I did so many other things; they think only of the 100-point game.

Kareem Abdul-Jabbar presents another example of the importance of scoring. He is the all-time top scorer in the history of professional basketball, and scoring is what he is known for. Jabbar is not going to be remembered for his four or five world championships. Every time he is announced, you will hear, "Ladies and gentlemen, here is Kareem Abdul-Jabbar, the number one scorer in the history of basketball." Scoring is, after all, what he was better at than anybody else, and when you get right down to it, he did score more points than anybody else. So, like it or not, that's the banner he must wave.

If we could induce today's athletes to be as animated during play as they are following each mundane catch or routine basket, we would have a performance worth paying to see. A lot of energy and effort goes into every post-play celebration—often more than the energy put forth in the play itself.

But maybe I'm missing the point here. Could these players' highjinks be more than just fun and games? Could they be "crazy like a fox," and have the right idea, after all? Our present day athletes are surely aware that the stuff that goes on *after* a play will be watched by every camera in existence. They realize not only that their actions will be in the camera's eye; they know, as well, that camera time brings popularity. Players are, furthermore, very aware that popularity translates into mucho money. Conclusion: they know exactly what they are doing—at least when it comes to making moolah.

*P. S.* I do want to apologize right now to all the players who are out on the court doing their best, and who are into the game for all the right reasons. There *are* some of you guys out there. But do you know what? There are only a very few.

# TWO

# YESTERDAY AND TODAY

| YESTERDAY'S CODE: | TODAY'S CODE: |
|---|---|
| JUMP HIGHER. | GIVE LESS. |
| RUN FASTER | GET MORE |
| BE STRONGER | BECOME RICHER |

The world has changed enormously in the last couple of decades. The world of sports has changed as well—and not always for the better. Change is constant and inevitable and is bound to happen in spite of anything we do, so instead of trying to stop it or slow it down, we might be smarter simply to try to reverse its direction, and move back toward the way we used to be.

It sure isn't anyone's fault that values have changed and that kids' dreams have become confused. The satisfaction that we used to get from doing something well, just for the pure love of it, has become tainted with money. We have a hard time nowadays figuring out which is most important, the love of money or the love of the sport. When I was a kid, we didn't have that problem. We played a sport because we loved it, even though we knew there was not very much money in it. Money just never was an issue.

In the early days, guys played because they loved the game of basketball. All they were interested in was securing a contract for as many years as they could get. The length of the contract was of the most importance because their salaries were about the same as what a school teacher earned—$4,000 to $7,000. Because most players were at that time college graduates, they could go out and get a regular job for more than they were earning playing basketball.

The system that prevented a young man from going into the pros until his college class had graduated was a good one for a couple of reasons. It helped to ensure that an athlete would be fairly mature by the time he entered professional ranks. It also meant that most of the early professional players were college graduates, and obtaining other employment was not usually a problem. Their choice of basketball as a career came from a real love of the game.

Then along came a brash young man, Wilt Chamberlain, who, in a short period of time, turned the whole picture around. During my rookie year, my salary, including bonuses, was six figures, an amount that at that time was almost unbelievable. When the size of my salary came to the attention of the media, other players followed along like sheep. Their attitude was, "If he is getting that kind of money, I want some, too." At that point we were off and running, headed down the path that would lead to Coleman, Kenny Anderson and Big Hog (oops, I meant Big *Dog!*).

Looking back, I believe I was justified in negotiating a salary of that size. I had played as the headliner with the Globetrotters, and my ability to draw large crowds all over the world had already established me as a proven commodity. What's more, I had drawn sellout and record crowds in high school, in the Amateur Athletic Union (AAU), and in college.

But let's set up some fairness parameters here. I am not here just to blast the other guys. I caused a lot of this stuff myself, and I did some of the same things in my day that I now complain about today's players doing. So, who is *better* qualified to know about badness than the one who, himself, has been bad?

## WILTISM

**THE MAKING OF MONEY IS ALL RIGHT, HONEY;**

**BUT MAKING THE TEAM FULFILLS THE REAL DREAM.**

I do not believe that most basketball players of today could handle the hardships and the pressures that were faced by players of yesteryear. Today's players probably deserve what they get (most do, anyway), but virtually none of the goodies they enjoy were bestowed upon us while we were playing.

Here are but a few of the "benefits" that were enjoyed by yesterday's players. Imagine having no trainers, or no first class airline seats. Did you ever try to fit a seven-foot-seven frame into coach-class accommodations? There was no limit on pre-season games. One year I played in close to thirty-five of these exhibition games while, today, seven games are considered to be too much. Long hours of travel were considered just a part of our typical working day. Climate-controlled buildings were unheard of then, and we had no king-size beds—no one cared about the safety of *our* heads.

Most of today's athletes are not aware of what we had to endure so that they could reap their bountiful harvest—nor do they probably care. Selfishness is definitely a characteristic of most jocks' mentality. A self-centered attitude has, I think, always been a flaw in our character.

The subject I want to address next is America's position in basketball. By our "position" I mean the way we are thought of in relation to other countries. In the '30s, '40s and '50s, we were so dominant that only *American* basketball was talked about. Have we been losing ground to the rest of the world? My answer to that question is "yes"—a resounding "yes."

I can think of several reasons for our loss of status. Players in the rest of the world are not only getting better, but more of them are playing than ever before. Just as we Americans are growing in our acceptance of games such as soccer, the world has taken the American game of basketball to heart. But at the same time that worldwide interest in basketball has reached its peak, we have begun to slip in our overall play.

This has not happened as the result of our cockiness or lack of care. Most athletes in any game will try to put their best foot forward whenever they are on the playing field or court. It has come about because the type of game Americans play has changed, although our opponents in most other parts of the world are playing the same game they learned from us in the fifties and sixties.

One would think that the rest of the world should be far behind us, since they are using the old regimes and the old fundamental ways of thinking about basketball. Unfortunately for us, such is not the case.

Our game used to be sound and functional—and now that kind of game is being used against us. Nowadays we use what we call a one-shoot (playground) style, a more freelance, run and shoot, haphazard way of playing the game which features show business more than taking care of business. And now, when you see us in the Pan-American Games, the World Games, or other international competitions, you will find that we frequently do not even place. That's right. No need to worry any longer about our not taking first place. Today we have a hard time winning *any* type of medal in international competition, most likely because we don't put our best foot foward.

Who should we blame for this? Maybe our amateur jocks could use a bit of schooling here. Perhaps they should take international tournament play a little more seriously and feel pride when they are asked to participate. No longer can we simply throw our guys on the court and expect to win. These young people must recognize that competition is now coming from every corner of the world, but if they participate, they will become much better for it. Intense competition can push players to their ultimate level of achievement.

If our coaches (at least those who are not currently tuned in to what is going on in international sports) were more attentive, they would see clearly that they are being confronted by nothing but good, old-fashioned basketball. They are having to deal with basic blocking out, pick and rolls, filling the lanes, and weak side back on defense. These and other goodies were important parts of the game when our coaches were growing up or first started to coach. However, over the years, our coaches may have forgotten about these elements of the game or, at the very least how to utilize them.

Pleasing the fans with "showtime" is nice, but the game is not entirely about showtime. It's about winning time, too.

Do you want a today-to-yesterday comparison? Take the last game of the season between the Indiana Pacers and the Cleveland Cavaliers. The Cavaliers lost the game to the Pacers, 98-89—a low-scoring game by most standards. One team had a total of 26 rebounds. Consider, please, that for about 10 of my 13 years in basketball, I averaged over 26 rebounds a game—*by myself.* If one guy's rebound average for a year can equal that of an entire team, you might get the feeling that something is terribly wrong, or at least a lot different.

Indiana had 45 rebounds in that game, something I had also managed single-handedly *(Wiltie, you're bragging again!)* while Cleveland had only 26 rebounds. Even so, the leading rebounder for the game was some guy with a big fat seven. Another player had an amazing five rebounds, and another, three. This scenario doesn't mean that only one or two guys were not hustling for the ball, it means that the whole damn team was not hustling. Period. And that's appalling.

The game was lost by a team that was out-rebounded by almost 20, a huge difference. It may be worth noting that in the third quarter Indiana scored only 17 points and Cleveland got an impressive 12 points. Now, if this is not high school basketball, you sure could have fooled me. And remember, this performance is *with* the clock. (We had no clock in my high school and college playing days.) In the game under discussion, Indiana had 61 attempts from the field for the whole game—61 attempts! In one game *(Wiltie, here you go again),* I made 66 shot attempts, all by my little old lonesome self. What a gunner I was! And I scored 100 points—a lot more than this whole team did. And you think the game hasn't changed?

In my playing days, we were out there *playing*—not seeing how little we could do, but how much. This kind of play took stamina and endurance. People realized then that basketball players had to be in tremendous shape to handle the pace of a good game. Today, with less effort in their play, and with timeouts being called every which way, a player need not be in particularly great shape, but the ones who *are* have become the game's superstars.

Though not quite as good as Chicago in a number of ways, Seattle was playing Chicago for the World Championship. Seattle, easily the best team in the West, and considered by many to be the second best team in the NBA, had been playing over .700 ball, but they were not expected to do very much against Chicago. The ratings were very low, and the TV people were saying that they expected this to be a ho-hum, blowout type of series.

We heard that Seattle had nothing going for them, and that they were, essentially, not a very good team. But how, I ask you, can you call a team that is playing over .700 ball "not a very good team?" Only in the NBA today is that possible—though, in truth, I believe they are right. Seattle was *not* a very good team. There weren't any really good teams out there except for one, and that one was Chicago, though we are only speaking here in relative terms.

As I observed the sick performance in the first half of the third game in Seattle when the Sonics allowed Jordan to shoot one unmolested shot after another, I became increasingly dismayed. I wondered whether the opposing team's fear of Jordan was due to a belief that if they were to come close to him or, heaven forbid, actually *touch* him, that they would be called for a flagrant foul? I have never in my entire life seen a superstar allowed to shoot so many free shots.

55

Often, when Jordan was shooting the ball, no one was within five to fifteen feet of him. How can a man who has that much ability and that great a reputation be left virtually alone on the court? It's a disgrace. George Karl and all the Supersonics should be lined up against a wall and shot with a basketball for letting this man have so many free shots at the basket.

If the Sonics were to complain about not being able to touch Jordan, I would respond that everybody should go to him just as hard as they possibly can. That's what I would have my players do if I were coach. If Jordan is so special that touching him is called a flagrant foul, then my whole team would just have to foul out. They would all probably be out after the first half, and there would be no game. We would soon find out how it would sit with the audience and the rest of the basketball world if everybody fouled out just because they played Jordan as they should.

George Karl was asked at half time about his team's lousy performance. Here is a guy who is a strong, hard-nosed player but, a typical coach. He comes up with a BS answer, "They played good defense, and with Michael Jordan's tremendous playing, blah, blah, blah."

Hannah Storm, when she interviewed Karl, should have come straight out and asked, "Well, George, what was so great about their defense if nobody was even guarding Jordan? Just what is so formidable? He's out there taking shots all by himself, and even then he's only shooting around 50 percent. It's not as though he's shooting 80 percent or 90 percent from the field. He's scored just 24 points, and he has made his last five shots. In other words, he was shooting a lousy 31 percent or 32 percent before he hit those last four in a row, and for those last four, there wasn't a guy within three feet of him. How do you explain that, George?"

I would like to have heard his answers to *those* questions. The usual coach's strategy is to take the easy way out and remove the burden from himself by telling us how great Jordan is, implying that no one can stop him. That's bull. No one on that BS team of his has the guts to even *try* to stop Jordan.

These teams were in a World Championship game, and one of them was down by 24 points on their own home court, outrun and outdone in every category. I couldn't figure what happened to Detlef Schrempf or to Gary Payton, who is the number one defensive player in the game today. "Number one at what?" you ask. "Number one at getting destroyed," is my response.

Then there was Kemp, the biggest in-and-outer I have ever seen. You never know when he is going to give you any kind of a game. These guys were truly laughable. This was not the performance of a team that belonged in a final championship series. Any halfway knowledgeable person who happened to be watching these games would tell you the same thing—but it's a lot harder to get an honest statement from a coach. A straight-from-the-shoulder guy would tell us after the first half of the game, "We were lousy. I have no idea why we played so badly, but believe me, something different is going to happen during the next half or these guys will not be playing. If something doesn't change, and soon, they are going to be sitting on the bench next to me." That's all he would have to say.

The Bulls' key player was Kerr. Picture this: the little guard gets a rebound and throws the ball down court where there is a fast break by Jordan and Pippen with one guy back for Seattle. Pippen passes to Jordan for a dunk shot. Jordan has already missed five straight shots, but this one is an easy lay-up, unmolested, on a fast break started by a guard who got the rebound.

Now, where were the Seattle Supersonics while all this was happening? They weren't on the boards (a Bulls' guard got the rebound) and they weren't back on defense.

Where were they? They were all standing in the middle of the floor picking their noses.

Is this all we can expect from a team that is supposed to be one of the best in the world? I am angry—really angry. In what should be a great basketball series, one team plays the game correctly, while the other gives absolutely nothing. When it's all over, people will shrug and say, "Well, they did get to the World Championship . . ." Sure, they did—but from that point on, they didn't do diddley squat.


I stood by and listened as my friend, Earl the Pearl Monroe, was interviewed during half time at the game in Orlando, Florida. I don't have to tell you how unique Earl was, and how great a player, so you'll understand that I watched the questioning with considerable interest. The announcers were trying to get Earl to talk about how great today's players are. They repeatedly asked leading questions about how he was enjoying the game, and wasn't it amazing what athletes are able to do today?

Earl wasn't about to fall into that trap. Being a real stand-up kind of guy, he never once gave the announcer the answer he was angling for, or even let on that he thought the players might not be doing all they should or could. Earl was *definitely* not about to say that these players were doing anything more special than what had gone on during the days when he was playing. He simply said, "Well, these guys are showing the way for the kids of the future. They have to be correct in what they do because people are going to be watching them."

Media people are always looking for us to tout the ball players of today, but they, in turn, are not willing to say anything about the guys of yesteryear. The announcer should have said, "Just as you did in your time, Earl, these guys are out there doing a job and helping to carry the game forward." In fact, he said absolutely nothing about what Earl had achieved personally, or what he had done for the game during his time. He only wanted to exploit Earl for his own purposes.

Earl is a guy from yesterday who accomplished wonderful things, and the interviewer showed a definite lack of class in not making the slightest reference to Earl's history, asking him only about today's game. The announcers seemed disappointed that Earl failed to rise to the bait and that he declined to spend a lot of time lauding today's athletes.

Earl took nothing from today's players, but he did find a way to subtly inform his interviewers that a few years ago there were athletes who were able to do the same things—perhaps even better. He was not going to say that the guys of today are the best ever, because he doesn't believe they are. He managed to send the announcers a clear message that, just because *their* purpose was to sell the game, they shouldn't have tried to make him part of their sales force.

If you could get each of yesterday's players into a private one-on-one conversation, I believe that most of them—though not all—would admit to being in a quandary about today's game. They would not be inclined to put down our current players (they know these guys have great athletic ability) but I believe they would tell you that they are not enthusiastic about the game today. I hear it over and over again: "These guys are not playing the way basketball used to be played."

We are not dealing here with a matter of ego. Yesterday's players just see a technically stronger game going down the drain, and showmanship taking its place. And fans, apparently, have accepted showmanship in preference to watching a purer form of basketball.

There may be no "correct" way of playing basketball, but there was a purer form, more technically correct, that was played in years past. Even so, to hear the players of yesteryear discuss basketball in front of a mic, where many of them often find themselves, you would think they were speaking of a different game from the one they talk about when they are *not* on TV (unless the person in front of the mic happens to be that old big-mouth, *Wiltie*).

Since most of my friends from yesteryear are of one uniform opinion that the game is not as good as it was back then, don't you think it would be to everybody's advantage if they were to say so? Why don't they let people know that they are not altogether happy with what has happened to the game that they helped to make such a great American institution?

I think that the players of yesterday should stand up and be counted. That's why I was happy that Earl Monroe did not back down and that, without saying anything negative about the game or the players of today, he stated his true feelings.

Of course, not every guy who is willing to say his peace has had a chance to do so. Not that I am afraid to be out here all by myself (hey, I've been here before), and it's not that the other guys are afraid. It's just that I would like to see more of those men who were contemporaries of mine stand up and let it be known that things are different today—and not all for the better.

I am reminded of a conversation I heard a while ago between Bob Cousy and Tommy Heinsohn. They were doing their usual announcing job for the Boston Celtics and Heinsohn, referring to an assist by someone on the floor, stated that ". . . assists are different today, ladies and gentlemen." He played with the great Bob Cousy, of course, the guy who may have been the greatest assistman of all time.

Yes, *Heinsohn* said it, not I. Assists are different today than when he was playing. He let it be known that you get an assist today for doing almost anything at all, just as long as you were the last guy to touch the ball before the player who scored the basket.

I am bringing up this business of assists only because I think we should recognize that the game has changed, and people may be deserving of more—or less—credit today than yesterday. Today's game is different, and it should be looked upon differently. So when we say that Cousy was the greatest assist guy of all time, we are talking only about his numbers, and we should be aware that his numbers may not have been credited in the same way that somebody else's were.

I am very proud of my own assist records, and I held a few of them. At one time, I held the assist record for a playoff game. This record has since been broken, but it was broken by guys from a new era when, as I said earlier, the guidelines were different.

I am not concerned about the record, but I would like it to be known that there is a difference. A rebound is still a rebound, but an assist is no longer an assist. Ask any of the old coaches or the old players; they'll all tell you the same thing. This is universally agreed upon, so why don't they let us know that players are rewarded for their achievements on the court differently today than they were in times past.

Arguments can, and do, go on forever about who are the better players, the guys of today or the guys of yesterday, and people use a variety of criteria in reaching their conclusions. I claim that many of the standards that are applied are erroneous. Percentages are used to show how well guys are shooting today compared to yesterday, and, as I have said before and will undoubtedly say again, the percentages are higher today because the type of shots that were given up in my day were very different from the kind that are given up today. The rules and regulations of the game have opened up the middle allowing players to drive in and get to the basket to dunk the ball without much opposition in the way of hand checking or illegal zones being called.

In my day, there was far more opposition. Players like Jerry West or Oscar Robertson, two of the greatest in the world, couldn't move successfully against players of Bill Russell's, Nate Thurmond's or Wilt Chamberlain's caliber, because their shots would have been blocked. But today, with zone defenses and so forth, Michael and the others can get to the basket more easily. I am not saying that they couldn't have made it under the old rules, but when it is easier, their percentages are going to be higher. These differences should be taken into consideration when talk turns to today's percentages and how these guys are shooting better today.

One thing is certain: I'll take almost any of the shooters of yesteryear over most of today's. Sure, Larry Bird and few other guys can shoot with anybody in the world at any given time, but I'll take guys like Jerry West, Bill Sharman, Bob Pettit, Dolph Schayes, Jerry Lucas, Oscar Robertson and many others, over anybody who ever picked up a basketball. I'd even stake my house on it.

You can forget about who you may think is the great shooter of today, Dennis Scott or Reggie Miller. These guys are supposed to be such tremendous outside shooters because they can make shots from the outside with nobody guarding them, but those are the kind of shots the guys of my day had to make all the time—*with* people guarding them. I maintain that only the three-point shot is a valid standard for measuring today's true percentages. Look at the three-point shot percentages and you will see that guys like Jordan are shooting around 30 percent.

When I was playing, most of the shots came from what is today the three-point area. The guards were all shooting two-hand set shots and one-hand stabs (as they called them) and shooting off of picks. All of these were basically three-point shots. Yes, and their percentages were between 31 percent and 43 percent.

Those stats have been thought of as poor, but in comparison with what the guys are shooting today from the three-point area, a different picture emerges. Average players are shooting only about 33 percent from the three-point area, and the good guys are shooting 40 percent. One player is shooting 51 percent, and another may be reaching 46 percent—but that's it. Most are down in the low thirties, and some are even shooting in the twenties.


Claims about the superiority of today's athletes over those of yesterday are heard around the world, and maybe there is some truth to them. But there is something I want you, the fans to understand, especially those of you who root so hard for your contemporaries. Back in the fifties and sixties, basketball players were allowed to do a lot more than they are today. (The same was decidedly true for football players of the fifties.) The change has not been the fault of our athletes. If anyone is to blame, it is probably the coaches or fans who demand too little from the great athletes of today.

There is nothing wrong with being a specialist, but in today's basketball game, and in a lot of other sports, they hire guys to do one particular thing and that one thing only. Rodman, for one, has taken the specialization principle to a new level. When he first started playing basketball, he did it all: he scored points, he played tough defense, he got some rebounds, he ran up and down the court, and he did all the other things that a basketball player is supposed to do. Then he decided that his forte was going to be rebounding, and he has since made himself a bundle of money and fame by getting the ball for his team, then letting someone else pass it, kick it, put the ball in the hole, or whatever else they choose. His only objective is to get the ball; the rest is up to the other guys.

That scenario, in my opinion, is a bunch of crap. For one thing, Rodman is capable of doing a lot more. For another, I believe that athletes should be given a chance to do all the things they are capable of, not restricted to only one or two functions.

Athletes used to learn the whole game, not just a part of it, and they were expected to perform in every aspect of a sport—to play the way games were meant to be played. No one was paid just to get three or four blocked shots a game or only to play point guard and pass the ball, or just to come in to play defense against a certain forward. Each player took the three-point shot when needed, or played a particular player; everybody had to do it all.

Let's look at the athletes who, during the last fifteen or twenty years, seem to have been the true "greats." Magic Johnson, Michael Jordan, Larry Bird, and Charles Barkley are the players who have impressed me, and many others, as the very best. And do you know why they are thought of in that way? It's simple, really. It's because they play the game in a complete fashion—the whole thing.

Charles Barkley will get you rebounds, he'll get you points, he'll try to play good strong defense and he takes no guff from nobody as he runs the court and does all the things that a basketball player is supposed to do. Magic Johnson led his Laker teams to five championships in the eighties, and played every position on the court from guard to forward to center. He rebounded well and he scored points. His defense was suspect, but at least he gave an honest effort in that direction. He did everything. And Larry Bird was, to me, the consummate pro of that era. He did it all in every respect, and he did it well.

Back in the old days, football players went both offense and defense. The great Chuck Bednarik of the Philadelphia Eagles was probably the last of that dying breed. The concept made sense, really. Which player could best guard a tight end or a wide receiver but another wide receiver—one who plays that same position? He knows the moves that are usually generated by his opponent because he makes those same moves himself. So, *he* is the one who should be out there on defense—if they would give him a chance to do so.

Instead, football has become specialized to the extent that a guy goes into the game only as a passer, or just to kick field goals, or to go for one inch on third down. You've got all these specialists who don't ever become full fledged players because they aren't given a chance to do so. My guess is that some of them would like to play the full game—go both ways, defense and offense—but very few are given that opportunity, and then only after they have become so magnificent at one thing that they have the clout to demand a chance to do something else.

During my era, we did it all. We did everything all the time. Anything less was considered a crime. Barkley, Magic Johnson and Bird have this in common: they do it all. That's why they are the true superstars of today's game.

Doing it all is what it takes to be the greatest ever, and if you were to ask the opinion of modern-day players, I believe they would agree. But whether today's players *want* to play that kind of game is another matter entirely. They have learned to be content getting paid for playing half a game, and might not want to go for any more. There is Deion Sanders, of course, and undoubtedly others like him, but because of specialization (and too much of it) you'll never have a chance to watch most of today's great athletes show the full extent of what they are capable of doing.

## MY FAVORITE QUOTE FROM CHUCK BEDNARIK:

*"Deion Sanders couldn't tackle my wife Emma— and she's 70 years old."*

Mark Heisler, a writer for the *Los Angeles Times*, wrote in an article on Wednesday, June 12, 1996, "In such a fantastic age, with popularity and press coverage increasing geometrically, it is hard to remember that there was a NBA before the 1980's, but there was . . ." He went on to talk about the Philadelphia 76ers playing and winning 68 games while losing 13, and described the league at that time (only 10 teams), and how often (about nine times in the regular season) the 76ers had to go against the great Boston Celtics, who had won eight consecutive world championships.

What Heisler failed to mention was that we didn't even have a home court that we could play on consistently. Where today's usual schedule calls for 40 or 41 home games, we played at home only 29 times.

We had what were called "neutral court" games, but these contests were often played on courts that were far from "neutral." In some of these neutral court games, the crowds cheered more for the team we were playing against than for us. If we were playing a neutral court game in Ohio and our opponent was Cincinnati, it would be Cincinnati that the fans were rooting for, of course.

But back to Heisler's article. He told of watching a game involving the Chicago Bulls, frequently said to be the greatest, and seeing Luc Longley, Ron Harper and another guy pass the ball around the perimeter, trying to find someone who could shoot. Out of their starting five, they couldn't find anyone other than Pippen—but at that moment in time, Pippen was on the bench. Jordan had already passed the ball off (for the first time, he said) and they had no shooter to pass the ball to.

How, I ask you, could this team be considered one of the greatest when, if Pippen and Jordan are not available, there is no one who can shoot the ball? Are the rest of the players really Jordan's "supporting cast" as he, himself, admitted in the earlier days when he wanted to infuriate his team? Heisler commented, ". . . maybe Jordan shouldn't have been the one who said that," but MJ *was* telling the truth. They were his supporting cast then, they are his supporting cast now, and that's all they are—all of which does not bring them even close to being one of the best teams. Heisler added that even Dale Harris, coach of the Lakers, admitted during a radio interview that his current team could not possibly compete with the teams of '67: Chamberlain's 76ers, the Laker teams, or many of the great Boston Celtics teams.

Most interesting of all, Heisler, in his article, pointed out that, ". . . at this time every year, toward the end of the season, they are always looking to canonize someone, because someone has to be the hero and the star." Last year it was Hakeem; everyone said he was "another Pippen," and the Houston Rockets were said to be the greatest team in the world. (It was also said that the Rockets would have a great run for quite a while, but you may have noticed that their run didn't last all that long.) Heisler was right: every year they must canonize someone and some team. Expect it, get ready, here we go again!

## WILTISM

**A KNOWLEDGE OF HISTORY IS GOOD FOR ALL OF US. IT HELPS US DEAL WITH TODAY AND PREPARES US TO FACE TOMORROW. THE MORE WE KNOW ABOUT YESTERDAY, THE BETTER WE WILL BE ABLE TO HANDLE THE PROBLEMS OF TODAY AND DODGE THE PITFALLS OF TOMORROW.**

**THIS OBSERVATION PERTAINS TO ALL OF LIFE. BASKETBALL IS NOT AN EXCEPTION.**

Forgive me for mentioning it, but hearing that we were lesser players is not ego gratifying for those of us from my era. Furthermore, this comparison is grossly misleading when today's standards and rules are used to make us appear to have been inferior. For history's sake, we need to look at the rules and regulations of today's game and put them into perspective before we can make a valid comparison of today's game with that of yesteryear, or compare today's players with yesterday's.

Take assists, for example. An assist is totally different today than is was in my time. Even the way an assist is earned has changed. You get an assist today just for being the person to give the ball to a player who scores a basket. Hell can freeze over before he scores, but you get an assist nonetheless, just as long as you were the last player to have the ball before he scores the basket.

Then there is the matter of shooting percentages. They seem to be way up there today compared with the percentages in my time. Today's game seems to produce much higher percentages, but only until you take a closer look at how players were shooting years ago, and where they were shooting from.

Jordan gets a lot of dunks, and often goes through without being touched. His performance in this respect is largely because of his own skills, but a major part of his success is due to the way the rules are now written. Because of rules changes, comparing Jordan's shooting stats with those of earlier players is like comparing apples and oranges. If these differences were taken into account, the true shooting stats might surprise many of today's fans.

If we were to use the three-point percentages of current players, we would have a more accurate comparison with the shooting of yesteryear. Why? Because most of our baskets then were comparable to today's three-point shots. Due to differences in the rules, the guys from yesteryear did not get in to the basket to slice, dunk, and get lay-ups as they do today. The current "no hand-checking" and zone defense rules keep the middle from being blocked up as much as before, and it is easier now for guys to get in for unmolested lay-ups, making for higher percentages.

You can't simply say that guys shoot better now than they used to. They *don't* shoot better. If the three-point line were used as a measuring stick, it might be seen that current shooting is actually terrible, and the players from the times of old might be recognized as the best marksmen in basketball.

For you people who think that points are not important and that they should not be used as a measure of basketball greatness, allow me to explain how wrong you are. Looking at points is still the number one way to judge whether a player is good, better, indifferent, or awful. The first thing anyone asks about a game is, "How many points did so-and-so get?" The only stats you may see in the paper are totals for the leading scorers. Often nothing else is mentioned, not even rebounds, and perhaps not even assists.

The leading scorer is *always* mentioned, and no one knows that better than Jordan. The additional points he earns on the foul line each game create the difference that has made him the leading scorer of all time. They give him an edge over other players whose shooting averages would be similar to his if he weren't the one who shot all the technical fouls.

There are other players, Karl Malone among them, who don't shoot technical fouls, but who are averaging 26 or 27 points a game. If they were allowed to shoot the technical fouls, and these were added to their stats, they would average as much as Jordan. If I had shot the technical fouls for my team, athough I was so bad they wouldn't have dared let me, and assuming I had attempted as few as five per game, at my little 50 percent rate I would have earned a lifetime average of about 34 points instead of 31, making my average the all time best. Points *do* make a difference.

I have just witnessed a playoff game in which the total at half time was 68 points—that's right, *68 points*— and that's not for *one* of the teams, it's for *both*. The final score was equally abysmal. That's an average of 34 points per team for the half, or 17 points per quarter. Hey, high school teams score more points than these guys did! Unfortunately, scores of this sort are becoming the rule rather than the exception. There just don't seem to be enough players who can score points any more.

When I told one of my friends that I was writing a book, he told me not to forget to mention the rituals that have become an expected part of today's game. We are talking here about the chest-thumping after each field goal, and the hand-touching and slapping after each trip to the foul line, whether the foul shot is made or not.

I'm not sure what these routines are all about or why they are universally done. I *am* sure that, even without them, the player in question knows that his team is rooting for him. Capers like these have the effect of breaking concentration at the line. What's more, they destroy the rhythm of the game. That bumping of the chest seems to me like some kind of Tarzan impersonation, a totally adolescent behavior—kids doing their thing.

Thinking back a few years, I can see it now. Picture *my* teammates coming up to *me* and slapping me on the hand as I stood on the foul line to make a shot. No doubt about it. I would have punched them out for interrupting what little bit of concentration I possessed.

We take for granted that professional athletes will score points and touchdowns, and that they will make simple catches. These are the things they are paid to do. The self-congratulatory capers that today's athletes perform after scoring a point or touchdown or after making a simple catch are the antics of immature kids, *not* the actions of true professionals.

The real greats among today's players still act like the true professionals they are; *no* shenanigans! Check out the actions of Barry Sanders of the Detroit Lions after a 60-yard run, or the behavior of San Francisco's Jerry Rice after he's caught a long pass. No show-off stuff. Just real pros, all the way.

---

## WILTISM

THOU SHOULDST ALWAYS REMEMBER THAT
FEELING TOO EMOTIONALLY HIGH AFTER A WIN
OFTEN BRINGS A DOUBLY DEEP LOW AFTER A LOSS.
AS THE WIZARD OF WESTWOOD WOULD SAY,
"STAY ON AN EVEN KEEL; THAT'S BY FAR THE
BEST DEAL."

---

Going back to basics is not a bad idea. Take, for
instance, the Portland Trail Blazer's Lithuanian player,
Arvydas Sabonis, a player who, in my opinion, should have
been named rookie of the year. After playing for 10 or 15
years in Europe, where he was an outstanding player, he
came here to play in the NBA, supposedly the *creme de la
creme* of world basketball. Here, at about 34-years-old and
in spite of two bad knees, Sabonis is tearing most of our
centers apart. He is able to do this because his play is
fundamentally sound.

Sabonis learned his game from old tapes of how we
used to play back in the '50s and '60s, and was taught by
European coaches who learned their games from us. Even
with a tired old body, he brought that old-fashioned game
over here where he has become a standout player. He has
done this at an age when most athletes have stopped playing
altogether, and with physical challenges that would have
kept most of us on the sidelines. Using a sound knowledge
of the game, he has made himself look better than most
players who are younger and in far better physical shape.

I frequently hear phrases spoken by sports figures today that, during my entire career of more than three decades, I never heard used by anyone. It is not uncommon nowadays to hear a player say, "One of us will have to go!" meaning, "It's either the coach or me. If he's here next year, I'm gone."

We also hear of coaches voicing similar sentiments during contract negotiations: "I want more money, a 100-year contract plus a good percentage of the ownership of this franchise." This happens, of course, only if they have won the Super Bowl or the World Championship during the past year or, perhaps, a number of years earlier as occurred with coaches Pat Riley of the Lakers and Jimmy Johnson of Dallas. These coaches apparently forget that by winning, they did no more than what they were hired to do: win—especially the big ones. If they expect more for doing only what they are paid to do, I wonder what they might be willing to give up when they don't produce that championship?

Today's professional athletes often appear to be looking for reasons to stay *off* the court. They take games off without hesitation, but grab that paycheck without reservation. It was different for me. I used to try to find every reason possible to be *on* the court—even when I probably should not have been there. This little tale will explain what I mean.

During one of my years in basketball I missed a good part of the regular season due to a ruptured patellar tendon (the major tendon in your knee) and ligament damage. I was in a full leg cast for four and a half months, but still managed to play in the post season, and helped to lead my team to the finals. (Unfortunately, we lost to the Knicks). I lost so much time that I actually have a hard time counting

73

this as a playing year, and still feel embarrassed to call it a whole season, although many of today's jocks would probably look at it differently.

I was told, after my injury, that I probably would not play again, or if I did, only after a couple of years. But thanks to a good team of doctors and a lot of hard work in rehabilitation, I returned to play at the earliest date I could, even though going back to the game so soon meant that I could easily get hurt again.

Many of today's athletes do not regard injuries in the same way. They won't compete with even the slightest injury. They are not about to risk shortening their careers — not with all the dough they're making these years. Come to think of it, maybe they are smarter than I was: I only wanted to play, but they're looking for the easiest way to stay.

## My "All-Time Best" Team

The next few pages are for those of you who have repeatedly asked me which team I believe to have been the greatest in basketball history. I am going to give you my choice and my reasons for making it, even though this is not an issue that I tend to get very excited about.

Two of the NBA teams I played on during my professional career have, at one time or another, been considered to be the "best ever." Actually, *three* of my teams earned that distinction. The third was the Harlem Globetrotters, a team that for a long period of time was considered the best anywhere in the world. (Actually, now that I think of it, there was a team that I played with when I was just fifteen that was also tremendously gifted with sensational players.) But of the two NBA teams, my personal choice has always been the 1967 Philadelphia 76ers.

My rationale for choosing the 76ers is very simple: it's all about *players, coaches* and *time*. First, let's talk about players. The 1967 Philadelphia 76ers were a far better team than my 1972 Laker team. Why? It's simple: I was five years younger as were many of the stars of that team. In 1972, I was a part of an "over-the-hill gang." A team that was picked by the experts to only finish fourth in our division, behind Golden State, Seattle, and, as I recall, either Phoenix or Houston.

The personnel of the 1967 Philadelphia 76ers were truly gifted. On our front line we had Chet Walker, six foot-eight, and the top one-on-one forward in the league. Our other forward, the epitome of what a power forward should be, was six-foot-nine Luke Jackson, two hundred sixty-five pounds of raw steel—no fat at all. Luke had an attitude to go with his physique, but had a soft and gifted shooting touch.

Our guards were Hal Greer and Larry Costello. Greer was one of the premier jump shooters in the history of the league. His jump shot was so effective, in fact, that he is the only man still remembered for shooting jump shots for his foul shots. Larry Costello was a tough, two-handed set shot artist who could shoot from anywhere on the floor, and he was also known to be an aggressive defensive player.

Off the bench came a gutty and torrid scorer, Hall of Famer, Bill Cunningham. Cunningham was *instant offense,* and he enjoyed his role like no other player I have ever known. We went half the season with only three losses, but then we lost Costello for the remainder of the season. His position was filled by Wali Jones, who became our heart and soul, as well as our stand-up comedian. Like Costello, he could shoot from anywhere on the floor and was a tremendous defensive player.

When I was young, I did play on other teams as gifted with pure talent, but those seven guys, with Alex Hannum at the helm, were, in my humble opinion, the greatest team to ever play basketball in the NBA.

P. S. No team in the history of sports ever achieved so much with so little as did the 1972 World Champion Los Angeles Lakers. The only true star we had was coach Bill Sharman. The rest of us just played above and beyond the call of duty—and then some.

I once heard a collegiate player say, while talking with a friend about the pro game, "You know, I've played against some pros and I can tell you, the pro game is not hard. Their game is like a one-on-one or a two-on-two. There aren't any real systems that one has to follow, so it's a very easy game to play."

This remark is indicative of what has happened to the professional game over time. Instead of being a game with a number of different things happening, it's helter skelter and bump and dunk—not really a system that one has to learn. Simplification may seem to have improved the game from a technical point of view, but it has been carried to a point where the complexity and intrigue that used to be there are gone.

When I thought about choosing my "greatest team," I quickly realized that the teams of the past were clearly superior to those of more recent years—and not because the athletes were that much better. The superiority of teams of the past was due to the type of systems we were allowed to play.

Fans today are looking for a far different kind of game. They want to see a show, and care little about the technical part of the game. They have accepted a lesser game from the jocks in exchange for more entertainment, and the entertainment they are paying for consists not of a good technical game, but a show.

If we want purely entertainment—a Globetrotter type of league—that's something different. We could have eight teams all imitating the Globetrotters and competing to determine who can outshine the others in showmanship. That's a different type of basketball, of course, but maybe it's something we should think about. A Globetrotter league. (Actually, it's almost here.)

Here are a few of the reasons why I claim that my time in sports was the golden era. In football they played both offense and defense—beginning to end, while baseball players had no trouble hitting at least three-ten. Boxers could move, jab, and take one on the chin. Owners cared more; to the players they were friends. The fans were behind us as long as we tried, and wanted us on their team until the day we died. Hockey players seemed to have no fear; we won't see another Rocket Richard or Gordie Howe for many a year. Today's players' attitude of "in your face," during my time simply had no place. Basketball players had style and zest, and made no commercials claiming they were the best. *You're right on, Wiltie—and there are 1,000 reasons more; but I'd better stop now before I become a bore.*

*To go with your food, here is some wine for thought: Vintage wine is made when the little old winemaker does his thing with grapes grown in the very best years—vintage years. In sports, too, there are vintage years, and many of the best sports grapes were harvested some years ago.*

I have just returned from the October, 1996 convocation that was held to celebrate the fiftieth anniversary of the NBA and to honor the fifty most outstanding people in the history of basketball. I am pleased to report, in case you missed the event, that I had the distinction of being among those so honored. I also participated as one of the panel members who voted on the list of candidates, though I must confess, in all fairness, that there were others on the voting panel: some other ex-pros, some sports writers, plus others who have been close to the game.

I was proud to have been included, of course, but I must tell you that some very deserving candidates were left off of the final list. Something is seriously remiss when Shaquille O'Neal, with only four or five years of pro basketball activity, was included, while Bob McAdoo, with his impressive credentials and many years of professional play, did not make the cut. And, unfortunately, McAdoo is just one of the several greats who, though they had most decidedly earned a spot on the top-fifty list, were overlooked.

Could that old bugaboo, politics, have reared its ugly head? I'll probably never know for sure. I stand by my own choices, however, and hope to discuss them later on during radio and TV interviews. Stay tuned.

Here is an example of how we "oldtimers" are treated with a definite lack of consideration. Through my attorney, Seymour Goldberg, I received today a request from Laura Adler of Independent Casting, asking me to make a cameo appearance in a movie—". . . as a favor with no money involved." The film is a Warner Brothers production that is tentatively titled, *Steel*. I am to do one scene with none other than Shaquille O'Neal. Ladies and gentlemen, I am sure you are quite aware of how much money Shaq is making (mo money and mo money—over $50 million a year, I hear), but I am to do this ". . . as a favor with no money involved." And, on my birthday no less!

## WILTISM

ALL YOU PLAYERS NOW BASKING IN THE SUN: IT WILL NOT BE LONG BEFORE YOUR DAY IS DONE. SO BE MORE RESPECTFUL WHILE YOU'RE IN YOUR PRIME; YOU'LL JOIN THE RANKS OF THE "ONCE-GREATS" IN TIME.

Here I am learning the game from the University of Kansas Coach, Dr. Phog Allen. Dr. Allen was taught by the originator of the game, Dr. James Naismith.

# THREE

## ME: NUMBER THIRTEEN

In this chapter, I'm going to talk about some of the players, coaches, owners and members of the press, singling them out by name and deed; but before I do, I'd like to tell you a little about yours truly.

First of all, and for the record, I admit my share of responsibility for a great deal of what has been happening in sports, as I most definitely made a contribution to the mess we are currently in.

In my early days of playing pro basketball, I had a reputation for being different. To many, being "different" meant I didn't get along with my coaches and the other players. I was considered a loner, and because I scored a lot of points, they thought I was selfish. In addition, because my teams didn't consistently win the world championship, I was thought to care only about my stats and nothing else.

It was said that I missed practices often, and I was accused by Dolph Schayes and others of practicing foul shooting less than I should. Dolph, who later became my coach, was fond of saying, "Anyone who practices one hundred shots or more a day could easily shoot 75 percent." While that might have been true for *him* (Dolph was a great foul shooter), for many basketball players, shooting 75 percent is not that easy.

But back to bad Wilt. I must confess that I *was* different, just as was implied by the title of my first book, *Wilt, Just Like Any Other Seven-Foot Black Millionaire Who Lives Next Door.* Different I will always be, no matter in what era, but now I want to talk about the characteristics that earned me a "bad" label in my day.

Money! I had it, I demanded it, and I commanded it. Yes, I was the father of the big dollar, and made six figures long before the rest. I recall that when I was only a high school kid working as a bellhop at Kutsher's Country Club in the Catskills (and making what I thought was big money) I told Haskell Cohen that I would make six figures when I got to the NBA. Haskell, then the publicity director of the National Basketball Association, promptly retorted, "You're crazy, Wilt. It will never happen."

As I approached my first year in the NBA, the highest paid players were Bob Cousy of the Boston Celtics and Bob Pettit of the St. Louis Hawks. Each was making $22,500—and those guys were the stars of the league! So how could someone like me hope to make six figures? No wonder Cohen said it was impossible. Yet I persisted, saying. "Where there's a Wilt, there's a way." And in my first year I did, indeed, sign a six-figure contract, with bonuses.

Until I came along, media coverage of basketball had been extremely limited. I helped to raise attendance by 28 percent in my first year alone, and brought the NBA to worldwide attention. For that reason alone, I felt that I deserved the salary I asked for—even though deep down inside, I didn't believe that *anyone*, including myself, deserved (or would ever be paid) that kind of money just for playing a silly game of basketball.

We didn't have agents in those days (at least *I* didn't have one), and when I first met with the guy they called "the mogul," Eddie Gottlieb, I was on my own. Eddie was an owner and one of the originators of the NBA, and we were there to talk contract terms. I had just finished a year on the road with Abe Saperstein and the Harlem Globetrotters for which I had been paid a great deal of money—$65,000. Knowing I could always go back to the Trotters was my ace in the hole in my negotiations with the NBA. (The newly-formed European league had made overtures to me as well, and I must admit that living abroad and playing in Europe appealed strongly to the romantic in me.)

Gottlieb and I sat down to discuss salaries and the number of years I should sign for. I told him at the very beginning, "One year, sir. Just one year at a time. You might not like me or my game, and I might not like you or your team." That was a fairly bold starting point for a young player.

As the numbers began to escalate, I couldn't hold back a grin, and then I actually began to laugh. I couldn't believe how much they were willing to pay. Gottlieb thought my laughter was an expression of disdain, and his offers went up, up and up. I was dealing with one of the shrewdest men in sports, yet when I emerged from the meeting I had acquired a reputation as being in a class of my own when it came to negotiations. (Perhaps now you can understand why I have mixed feelings when I read the salary numbers that are reported for some of our present day stars.)

Yes. I, too, was one of those bad kids. But I was different. I always made a point of waiting until camp time was almost at hand before starting negotiations for my new contract. My reasons were sound. I would hem, haw and hedge until training was at least half over before coming to terms with the team owner, thus missing all those boring twice-a-day practices. Getting in shape was never an issue because I played basketball all year around. Each year after the NBA season was over, I joined the Trotters, and I also played in the schoolyards of many of the major cities of this great country.

Don't get me wrong. To a certain extent, I did enjoy practicing. I also got egotistical pleasure in performing with my teammates—showing them how fast I was by beating them in sprints, and always outdoing them in the various exercises the coaches had us go through. I even enjoyed shooting foul shots in practice, making nine out of ten most of the time. I really *could* shoot free throws; I just couldn't consistently make them during the games. If you don't believe me about all this, ask some of my old teammates: Tom Gola, Paul Arizin, Guy Rodgers or Al Attles. (I think they are all still alive, but "old timer's" memory may have set in for some of them.)

I'll admit that I missed some of our pre-season practice sessions (a result of my leisurely approach to finalizing my contract each year), but I earned a reputation for not showing up to practice at *any* time, or for coming to practice only when I wanted to. That's just not true, but the myth has persisted, nonetheless.

The belief that I consistently dodged practice sessions was bolstered one morning while I was playing for the Philadelphia 76ers. I did not show up for what was called a "shootaround" that had been called by Dolph Schayes, my head coach. A member of the press who happened to be there asked the coach where I was. At that time I was living in New York City and commuting a hundred miles or so every day for games and practices.

On this particular occasion, I had asked Dolph if I could be excused from the shootaround so that I could get some much-needed sleep before the evening game. Since the practice was going to be only a 15 to 20 minute shootaround and the game that night was to be in Philadelphia, Dolph had agreed. He was aware of my sleeping habits and knew that the request was not out of line, but for some odd reason, when asked by the reporter why I was not at practice, Dolph said that he didn't know. This remark, when reported in the press, only added fuel to Wilt's no-practice myth.

I should point out in my own defense that, although I didn't consistently enjoy practice, I did adhere to the rules and regulations of the coaches I was involved with. This, of course, is not true of many players today.

Before I forget, here's one more story about Dolph Schayes, the coach who forgot to tell the press that he had given me permission to miss the shootaround. Dolph was, himself, a basketball player of great renown, and it was he, during his playing days, who was quoted as saying that anyone with the right practice habits could shoot 75 percent from the foul line.

Dolph became my mentor on the foul line, and either before or after each practice session we would shoot and shoot, and shoot. I shot brilliantly in practice, but unfortunately, during that season I posted my most horrendous foul shot percentage—something like 37 percent (15 to 20 percent lower than before Dolph became my mentor.) Who knows; maybe I was just trying to show him that he didn't know beans about practice making perfect. *But thirty-seven percent; can you believe that, Wiltie?* No, I can't.

After that foul-shooting debacle, I even went to a psychologist to see if *he* could help me. I was in therapy for a couple of months, going once a week for two-hour sessions. The result: he became a brilliant foul shooter, and I learned how to analyze people.

I freely confess to a number of bad-boy acts, although I never pulled one quite like the incident, reported in *Sports Illustrated*, that involved a New Jersey Nets practice session. Reasoning that they were only going to shoot the ball for a short while, and since no running is required for shooting, Kenny Anderson refused to tie his shoes during practice. This is nothing but childishness: "I don't want to tie my shoes, Mommie." These guys aren't bad—just kids. You give them a slap on the rear and send them to bed without their favorite girlfriend.

The idea that I was an intimidating player is a bunch of bull. Intimidating to whom? To the other teams, perhaps, but never to players on my own team. To them, I was only a teammate who stood ready to do whatever was needed to win. That's why I was willing to pass the ball off, taking only a single shot in some games. *As long as we won, that was the fun. It didn't matter whether I took sixty shots or one.*

One final item relative to my bad boy image. It was said that I did not like my coaches and that I got them all fired. That's the one that hurts the most.

I had a number of coaches—seven to be exact. The first was Neil Johnston of the Philadelphia Warriors, a good basketball center. At the time he started coaching, Neil had maybe a year or two of pro basketball playing left in him, but I was to become his replacement as center.

You need to understand, that during my playing days, owners felt a strong obligation to their players. I dare say this kind of thinking by owners is pretty much obsolete today, but in that era they made sure that things were all right in their player's lives. So, knowing Neil would get very little chance to play behind me, Gottlieb, the owner, gave him the chance to become coach of the team. Neil's coaching job was meant to be temporary—just long enough for him to make some money and get on his feet financially. He was hired to be fired in two seasons, no matter who was on the team.

This plan turned out to be a big mistake. Neil's selection as coach was doomed from the start. (Gottlieb admitted as much to me later, saying he would always regret his decision.) What Gottlieb did not realize at the time was that, of all available coaching choices, Neil was the one who would be the least enamored of me. I had played against him a few years earlier, and used to consistently kick his butt in two-on-two or three-on-three pick-up games. Unfortunately for our relationship, Neil was at that time the leading scorer and rebounder in the best basketball league in the world—the NBA—and I was still in high school, just an upstart kid. I was blocking his every shot and scoring at will at the other end—not a good way to make a friend! It doesn't take an Einstein to figure out that some years later, when I took over his job as a leading scorer and rebounder, I wasn't going to be his favorite player.

Frank McGuire of North Carolina University became my second coach. I learned to love McGuire like a father, brother and friend. He was the first professional coach who understood my unique problems and talent.

McGuire had been the coach of the North Carolina team that had beaten my Kansas team for the 1957 National

Championship by one point in the third overtime. We often used to talk about how he used four Tar Heels to guard me during most of that game, and on offense employed a stalling tactic with the ball. He told me that he had said to his team, "All we have to do is stop Mr. Chamberlain, and we can win this game." That is precisely what they focused on, and the rest is history. They won, and even though North Carolina had been ranked number one in the nation for the entire year, that was the beginning of my being tagged a "loser."

The Warriors were on the move and learning how to beat the great Boston Celtic teams when, unfortunately, both for Frank McGuire and for me, the team was sold to San Francisco. We had just posted a 30 and 10 record for the second half of the season, and we lost in the seventh game of the playoffs by just one point. We were looking forward to taking revenge during the upcoming season, but it was not to be. McGuire did not choose to follow the team to San Francisco, believing that the move would have been too hard on his son, Frankie, Jr., who had cerebral palsy.

The San Francisco group who bought the team had difficulty finding a good coach who was willing to relocate in California. Eventually, they talked to Bob Feerick, an ex-player from Baltimore who was living in San Francisco at the time. They asked him to coach the team for a year while they found a more permanent replacement. Feerick really did not want the job, but he did like the people who were asking for his help, so he agreed to accept their offer.

Feerick and I had a great relationship. Admitting that coaching was not his forte, he often told me, "Wilt, if it weren't for you, I don't know what I would do. You have helped me on and off the basketball court." Though I knew coaching was not one of his talents, I really liked Feerick. Just as with McGuire, I acquired a good friend, and when he left the following year, I knew I had lost someone close and dear.

After Feerick, the owners brought in "The Sarge," as we called him. I'm talking about none other than Alex Hannum, another ex-basketball player. Hannum had proven himself a great coach by winning the world championship with the St. Louis Hawks. He was tough and knew his stuff. We had our off moments, to be sure, but for the most part we got along splendidly because we had so much in common, both on and off the court. We both liked fast cars and fast boats, and we had fun together. When I was traded to the 76ers to play under Dolph Schayes, he followed a year and a half later to become the coach who led our team to a world championship—my first.

After the heartrending end of the 1968 season, I was ready to give up basketball, so I packed up and moved to the west coast to make a new start. My parents were living out there, and I enjoyed Southern California. There I met Jack Kent Cooke, owner of the Los Angeles Lakers. Jack talked me into playing for him, even though I wasn't sure how it would work out. Elgin Baylor, Jerry West and I would be on the same team, and with all of us being, as you might say, in the twilight of our careers, I had some misgivings.

They had a coach by the name of Butch van Breda Kolff. I think I may have called him, "Butch the Dumbkoff," but I no longer remember. (I've spent years trying to forget him.) Butch, as it developed, didn't care very much for me, either, and was not happy that I had become a member of the team.

From the very beginning, Butch and I were like oil and water. In our first press conference a reporter asked him, "How are you going to deal with Mr. Chamberlain? Do you think he'll be a problem?" Butch responded, "There will be no problems. I know how to handle him." I retorted, "You don't 'handle' people; you 'handle' animals. You *work* with people." From that moment on, I knew we would not get along, but I tried to do what I was asked to do. During that first season, Elgin Baylor's and Jerry West's averages stayed the same or rose, but my scoring average plummeted as I tried to help the team by doing other things.

After two years, Coach van Breda Kolff's contract was terminated and Joe Mullaney, a college coach from the east was brought in to coach the team for one year. Joe didn't enjoy being on the West coast, and returned to the east after he had fulfilled the terms of his one-year contract.

Then came Bill Sharman, the great former Boston Celtics guard. He and I had a wonderful time together, in spite of his wanting me to do a number of things that I downright didn't appreciate, unpleasant things such as getting up early in the morning for shootaround practices. In the end, however, we worked it all out, and we remain friends today.

That's my story on coaches. I never asked any owner to fire a coach and, unlike players of today, I *never* told anyone—owners, management or the media—that I wouldn't play if they didn't send some coach away.

On the other hand, as you probably know, many of today's athletes are rumored to have brought about the dismissal of their coaches. You will recall that even our great Laker leader, Magic Johnson, when he experienced problems with a coach in the '80s, made his feelings known—and the coach had to go.

I never believed in the practice of challenging owners either to trade me or to fire the coach. In fact, I was so sensitive about the firing of coaches that before we made the deal with L.A., when I was asked to stay and coach the

76ers, I refused, knowing that Alex would have to be dismissed. Because Alex was a friend of mine, I could in no way consider accepting that honor. Actually, at that time in my career I needed his kind of coaching. He was strong and intelligent, had little or no ego problem, and, as far as championships were concerned, he had been there, himself.

The stories of my having coaches fired are just not true. They are myths, and an unfair rap.

This is probably as good a place as any to talk about a more recent incident, one that added a postscript to my bad boy image. Five years or so ago, in a book I wrote titled, *A View From Above,* I had the audacity to use, as a figure of speech, the round number of 20,000 to illustrate (in a non-literal manner) that I had been involved in the world of sex in a way most men only dream of. I was not graphic, nor did I name names; in fact I said very little. As a writer, my aim was to get my point across—but in this case I may have overdone it. I indulged in hyperbole, deliberately choosing a number that I knew would get attention. Unfortunately, with the help of the media, every dunce in the world (especially those who found time to read *only* those few lines), took the number quite literally, not realizing it was a figure of speech.

I spoke as I did about that aspect of my personal history for two reasons. First, it was a way for me to avoid a more graphic description of my sex life. Second, I used it to move into a discussion of how sex rules the world. The number was never meant to promote promiscuity, especially on the part of today's youth.

The chapter as a whole dealt with a variety of relationships: the institution of marriage, mothers, feminine beauty, and integrity (among other things). I should have been more concerned about how my use of that figure of speech would be perceived, but in my defense, I suggest that those who read my book take note of that chapter's final two sentences: *"Most men would think it a great achievement if they could make love to a thousand different women. But I've come to believe the greater achievement would be to make love to the same woman a thousand times."*

I believe these words as firmly today as I did when I first wrote them. They are the essence of the point I really wanted to make, of course, but media people weren't interested in focusing on *those* words. They were overlooked as not worthy of media attention, coming from the likes of bad boy Wiltie. I should have remembered that no one roots for Goliath—and no one tells the truth about him, either.

I wouldn't for the world have denied the media an opportunity to have a good time at my expense. I do want them to know, however, that while they had fun with my twenty thousand encounters, *I* enjoyed them a lot more than the media did!

Peace!


P. S. I feel that I owe a sincere apology to any of my readers, fans or friends who may have thought that I used my book in bad taste in order to glorify my sexual exploits. That was never my purpose. I especially apologize if I have offended, even slightly, any of the women I now know, or those I have known. Though many among you were, in appearance, "a number," none of you were ever just a number to me.


Bad or good, everything has a beginning. There have been many individual stars in team sports, but I stood out literally and figuratively in an era when sports were beginning to make their tremendous impact on society. For better or for worse, I had a strong influence on how things played out in the sports world, and my actions were, in many cases, responsible for starting the trends that now cause us concern. Here is an example of how these things happened—an item that may have escaped your notice.

My sleeping habits were always much different from those of my fellow players. NBA games were usually over between 9:30 and 10:00 p.m. After 48 minutes of play (my customary pattern) I finished most games still wound up and unable to eat. Because it was thought best not to play on a full stomach, most of us avoided eating during the four hours before a game, waiting until after the game. But at the end of a game, I was never in a mood for food. I needed two or three hours to unwind, and it was usually midnight or 1:00 a.m. before I felt hungry and ready for a meal.

Unfortunately, after stuffing myself I couldn't sleep. I did a lot of reading (there being very few late shows on television in those days) or played cards and other kinds of games until three, four, or five o'clock in the morning—every morning. Then, for obvious reasons, getting up at seven or eight was just impossible for me. (That is why I fought the morning stuff.)

My time schedule in no way matched that of my fellow players. No one else made a habit of going to bed at five o'clock in the morning as I did. My eccentric sleeping habits, in fact, required that I have a single room. What player would want to be in a room with me while I was playing cards with the lights on at four o'clock in the morning?

When I started playing pro ball everybody, coaches and all, had roommates when the team was traveling. We had no trainers or business managers, but two to a room was the required arrangement. In view of my terrible sleeping habits, having a roommate just wasn't going to work. I let this be known to the owners and they made an exception in my case. (This is where I picked up the reputation of being a loner.)

Management gave all sorts of reasons to the rest of the team for why I was given solo status. They said my height required two beds (leaving no space for a roommate) and a lot of other such nonsense. Of course, these reasons were believed by no one, especially since there were other players on my team who were only an inch or two shorter than I was. In fact, many *taller* players on other teams had roommates.

My getting solo quarters caused a quiet rebellion by my teammates who began to request for themselves a single room like Wiltie had. Management was in a bind. So as not to show favoritism, they said, "Well, you guys who want to get a single may have one, but, like Wiltie, you'll pay the difference over the double-room price." Most of the players on my team were willing to pay their half-share difference and welcomed this opportunity for privacy. But some, for one reason or another (perhaps because they were cheap), chose to have roommates.

In my day, a professional basketball player didn't make much more, on average, than a good school teacher. That's right; they were paid $5,000 to $6,000 a year (or in this case, a season). That is hard to believe, I know; but what a difference a day or so makes!

All of this leads me to the main reason I accepted a major part of the responsibility for the downward spiral of professional sports—at least for the part that involves money. As I have said before, I demanded it, commanded it, and got it. Then, when others read about what they thought I was making, they, quite naturally, wanted more for themselves. The satisfied players who until then had been happy just to be playing pro basketball instead of working a nine-to-five job, all of a sudden became more interested in the dollar part of a contract than in how many years they could sign for.

I still get a kick out of the story about my friend (and by far the most valuable player on the world championship Boston Celtics team), Bill Russell. He made it known to his owners that whatever I made, he wanted a dollar more. That's right: one dollar more than whatever amount I signed for. When that number was announced as a whopping $100,000, the next day's Boston Globe headlines read, "Bill Russell Signs for $100,001, Making Him the Highest Paid Basketball Player in the World." That, I presume, pleased everyone concerned. Of course, I enjoyed my little private joke, knowing that I had actually signed for close to three times that amount.

Whether that was truly the amount they paid Bill is not the issue here. The point I am trying to make is that this incident started the "I am better than you because I am making more than you" syndrome.

There are certain comments that I hear over and over again. One of those that comes up most frequently refers to how much money I could have made if only I had come along a few years later: "God, Wiltie, you were just born a little too soon."

I used to reply that I was quite satisfied with having been born when I was. As it was, I made a great deal of money. Taking into account inflation, and all other things being equal, I did better than all right. But every once in a while, when I think of Patrick Ewing making eighteen-plus million in a season, it does occur to me that he is earning a quarter of a million dollars per game—*per game,* ladies and gentlemen. I didn't average that much *per year* in all the 14 years I played, even though I was the highest paid basketball player of my time.

Although dollars alone cannot—and do not—reflect the true value of an athlete, in my case the salary I was paid helped to point out something I've always been proud of: the consistency of my performance from the day I entered the league until my very last contract. From day one until my basketball-playing career was done, I was the league's highest paid player—a record no one else has ever matched.

I earned in my first year four or five times the salary of the highest paid players of that time. And, even though new superstars such as Kareem Abdul-Jabbar had made their entrance at the time I left professional basketball, I was still earning four to five times the salary of the other highest paid players. In order to command that kind of income, I had to consistently maintain a standard of excellence that fulfilled the expectations of myself and others.

Still, in all of my 14 full years put together I didn't earn as much money as Patrick Ewing makes in ten games. Ten games! Just in case you were wondering, and to save you some figuring, I played in about 1200 games, play-offs included. That means that Ewing makes more for each *game* than yours truly made in an average *year!*

*Hey, Wiltie, how much do you think you would you have made today? You weren't a bad player, and you filled the arenas wherever you went. You even drew people on street corners who came to watch your every step. And conversations would change (as they do even today) when you walked into a room. No matter what the subject might have been, talk would immediately turn to height and basketball. You truly had the ability to get people to focus*

96

*on you and whatever you were involved with. This quality is called "drawing power."*

I do wonder what someone like Wilt Chamberlain or Babe Ruth could earn today, and from time to time I have tried to estimate what my services might bring in today's market.

I could start with the $2.5 million per year that John Koncak was paid a few years ago when he became a free agent, then compare *his* stats with *mine* for one of my good years. (To be entirely fair, since Koncak has never won anything, I'll use one of my non-championship years.) Then, on a pro rata basis, we could come up with what I might have been worth.

Oh, man!! When Koncak got the $2.5 million a year contract, his stats were three rebounds and four points a game. My stats were approximately 15 times greater than his in these two areas alone, never mind blocked shots and assists or intangibles such as drawing power. Multiplying his salary by 15 times equates to $37 million a year. But in today's "kiddy jock" world, the owners would first offer me $185 million for five years. That figure would prompt me to roll my eyes, stamp my size 14 1/2 Nikes' (the average size shoe worn by NBA players today) and reply, "Are you kidding? I won't get out of bed for less then $200 million." (Note: the key word in my retort is "kidding;" we are back to that kid stuff again.) I would also remind them that because I am already making $50 million a season from my Nike contract, I really don't need them anyhow.

All kidding aside, what owner in full possession of his faculties would pay Koncak that kind of money just because he became a free agent? Matter of fact, who would give a damn? The only money he'd ever receive from me is Greyhound fare to anywhere, just as long as he got out of my hair.

I received a Christmas card last year that had on its front a picture of three people at a sports event: me, the guy who sent the card, and one of his friends. In the note that accompanied the card, the sender wrote that he didn't recall a front line (two forwards and a center) of any of the present 27 teams in the NBA that had averaged as much in the current year as I did in 1962—50.4 points and 25.5 rebounds a game for the entire season. *That is not me bragging, WIltie. It's just my friend bringing out a fact about today's game and players.*

Here is some data for you basketball buffs, just to let you know what Wilt Chamberlain was in his prime.

Take a guy who scored one-third more points than the great Michael Jordan; had twice as many rebounds as Dennis Rodman; and, playing center position, was high on the assist list for many years. He even led the league in assists for one of those years, a feat never accomplished by anyone other than a guard. (Remember, neither Rodman or Jordan ever led their own team in assists—never mind leading the league.) Summing it up, this player each year topped the best of his contemporaries in the three or four areas that are considered most important.

According to Harvey Pollack's unauthorized stats, this guy, Chamberlain, doubled Bill Russell's blocked shot total (official block shot records were not kept until a year after Chamberlain retired), and he led the league in field goals during 12 of his 14 years in NBA basketball, placing second one of the other years, and third or fourth in the remaining year.

His endurance credentials were superior to those of anyone in any known team sport: one year he averaged 48.4 minutes of play per game, and after playing 51 consecutive complete games, he missed only six minutes of the 52nd. And during all this time, he never fouled out of a game.

That was Wilt in his prime.

In case you contemporary basketball buffs might be thinking that I had no competition, following is a list that includes every center I played against. Those on the first list are the players who have been elected to the Hall of Fame. (Some of these men were voted in after my retirement in 1973-74, but I had played against all of them.) The second list includes the names of greats whom I have competed against, but who have not been honored by Hall of Fame status (though, of course, they may be elected at some time in the future.)

Hall of Fame Honorees

Clyde Lovellette

Bill Russell

Kareem Abdul-Jabbar

Bob Lanier

Bob McAdoo

Dave Cowens

Walt Bellamy

Wes Unsel

Nate Thurmond

Bob Pettit

Elvin Hayes

Jerry Lucas

Dolph Schayes

Other Greats (Potential Honorees)

Spencer Haywood—a great all-around basketball player

Johnny "Red" Kerr—the most intelligent center I ever played against

Paul Silas—a tremendous rebounder

Elmore Smith—one of the all-time best shot-blockers

Clifford Ray—led the Golden State Warriors to their first World Championship (he took over for Nate Thurmond who couldn't quite do it)

Clyde Lee—a capable center

Bob Rule—a fine all-around player

Leroy Ellis—fast and athletic

Zelmo Beaty—an all-around great center

Wayne Embry—as strong as they come

Kenny Sears–a superb shooter

Walter Dukes—the first seven-foot, fast, athletic-type center in the NBA

Thomas Boerwinkle—an imposing Chicago Bulls center

Even though the players on the second list never made the Hall of Fame, they were great centers. But how could you newer fans ever know about them? Present day media and announcers never mention their names or tell you about their games. That is why it is important that announcers and fans learn our history.

This list as a whole should give the skeptical reader a fair idea of the caliber of Wilt Chamberlain's competition, yet many of today's sportscasters claim that I had no one to face when I was playing. Come to think of it, there have been few Hall of Fame centers, if any, whom I did *not* play against. And we didn't play each other just once or twice a year; we played some 12 or 13 times during a given season.

I don't know of an athlete who has faced tougher competition. In the minds of many, Bill Russell was the winningest and greatest defensive player of all, and Kareem Abdul-Jabbar is the leading scorer and number one All-Star of all time. These two players alone should be enough to establish the level of my competition.

Someone should tell the world about the greats of yesterday. It's a shame that we hear no consistent reminders of their prowess from the media. Too bad, as well, that there is no available footage of their games.

Why do people always stare and give a hard time to tall people, but not to heavy people? My theory is that when you are tall, most people have to look up to you whether they want to or not, and that pisses them off.

I like being tall. It puts me farther away, literally and figuratively, from so many assholes. Another advantage of being vertically gifted is that, since hot air rises, a tall person is always going to be warmer than anyone else. (If it gets too warm, you can always sit down.) And, as an added bonus, in an elevator, your nose isn't always in a smelly armpit, although other people's noses may be in yours).


Life has always been recursive and circular, which I find rather ironic, since I am a part of the history I am writing about. Let me explain what I mean.

Since the beginning of time, the establishment has opposed ideas which they didn't fully understand or which threatened their beliefs. Galileo almost had his eye plucked out because his use of the telescope threatened the beliefs of the church. His stars were not in the kind of heavens that the church wanted people to believe in. For this and other reasons, his life was often threatened.

My life has never been in jeopardy because of the things I did, but they did try to stop me in other ways. There were even headlines proclaiming that I was the possible ruination of basketball. Out of fear that this could happen, they took out of the game some of the things that I was able to do best, and rules were put in place to keep me from doing the things that were in my power to do.

Changes were inevitable from the time I first started playing college ball, and started right after the first three games of my sophomore year. (Freshmen were not allowed to play varsity ball.) The University of Kansas, my team, won easily. It was then that the opposition knew they could not contain or control what was in my power to do. I averaged nearly 50 points in those first three games, and completely demoralized the opposition by grabbing balls out of the air on defense, a move that was rather like blocking a shot and rebounding at the same time. They (the powers that be in basketball) knew that unless something was done, for the other teams, basketball would be no fun—and they started their legislation against yours truly. To keep me away from the ball, they tried it all; but the boring result was a constant stall.

Here are a few of the goodies that were initiated over a period of years in order to put clamps on my abilities. First, the "widening of the lane" rule. No, the lane wasn't always 18 feet wide; it used to be about half that size. (As a matter of fact, they've changed its dimension twice.) They thought the wider lane would keep me farther from the basket and prevent my being such a prolific scorer. But the majority of my scoring was not being done close to the basket. So, after I had scored 38 points a game during my second year as a pro, the NBA widened the lane a second time, this time to 18 feet. They thought that might be the answer to their problem, but they were doomed to disappointment. I went from 38 points to 50 points a game. And if that doesn't tell you something, nothing will.

The year before the second lane-width change, they took away offensive goaltending. For those of you who don't quite understand what that term means, let me explain. When a player tosses a ball in the direction of the basket in order for Shaquille O'Neal to go up and dunk it, that's called a lob-pass. In my day, we used a similar move. My teammates used to actually shoot the ball so that I could go up and get it. That way we had two chances to score: either the first player made the shot, or I grabbed the ball, myself, and put it in.

Have you ever seen Shaquille O'Neal shoot jumpshots like this? I don't think so!

103

This was a move which required both jumping ability and timing. Since I excelled in using it, the maneuver was outlawed. No longer, except in international basketball, can one offensively goaltend or touch the ball on the rim.

Figure for yourself how high this sergeant jump is as I casually look down on a bar that is almost 7 feet high. This award winning shot from the Brussels, Belgium World's Fair shows me over 4 feet off the ground. But was I going up or coming down? Think about it when you hear that Air Jordan has a 41 inch sergeant jump.

A year earlier, back in my college days, when my teammates took the ball out of bounds from behind the basket, they would throw it over the backboard. I would jump 50 inches or so off the ground to guide the ball into the basket or dunk it as it came over the backboard. No one else could come close to touching the ball. You-know-who (the powers that be) knew that something had to be done about *that* play, so they outlawed "passing the ball over the backboard." No longer could a player pass the ball from behind the backboard before throwing the ball inbound. He had to first move to one side of the backboard or the other. The backboard could not be used as a shield, and Wilt Chamberlain could no longer jump up and have the ball all to himself.

Another rule change deprived me of using one of my other skills. They disallowed dunking from the foul line, a maneuver that required not only a great deal of agility, but considerable jumping ability. I sometimes laugh about this one today, but in another sense, I still feel angry about it. In college, I was a world class high jumper and triple jumper, and, as a result, I had a unique way of shooting free throws. I was able, from within the half-circle and behind the foul line (which is 15 feet from the basket), to jump-glide through the air and put the ball into the basket before my feet touched the floor. That was considered a legal play as long as the ball went through the hoop before the player's feet touched the floor.

When it became known during my freshman year that I was able to dunk the ball from behind the foul line, they knew that something had to be done or I would be able to make 99.9 percent of my free throws. So, they outlawed dunking the basketball from the foul line when shooting free throws. As no one else had been able to dunk the basketball from inside the half-circle, it was fairly clear that this rule change was a direct jab at my own personal chin.

I would have thought that almost everyone would enjoy watching a young, skinny, seven-foot college player perform this feat, simply as an exhibition of athleticism. The pros at that time were drooling to have me join them to do just that. Instead, I went to the Globetrotters where I had fun dunking the ball from wherever I pleased.

We've recently seen the likes of Jordan and Dr. J do an increased amount of dunking the ball from around the foul line. They go back to the half court line, run, then make a running jump to dunk the ball. Those explosions bring the crowds down out of the stands. They have used this maneuver to win slam-dunk contests at the NBA All-Star games, scoring perfect tens before enthusiastic audiences.

*As a freshman, I did this 10 or 15 times a night, but then they said, "That is not right!" even though Kansans watched with delight.*

I sit back and smirk when I see this move being executed by Brent Barry. He won a dunking contest by doing it my way—a dunk from just behind the foul line. Of course he had to get momentum up by going to the far end and sprinting the length of the court before taking off. (Dr. J and Jordan were over the line when they took off to dunk the ball, which would have made the foul shot no good.)

Strangely enough, it was a non rule—the no-clock rule—that gave me the most problems. Under this regulation (since there was no clock) the teams that faced me were allowed to hold the ball forever, and ever, and ever, and ever—amen. As a result, many times during my sophomore and junior years in college, game scores were in the '30s and '40s The opposing teams knew, and they were right, that the only way they could possibly win was to hold the ball. In their place, I would have done the same thing. But this was no longer basketball for me. All I could do was play "go find the ball." I did just that, and even under those conditions, we won a great many games.

I had other problems, as well. When they weren't holding the ball from me on offense, they were using three and four people to guard me on defense. Even so, I was able to average 32 points a game, standing second in the nation one year and third the other. I led my team, the Jayhawks, to a one-point triple-overtime defeat of the number-one team in the nation, North Carolina, even though that team, like all the rest, held the ball as much as they were able and used four men to guard me the entire game.

None of the other great athletes, not Adbul-Jabbar (at that time, Lew Alcindor) or Bill Walton of UCLA, had to worry about the opposition holding the ball against them or about being guarded by four men at a time. I remember watching Bill, in a game against Memphis, score an unbelievable string of field goals—something like 21 out of 22—the greatest shooting exhibition I have ever seen by a college player. And the dumb SOBs' playing against him wouldn't put even two guys on him—only one. He literally tore them apart. The same thing is happening right now with MJ. Instead of putting four guys on him, opposing teams persist in trying to guard him with just one. Will they ever learn?

Here is a P.S. for those of you who criticized my foul shooting (though you had a perfect right to do so). I grant that in the pros I was one of the worst foul shooters ever to come down the pike, but if you had been able to see some of my high school stats you would have been sure that it was a different Wilton Norman Chamberlain who was shooting fouls. I shot 85 and 90 percent in many, many games. Not only do I have the stats to prove it, I have the clippings as well.

When I came into the NBA, there was a rule allowing a player to waive the foul—to choose to shoot it or not. (Logically enough, this was called the "waive-foul rule.") It was put in place to discourage the fouling which had become excessive in the latter part of many games. Knowing, as you do, that in the pros I was *not* renowned as a foul shooter, you've probably guessed by now what happened. They did away with the waive-foul rule.

Sorry, Shaq (and other less-than-perfect foul shooters); the fans are forced to watch you miss and miss—thanks to repeal of the waive-foul rule.

---

## Wiltism

**I HAVE RARELY REGRETTED THINGS I HAVE DONE, BUT I HAVE OFTEN REGRETTED THOSE LEFT UNDONE. I AM WORKING ON CHANGING THIS.**

---

A word or two here about records. While I was playing, there were only five major record categories: rebounding, assists, field-goal percentage, foul-shooting percentage and scoring. I led in three, and sometimes four, of these categories during almost every one of my 13 full years (14, if I count my injured year, in which I played only 15 or 20 games).

As I look back, I am always amazed that I was so consistently able to win at least three out of five of those leading honors: scoring, rebounding and field goal shooting percentage. I once even led the league in assists—my favorite record. Why was this one so special? Because it has never before or since, been won by anyone other than a guard. It is not hard to understand why this is so. A guard, after all, controls the tempo of the game and where the ball is sent. This means that, while a guard may have had the ball close to ninety percent of the offensive time, I, as center, might have had the ball only five percent of the time.

Michael Jordan has never led his team in assists, although, for a guard who is able to control the ball, this would not seem to be that difficult a feat. I, being a center, had limited opportunity to pile up assists. *That* is why I am so proud of the year I earned the assists record.

I want to sincerely congratulate Michael Jordan for achieving eight consecutive scoring championships and for breaking my record of seven in a row. Strangely enough, though, I got more ink out of his approaching my scoring record during the last two or three years than I ever got while I was setting it. Many of my records have been broken, and many are still alive, but the only real attention I have ever received from most of them has been when someone else was approaching or about to break them. Then those records are useful in illuminating the record-breaker's career, and helping people to realize how truly outstanding a player he is.

Funny, though; when I set my 100 records, no one used them as a barometer to establish *my* greatness. It would always be said, "Oh, yeah, but he didn't win any world championships; Bill Russell won them all." Yet now, breaking one of my records is highlighted as one of the greatest things a player could possibly do.

It's ironic, too, that my records weren't even used to illuminate some of the things that I did exceptionally well. They weren't reported in such a way that people were even aware of what had been done. When I got 55 rebounds in one match (which I think is a pretty tremendous record), no one read in the headlines about it. I didn't make the cover of Sports Illustrated, either. But now, when Rodman gets 20 rebounds, it's headline material.

To be honest, I don't have a clue as to who held the record before I got the 55 rebounds. I might even have broken one of my own records, or maybe Bill Russell's. I don't know, and neither does anyone else. It's a fact of life, I guess, that until somebody approaches a record, you hear very little about it. Case in point: I'll wager you didn't know I owned that record until I told you about it just now. And if you did know, I'll bet you can't tell me what the record was (and I'm not going to tell you).

Whether it was Kareem's breaking my scoring record, or Michael and his team's breaking my team's win-loss record, I am certain you heard about it over and over again. In fact, when Kareem broke my scoring record there were parties of all kinds. I went, myself, along with the rest of the world, to an affair at the Forum as he received gifts and congratulations for his incredible achievement in breaking such a daunting record. (When I set the record, I didn't get as much as a popsicle.)

## CONTROLLING THE GAME

One of my reasons for writing this book is to bring to those who read it my opinions about the accomplishments of certain players and how they have contributed to the game of basketball. I will, at the conclusion, select my personal All-Star team. But before that happens, I have some comments to make about the qualities that make a player valuable to his team.

First among these qualities is the ability (possessed by only a limited number of gifted basketball players) to take over control of a game. This capability is of inestimable value to any team. There are, however, only three ways that a game can be taken over: a player can control a game with his great offense, his great defense, or his superb control of the boards. Mastery of even *one* of these is something special. Mastery of two would be phenomenal, and I can think of only one person who was truly a master of all three.

Let's talk about the athletes who qualify for game-control laurels in one or two of those important elements.

110

**Bill Russell** was one of the greatest—at least defensively—and was revered because his teams won so many impressive world championship games so deservedly. There was no argument about it: although it takes more than one person to earn world championship status, Russell was most definitely the hub of his teams. He was tremendous on defense (he could control many games with his defensive skills alone) and his control of the boards must be acknowledged in addition to his defensive and offensive abilities. His rebounding was second to none. Bill fell down only in the scoring department. He was a *good* scorer, but never a scorer who one could say controlled a game. Giving him two out of three—defense and control of the boards—is probably as high as you are going to get, at least from me.

Surprisingly, the guy in today's game who stands above all others in my view, is not **Larry Bird** (though he *is* my favorite player). Bird could do it on the scoring end, and his presence plus the many other things that he did gave his men a great deal of confidence. He was a good defensive player (though not a great one) and a really good rebounder, possibly a truly great one. He did all those things really well, and scored as well as anyone, especially when scoring is most needed. But as for taking over a game with any of these, except in scoring for a short period of time, I don't think so.

But **Sir Charles Barkley,** on the other hand, is (when he wants to be) the type of guy who can dramatically take over—and you know it when he does. He is able to get 20 rebounds and 25 points, so he definitely merits credit for two of the three elements of control that we are talking about: scoring and rebounding. He plays a respectable type of defense, as well—probably as strong a defense as almost anyone in this era, at least to the degree that he doesn't embarrass himself or his team.

Although Sir Charles gets check marks for control in two categories, his do not carry the weight and worth of William Felton Russell's two categories, in my opinion. Sir Charles, in his two areas of strength, doesn't quite match Russell's dominating ability to control a game.

**Michael Jordan** is, I think, a good candidate for consideration on our game-control check-off list. As everyone knows, he is tremendous offensively, and well able to take over a game in that department (we have seen him demonstrate this a zillion times). Yet I have always been more impressed by his earnest effort on defense where he is an extremely gifted and diligent worker.

But even though Michael is a great defensive player in the mold of K.C. Jones of the Boston Celtics, Jerry West of the Los Angeles Lakers, Walt Frazier of the New York Knicks, or Joe Dumars from Detroit, he cannot shut down the center to control a game as Bill Russell could. Therefore, he is not going to get a defensive control factor credit from me. Furthermore, he most surely has never proved that he can lock up the boards in such a way as to be considered a sensational rebounder. So, Michael gets one mark: for scoring.

There are three other players who, like Jordan and Bird, had the ability to take over a game through their scoring ability. **Elgin Baylor, George Mikan, and Magic Johnson** could control through a dominating offense, but they, like Jordan and Bird, cannot qualify for control laurels in the other two categories.

## I CHOOSE MY ALL-STAR TEAM

Now that we have covered the matter of game control and looked at the players who could take over a game in one or two ways, let's get down to how I'd go about the process of selecting my own All-Star basketball team.

The first step is to get past all the baloney and hype that star athletes have been given by PR guys and the media, and get down to the basics of offense and defense. *That,* after all, is what the game is all about. I would look at each candidate in terms of what they could contribute to those two aspects of the game, not forgetting, of course, the special value of a player's being able to take over control of a game.

Somewhere along the line, someone came up with the idea that specialization is more important than giving an athlete a chance to do it all. But my selection system is based on the belief that players should be gifted enough to play both offense and defense, and should be allowed to do so. Therefore, I award points for a player's ability in *both* areas.

For all of you basketball buffs who love making and discussing comparisons of players, I have created an instrument to help you out: Wiltie's 50-Point Barometer, otherwise known as the "Wiltometer." Here's how the Wiltometer works. For each athlete I would ask, "Is he a controlling factor when he's in a game? And how well does he play defense and offense?" If a player can play either defense or offense as well as it should be played, or as well as his position allows him to play it, he could get the maximum of 50 points in either area or in both.

**Bill Russell**, for example, would get the maximum in defense points. Surprisingly, he played team defense better against opposing centers such as Bellamy (who delighted in playing against Bill, and played him almost at will). But basketball *is* a team game. (A principle that applies to offense ratings, as well.) So, Bill gets 50 points for defense.

For offense, I give Bill about 30 points. Thirty points may seem rather high, but let me tell you my reasoning. First of all, he averaged about 16 points per game, a nice little average. That factor alone, however, would only give him about 20 or 25 points on the offensive end. But because rebounding is both offensively and defensively counted (depending on which end you get the ball at), and because Bill was such a tremendous rebounder, he gets some extra points. Furthermore, he was almost always in the top ten in assists, a feat unheard of for a center.

Wilt vs. Bill Russell

Bill was also a very good assist man, for a center. This is something that most people do not know about Russell, but if you look in the record books, you will see that almost every year his name was high on the list of the assist men of his era. So he gets some more points in offense for being an assist artist. Russell garners a total of 80 points

114

which, as you will see, will be very high on my scale—a score that anyone else will find it hard to match, or even approach.

The name that always comes to me when talk turns to all-around guys is **Oscar Robertson** (the "Big O"). During my day, everybody said that, pound for pound, Oscar was one of the best—if not *the* best—players out there. They didn't literally mean "pound for pound." They were using the expression as they would in comparing boxers. (Comparisons of a heavyweight versus a bantamweight or a middleweight, for example, have to be made "pound for pound.") In Oscar's case, comparison "inch for inch" would have been more appropriate because he was actually a very big guard compared with his contemporaries Jerry West, Hal Greer, Bob Cousy, or Walt Frazier.

As far as weight was concerned, Oscar may actually have weighed as much as some of the taller forwards or even some of the smaller centers. But, great as he was, he doesn't rank up there with Russell as an all-around player. I would give him an unhesitating 50 points for offense from a guard position. He could score as well from that position as any guard I know, Michael Jordan included.

As a defensive player, Oscar Robertson was not outstanding. He was, in fact, almost minus in that department. He *was* a very good rebounder and, because rebounding can be either defensive or offensive, we have to give him some points there. His assists added to his offensive game (one of the reasons he got 50 points for offense), but not to his defensive game. He did make a few steals, which helps him a little bit on defense, but I cannot give him any more than 10 points—15 at the very most.

Oscar's 50 plus 15 comes to 65 points, a long way from Russell's total. As a matter of fact, I think there are a number of guys who would rate higher than the Big O–even **Jerry West**, one of his contemporaries.

Jerry was a tremendous offensive player, but only 45 points' worth. He in no way matched Oscar's assist type of game, nor did he rebound nearly as well. He was, however, the leader in point making and a scoring threat whenever the ball was in his hands. As a pure shooter and an offensive player, he was almost second to none, especially at playoff time.

Defensively, Jerry was one of the good guards, and because he was noted for being a fine defensive player they had him play some of the tougher guards on opposing teams. His forte was stealing the ball—six, seven, or more times a game—a feat that is unheard of these days. So, I'll give him a good 30 points on defense, bringing his total to 75 points. That's five points below Russell and ten above Oscar Robertson.

A more contemporary guy worthy of consideration is **Larry Bird**, who deserves a place on this list because he has brought so much to the game of basketball. He stands out, especially, as a forward, and he made a major contribution to the Celtics' winning tradition. In the forward position, he very much resembled Jerry West in the guard position. Though he wasn't a tremendous defender, he was always tenacious.

Larry was a scorer supreme, worthy of a place on anybody's team. He could pass the ball well and, as a forward, he was a better assist man than Jerry West was as a guard (as far as that aspect of those positions can be compared). His rebounding was definitely adequate, and I would say that he was a better rebounder from the forward position than Jerry was from a guard position. For the most part, he played the forward position as well as it should be played, and he gets 45 points as far as offense is concerned.

For some reason, forwards never seem to be as great in defense as the guards or centers, and Bird was no exception to the rule. He wasn't one of the game's better defensive players, but he was up there with some of the best. Bird worked hard at what he did. Furthermore, he was not a guy who would ever give up. He consistently made his presence felt, even defensively. Altogether, I would give him roughly the same defensive marks as I gave Jerry West—25 to 30 points—bringing him to a total 75 points on my scale.

Keep in mind, as you are reading this, that we are looking at a number of things that, put together, make a basketball player. We are not talking merely about ballhandling, the ability to steal balls, or other little things that contribute to the making of a great basketball player. Bill Russell, for example, wasn't a great ballhandler—not like Jerry West, Oscar Robertson or Larry Bird. And none of these guys was as great a ballhandler as many other players. We are focusing, rather, on something more basic: the intrinsic qualities that seem to come naturally to certain great athletes who make a truly significant contribution to their teams. We are awarding points for the ability to do what an ideal player in that position should be able to do—not what people *think* that they should be doing (show time ballhandling, dribbling between their legs, and the like).

However fantastic a seven-footer handling the ball may appear to be, and no matter how many comments he inspires—remarks such as, "Oh man, he's seven feet tall, and he can dribble the ball!"—we should always remember to ask whether *that* is what he is being paid to do. Is bringing the ball up the court what is really important to his team?" Russell did the tasks that he was supposed to do for his team, and bringing the ball up the court was not one of them. So, let's not get confused. We are giving points here for how close a player comes to accomplishing what he is *supposed* to do. (You might find it interesting to keep this in mind during your Monday-morning quarterbacking discussions.)

Now, let's talk about the contemporary great one, **Michael Jordan**. Many people consider him the best, even though I often hear announcers claim that Scottie Pippen is today's top all-around player. (We will deal with Pippen after we discuss Jordan.)

I think people are in awe of Jordan because of *how* he does some of the things that he does. But keep in mind that, no matter how he does it, a basket is still only two or three points, not four or five. They don't give MJ extra points just because he adds his great flair to whatever he does. With Michael, it's usually show time (let's face it, that *is* important to many of his fans), but even so, he has to be given 50 points for offense in the guard position. As point guard, or whatever kind of guard you want to call him, it's not his job to control the ball, but control it he does—and he does so admirably. Above all, Michael scores points. He scores them when points are needed, and he does so as well as anyone else who ever played this game.

Surprisingly, though, Michael is a terrible assistman. His assists record should actually detract from his offensive score. Why should this be? It's because, as a guard, he handles the ball more than anyone else, yet he has one of the poorest (if not *the* poorest) ratio of assists per time playing of anyone who has ever played the ball-controlling guard position.

I would even go so far as to say (and this may shock most of you) that Michael should be docked five points or so for his inability to record more assists during the time he controls the basketball—and the numbers confirm my decision. I think he *could* do better; he just doesn't. (Here is an item of information that should put what I am saying into perspective: The Big O, who averaged 10 assists per game for his entire career, had a career scoring percentage only two or three points below MJ's.)

In spite of all this, I am still going to give Michael the full 50 offensive score because no other guard has ever, for a lifetime, averaged as many points as he has. However, I am going to deduct 5 points for his shooting percentage. Anyone who shoots as much as he does, and gets as many dunks and lay-ups, should shoot a higher percentage than 30.7% from the three-point range. For your edification, if Barkley shot as often as Michael, he would easily be the leading scorer. Get my point?

I like Michael's defensive game best of all. He does as good a job here as any guard, no matter who he's playing, He doesn't have Russell's ability to shut down a team, but he is able to bring about mayhem for the opposing guards, especially when his team is in a pressing mode.

MJ's defensive game does have limitations, however. His ability to steal the ball pales in comparison with that of Jerry West, K.C. Jones, Walt Frazier or Joe Dumars. Even though his jumping ability is well documented, and he is much taller than Robertson or Barkley, Jordan doesn't come close to these two when it comes to rebounding. (Believe it or not, on the boards, short old Barkley out rebounds the taller, built-for-basketball, high-jumping, strong competitor, MJ.) Therefore, in comparison to a Bill Russell, Michael gets no added defensive points for rebounding.

Putting all the parts of his defensive game together, I give Michael at least 35 points. As a guard, he is right up there with the best. Thirty-five to forty points, added to the 45 for his offensive game, gives him a total of roughly 80 points. There is the one other factor that must be considered, however: the ability to control. Russell can control a game in two areas, rebounding and defense, whereas Jordan can control it only from the offensive end. Therefore, even if Jordan had a higher point total, the nod would still go to Russell. But, oh boy, don't get Wiltie talking about the level of competition that Bill Russell had to contend with compared with what MJ has to face!

Now, let's talk about **Scottie Pippen**, Michael's running buddy. According to many of the announcers and color guys, Pippen is the greatest all-around player in the game today, and is able to do more things than Jordan can do. (Everyone is entitled to their own opinion, after all.) Pippen *is* a better rebounder and a better assistman, but he is *not* a better scorer, and he is *not* a better defender. (As good as MJ defensively, perhaps, but not better.) That's two out of four in Pippen's favor, plus one tie.

Scottie Pippen, however, does not have the ability to take over a game in any one of the major game-control categories, whereas MJ is able to do so in scoring. My judgement is to award Pippen 35 points on offense, perhaps going as high as 40, considering his rebounding, his scoring and his assists. He averages only 20 or 21 points a game, though his average rose some before Jordan's return. On defense, I would also give Pippen 35, making a total of 70 points.

This point total puts Pippen higher as an all-around player than many of the greats, including Oscar Robertson, and leaves me with some residual feelings of discomfort. Why? Whereas Oscar was willing and capable, does Pippen *want* to shoot the ball in crucial situations? I don't think so. (To catch my drift, check the playoffs of '96.)

Now I invite you to use the Wiltometer 50-point scale to compute ratings for players of your own choosing, perhaps picking one from the past and one from the present. See how your own figures come out. Magic Johnson might be a good present-era choice, and Elgin Baylor as a player from the past. I'll walk through a few point figures with you just in case you have a problem with the process. Here we go.

**Magic Johnson**, in addition to being a well-loved sports figure, helped to lead the Los Angeles Lakers to five World Championships. Now that, in itself, is a confusing statement. The fact that your team won a World Championship doesn't necessarily mean that you are a better player than someone who was on a team that lost out. There are any number of players who, though they play just as hard and give just as much, will never be part of a World Championship team. On the other hand, there are guys on World Championship teams who haven't given diddley squat.

Offensively, Magic Johnson is one of the greatest assist guys of all time. I should comment once again, however, that the definition of what constitutes an assist has gotten out of hand lately. Ask anyone, Coach Wooden, Bill Russell, Jerry West, Tom Heinsohn, Bob Cousy or any ten-year-old kid who follows the game. They all know that if you give the ball to a player who takes a notion to run around the corner for an ice cream cone before coming back to shoot a hook shot from the corner after dribbling the ball around the circle for an hour—you get an assist. That's how it is today.

OK, so the way assists are credited is a bit screwed up. Nonetheless, Magic is a good offensive player, a great assistman, and he scores points when he needs to. Playing the guard position at six-foot-nine has helped him in a number of ways. I don't know why smaller guards aren't able to easily take the ball away from him; he is *not* a fantastic dribbler—at least not in comparison with Guy Rodgers or Bob Cousy. He couldn't carry these guys' lunch boxes, yet he has performed well enough to be considered "magic," and he does a good job. I would give him 43-44 points on offense.

As far as game control is concerned, if Magic is going to take over a game, he has to do it offensively, because he sure can't control it on defense, where I think he's terrible—a literal zero. But he is a good rebounder (as he should be at six-foot-nine) but not good enough to take over a game. So I'll give him 15 points for his rebounding from the guard position. When we add these 15 points to the 40 for his offense, we arrive at only about a 55-point total for Magic Johnson.

On second thought, maybe I'm being too hard on Magic. Could be he deserves 20 points defensively, which would give him a total of about 60 points instead of 55. In either case, his is not an outstanding number compared with the score totals of the truly great players.

I want you to do the other great ones yourself. My guess is that you will be surprised at the numbers you come up with.

Here is something that may not have occurred to you. **Walt Frazier**, who played for the New York Knicks back in the early '70s, was amazing as a defensive player. He helped to lead his team to two World Championships, and was unparalleled defensively, unless you want to talk about K.C. Jones. In fact, these two are probably my all-time favorites.

Frazier, good-sized at about six-foot-five, played defense in a rugged, intelligent way. He was also a natural leader by example, and he played that way. He wasn't a tremendous rebounder or assistman as a guard, but he *was* a tremendous defender in that position. So, in defense, he would get 42-43 points. He couldn't control the defensive end as someone like Bill Russell could, but he did his job extremely well. Offensively, he was quite adequate but that's the best I can say for him because, as I said before, his assists were not that good. He gets 17 to 25 points offensively and with his 43 to 45 points for defense, he's in the 70-point range.

Then there is **Julius Erving** ("Dr. J"), another player who was the favorite of many fans. It appears to me that gaining "favorite" status seems to hinge on a player's ability to do certain things in a special and amazing way—to bring something more than just two points to a basket—and Dr. J was able to do that just as Jordan can. In the old days, Elgin Baylor, Earl the Pearl Monroe, and the late "Pistol Pete" Maravich had the same kind of quality. Players like these can bring you up out of your seat to exclaim, "Wow!" even though they may only have made two points or one rebound. Great as Dr. J was, you will see what I mean when you measure his talents objectively.

Offensively, as a forward, I would have to give the nod to Bird. He could do it outside as well as inside, whereas Dr. J. had to get inside to do most of his magical stuff. That detracts from his value as an all-around forward. Also, for a guy who could do so many things in the air, he was surprisingly weak as an assistman and rebounder. Altogether, I can't give him any more than a 40-point score on the offensive side.

Defensively, Dr. J was just so-so—possibly more negative than positive. Defensively, just as in offense, he wasn't a good rebounder, and he didn't steal that many balls. Because his flair added something undefinable to everything he did, he created the illusion that he had achieved much more than two points or one rebound. That's why people have said that he was the greatest, and I don't blame them for that. He was a joy to watch then in the same way that Jordan is today. But he doesn't merit more than 10 or 15 points defensively, bringing this guy, who many people considered the greatest at the time he was at his best, to a total of no more than 55 to 60 points.

Speaking of amazing feats and amazing players brings to my mind the most amazing basketball player I have ever known. I have seen this man play in thousands of games—that's right; *thousands of games,* ladies and gentleman. I played *with* him in a great many of those games, and also watched him via television. Not only did he make me laugh until I almost died, he did things I couldn't possibly explain (and I won't even try). He had to be seen to be believed. He was so good, in fact, that people thought everything he did was a trick such as magicians perform. He wasn't a magician, however, and he wasn't an illusionist. Everything he did was the product of pure skill. A magician or illusionist makes impossible things look real, but he made real things look as if they were done by magic. What a gift! I am talking, of course, about **Meadowlark Lemon** of the Harlem Globetrotters.

Question: What other professional basketball team did I play with other then the Harlem Globetrotters, the Philadelphia and San Fancisco Warriors, the Philadelphia 76ers and the Los Angeles Lakers?

Answer: Meadowlark Lemon's Bucketeers (not to be confused with Erol Flynn, Captain Hook or Long John Silver.)

There were two other incredible guys on the Trotters who, if they had been given a chance to play in the NBA, would have been outstanding pros. (They were prevented, of course, by the color thing back in the early days.) **Curley Neal** was somewhat more contemporary than Meadowlark, and I had the opportunity to play with him many times. Curley was a tremendous basketball player, and could very well have been an outstanding guard of the Isiah Thomas type. (Thomas played with the Detroit Pistons.)

But if you're talking about players who had flair and the ability to bring you out of your chair, you cannot overlook **Marques Haynes**, a dribbler for the Trotters back in the early '40s and '50s. Haynes was still playing during this decade, in fact, traveling the world with a team of his own until he was in his mid-sixties. What Haynes could do with a basketball could *not* be described. It had to be seen, and even then was still almost unbelievable.


One last word about controlling the game. Just so that you have it straight, let me repeat that there are three factors to consider: rebounding, defense and offense. I am not referring to the way the *pace* of the game is controlled by the players who control the ball—the guards. I'm talking about players who can use one of these three aspects of the game in such a way that they are able, when needed, to take their team over the hump. These players become invaluable assets to their teams.

When Michael Jordan says, "Hey, give me the ball on offense; I want it, and no one is going to stop me from scoring," you give him the ball, and that's what he does. And when Bill Russell commandingly takes the ball off the boards and gives it to his team (and does almost the same thing in the same way on defense), *that* is what I mean by controlling the game. It is entirely different from the way a guard controls the *tempo* of the game.

Remember the three control elements: rebounding, defense, and offense. Only one guy has been known to control all three. (If that's not obvious to you, it is to me.)

## My Wiltometer Team

Here are the ten players I have selected, based on my ratings, to make up what I will call my "Wiltometer Team." My choices are based on their ability to take over a game and to control it, and their combined scores on my 50-point scale. Considering all the above factors, nine players are unquestionably qualified: **Bill Russell, George Mikan, Jerry West, Elgin Baylor, Oscar Robertson, Magic Johnson, Larry Bird, Michael Jordan and Sir Charles Barkley**. But when I get to the tenth member, I have some misgivings.

Perhaps **Hakeem Olajuwon** should be included, though I'm not quite sure where he fits in. He is tremendous as an all-around threat, and he rebounds well, though not as well as some of the great rebounders. He doesn't even rebound as well as Charles Barkley. He scores well, but doesn't stand out as a shooter, even though he has had 40-point games. If you put a couple of guys on him or take the ball away from him, you can get away with it because his passing skills need to be honed and his in-depth knowledge of the game is somewhat limited. Altogether, I'm not quite sure what to say about Olajuwon except that he possesses a great deal of athletic ability and, playing with the teams that he has been with, he has been able to put it all together and make it happen.

Based on the Wiltometer scale, I would probably choose **Walt Frazier** of the New York Knicks in preference to Olajuwon as the tenth member of this controlling team. **Kareem Abdul-Jabbar** should be in there, as well. He, too, would be a better choice than Olajuwon, though including him would make eleven team members instead of ten.

I know many will ask, "Where is **Shaquille O'Neal**?" My answer is that we can't put every good basketball player on this list. We are focusing here on the control factor—a player's value to a team in terms of his ability to control a game. Shaq, as a matter of fact, proved last year that he may not be as valuable to his team as has been thought. When he was unable to play in the first 28 or 30 games because of an injury, his team played almost .800 ball without him. And when he came back, they played no better at all. I know that Shaq is an imposing basketball player, but I am not completely convinced of his value on my Wiltometer scale.

## An Alternative Rating System

Here is an even easier system to have fun with while rating your basketball greats. It can be used anywhere, and could increase your knowledge of the game. The basis of this system is the generally accepted statement that a good offense will beat any defense. I believe this to be true, and will prove it to you.

Basketball is essentially an offensive game, and everything a player does has as its ultimate purpose getting the ball into the basket. The value of a great offensive player lies in the need for the opposing team to use more than just one defender to guard him This results in a couple of players being left unguarded under the basket. That fact accounts in large part for the importance and value of a strong offensive player.

What makes a player an offensive standout? Just three elements are important here: per-game point average, average number of assists per game, and rebound average. Because assists, by definition, lead to scoring, they are among these important factors. And possession of the ball is a prerequisite for scoring which is why rebounds are included.

Only three stats enter in the scoring of players on this scale: point average, assist average, and rebound average. Once you add these up, point for point, you can arrive at a per-game total for any given player. To qualify for this process, a player must have played for at least nine years. The older a player becomes, the less impressive his numbers are apt to be, of course. (Longevity does have an equalizing effect.)

This is a totally objective system for creating a composite offensive average for a player of any era. Emotions do not play a part here, only the stats accrued by the listed players during their NBA years.

Some people award two points for rebounds in the belief that keeping the ball from the opposing team is worth one point, and getting it for your own team is worth another point. The **Total Worth** column in the chart below shows a total player value computed both ways. The first total includes rebounds as worth only one point, and the second (italicized) figure includes the extra rebound point. As you will see, the two-point rebound results in dramatic changes in the relative standings of the players. Bill Russell moves from the sixth position to number one, and Bellamy moves ahead of the great Oscar Robertson.

| Name | Years | Points | Assists | Rebounds | Total |
|------|-------|--------|---------|----------|-------|
| Elgin Baylor | 14 | 27.4 | 4.5 | 13.5 | 45.4 / *58.9* |
| Bob Pettit | 14 | 26.3 | 3.0 | 15.0 | 44.3 / *59.3* |
| Oscar Robertson | 14 | 25.7 | 9.7 | 7.7 | 43.*/ 50.8* |
| Michael Jordan | 9 | 31.0 | 5.0 | 6.7 | 42.7 / *49.4* |
| Kareem Abdul-Jabbar | 20 | 24.6 | 3.6 | 13.8 | 42.0 / *55.8* |
| Bill Russell | 14 | 15.1 | 4.3 | 22.4 | 41.8 / *64.2* |
| Larry Bird | 9 | 24.3 | 6.4 | 10.0 | 40.7 / *50.7* |
| Charles Barkley | 9 | 23.5 | 3.7 | 11.4 | 37.7 / *49.1* |
| Walt Bellamy | 14 | 20.1 | 2.4 | 15.0 | 37.0 / *52.0* |

Only one truly contemporary player, Michael Jordan, appears on this list, and you'll note that he is not at the top (which *doesn't* mean the list's a flop). All the rest are from days gone by, except Bird and Kareem. This serves to illustrate one of my gripes with the media: they do not let the fans know the real worth of yesterday's players.

The name that appears at the top of this group may come as a surprise to some, but not to me. And do you find it interesting that Bill Russell, the defensive giant, appears on this elite offensive list?

There may be other players whose names you believe should be included in this illustrious group—players such as Magic, Hakeem, or Pippen. One day when you feel like having some fun, use this system to find out why these others didn't quite measure up.

*Wiltie, I don't see your name on the list. Why not?* I'll let you figure that one out.

## Some Last Thoughts

We were in a playoff series with the Boston Celtics and I had scored nine points in a row, putting my team in a winning position, when Havlichek stole an inbound pass, enabling the Boston Celtics to win another seventh game from us by a point or so. I lost about four other seven-game series by a total of only 9 points, all told. If those 9 points had gone in my direction rather than against me, I would have had four more world championships, and I would have been perceived as a different player.

Jordan has been in situations not so different from those I found myself in, but in his case, Bill Paxton bailed Chicago out with two heroic shots that gave them two of their championships. That outcome would not have changed Jordan's view of the game or people's view of Jordan—he would have been the great Jordan in any case.

But he was fortunate to be on a team where someone else made the crucial baskets that gave him two additional championships and a winning image.

I recently ran across a clipping about my having had a fairly good game in Syracuse. It was not a big article, but it mentioned that I had scored 44 points and got 45 rebounds. In today's game, 44 points and 45 rebounds would not only get you headlines, it would get you another commercial. Mo' money, mo' money, mo' money!

The media would have you believe that it was my strength and size that made me impressive. They forever try to compare me to Shaq, though in body size, I was built more like Pippen or MJ in my early days.

Strangely enough, there *are* some parallels between Shaquille and me. *I sang a rock and roll song on TV, and he's a rapper as you can see. I did commercials, varied and many; he does commercials and makes aplenty. Foul shots—neither one of us can make any. Both Shaq and I now wear no hair, and that's about all I can find to compare.*

Yes, I grew to be seven feet tall, but I was blessed in other ways as well. I had the strength to put a shot. I was Philadelphia's high school shot put champ for three years, and NCAA freshman champion, beating out the great Al Orter (four-time Olympic discus medalist). I had enough speed to run, and would challenge anyone. As a college runner, I was beaten only once, and that was by my roommate, Charlie Tidwell, who was considered the fastest in the world.

When you are seven feet tall, people don't think of you as a jumper, but I have yet to see anyone who could get up off the floor as I did. (See if any of today's leapers can pick a quarter off the top of the backboard!)

In case you are convinced that I looked like Shaq, study this picture taken at the beginning of my pro career.

*When I played with the Globies, who specialized in jumping high, they'd sit back and watch me jump to the sky. Everyone's familiar with Kareem's hook, but few know that my jump shot was one of the best in the book. Michael and Shaq dunk more than I did on any given night, because I was shooting jump shots, hooks and finger rolls while*

131

*the defense held on tight. I was a center in the NBA, and this is the way I had to play: with my back to the basket—that was the right way. They could put me anywhere on the floor, and I was able to do more than just score. Here is one thing I want you to know: my defense was really the heart of the show. I was able to pull balls right out of the air, but my opponents thought that wasn't fair. So, goaltending became the call for them all—anything to keep me from taking that ball.*

Do you think I'm bragging? Well, if you were a painter, wouldn't you want people to know that a work of art was *your* rendering on the canvas, and not some other schmo's? I would rather be bragging than ragging on people as is the pastime of many athletes today.

The Greeks believed in a "strong body and a strong mind." I drove non-stop from Philly to L.A. many a day—body and mind working together all the way. Some climb mountains—that's their high. Others find theirs in the beauty of a butterfly. I found mine in the challenge of driving my car at speeds approaching 150 miles an hour on my trips across the country.

My highs have always come from challenging myself. Win, lose, or tie—I don't give a damn—but I must try.

## WILTISM

**SPORTS AND LIFE ARE BUT ONE AND THE SAME: IF PLAYED RIGHT, EACH IS A WONDERFUL GAME. IN BOTH, WE SHOULD BE LESS SELFISH AND A LOT MORE GIVING, AND HAVE GREATER RESPECT FOR ALL WHO ARE LIVING.**

This is my ultimate dream car! It took me 11 years to design and build it.

It's strange how certain basketball "facts" have changed over time - physical size, for example. I've grown from an even seven feet in height to seven feet plus many more inches. And the aspect of a player's game that he or she is remembered for today may be entirely different from the aspect of their play that was considered most outstanding at the time they were actually performing.

Who is responsible for these changes? Only the media has the power to bring about such shifts in the public's perception of athletes over a period of time.

My game was seen very differently during my playing years than it is remembered today. The early-day sports reporters were most impressed by my defensive game, but over the years, though reality hasn't changed, perception has gradually shifted. The consensus nowadays is that I excelled on offense, and that Bill Russell was the outstanding defensive player of that era."

The articles which follow illustrate clearly the error of this shift in perception, and will show that I was recognized from the very beginning for my defensive game.

These reprints of articles from the past will show clearly how perception and reality can part company over time. You will see that Bill Russell was not the only great defensive player of his era, and that from the very beginning, I was strong defensively as well as offensively.

You have been misled by the media—but how were you to know? And today they are doing it once again. They are pulling another snow job, leading you down the primrose path of myth and misperception as they try to convince you that Shaq is very much like me. Folks in the media have always dealt with me as a big and powerful 235 pounder, never as the skinny kid I actually was when I started in the pro game. What else other than my lanky frame and slender build would have prompted them to call me "Wilt the Stilt?"

Here is a question for which I've never found a satisfactory answer. Maybe the media can help me out here.

In news headlines and articles, I was consistently pitted against the same five or six players. Sports section headlines always seemed to portray me as dueling against Bill Russell, Walter Dukes, Elgin Baylor, Walt Bellamy, Nate Thurmond, or Kareem Abdul-Jabbar— all men of color.

It has always seemed to me, however, that the players who were actually most comparable to me—the logical ones for me to have been measured against were Bob Pettit (the league leader in scoring when I entered the NBA and the rebounder who was second only to Bill Russell) or Dolph Schayes (the six-foot-nine-and-a-half perennial star of the Syracuse Nationals - now the 76ers-who was later to be my coach).

I have never figured out for sure why I was rarely, if ever, mentioned in relation to the latter two athletes, but so often compared with players in the first group. Would this have had anything to do with color?

Even after my retirement, every great center of color was compared to yours truly: Kareem Abdul-Jabbar, Ralph Sampson, and now Shaquille O'Neal. But oddly enough, Bill Walton (the only great center of that time who was not of color) never inspired such comparisons, even though he played more like me than did any of the other centers. Perhaps some media wizard can tell me why this should be so.

They call him Wilt the Stilt and colleges fought ruthlessly to get him. Next week he starts to play for Kansas and after seeing this seven-foot superman in action, experts ask...

# Can Basketball Survive Chamberlain?

### BY JIMMY BRESLIN

Wilton Chamberlain, a seven-foot basketball player with the catchy nickname of Wilt the Stilt, is only a sophomore at the University of Kansas. His intercollegiate playing career doesn't start until next week. Yet because of this twenty-year-old Negro athlete, many basketball authorities have already conceded the next three years to Kansas. They expect Chamberlain to be even more dominant than Bill Russell, the six-ten Negro ace of San Francisco's two-time national champions.

There was a brief flurry of speculation that the advent of the Chamberlain era might be delayed when Wilt underwent a throat operation in October. However, the surgery was described as minor and his recuperation as excellent. He was back in action by the time basketball practice started on November first.

Wilt the Stilt has had an advance build-up to compare with that of Clint Hartung - remember him? - who was hailed at the New York Giants' training camp in 1947 as the greatest all-round phenom ever to put on a baseball glove. The Hartung fanfare reached such proportions that veteran scribe Tom Meany observed dryly, "Hartung shouldn't even bother to play. He should report directly to the Hall of Fame at Cooperstown."

In the case of Hartung, whose superman reputation sprang up in Army baseball, it was all an illusion. He turned out to be a performer of limited talents. This won't happen with Wilt Chamberlain. There is no real question about his ability.

137

# Can Stilt be Stopped?
# Sure, Freeze the Ball

CHICAGO, Dec. 4 (UP) - Wilt (The Stilt) Chamberlain Kansas' seven-foot basketball center, is good now and will get so much better that he'll probably change the style of play against the Jayhawkers, Northwestern coach Waldo Fisher said today.

Fisher's team, with three sophomores, was an 87-69 victim of Kansas last night as sophomore Wilt from Philadelphia threw in 52 points in his collegiate debut.

"He's probably the toughest guy I've ever seen to stop when he's got the ball," Fisher said. "I think the guy's going to improve, or can improve, on defense, and I think he'll do it.

"But on offense, they're going to do a lot of things to try and stop him. I don't know how you can do it without fouling. He's so much higher than anybody else that you just can't stop the ball from getting in to him under the basket.

"And he's a guy capable of staying under the basket and getting the ball. By that I mean he can stay five or six or seven feet away and it's just a jump shot for him from the distance. He doesn't even have to step in."

"What this is going to do," he said, "is cause low-scoring games. A team playing them is going to hold the ball and pass up good shots for cinch ones. Their reasoning is going to be, 'We've got to hold down his scoring and how are we going to do it best? - by keeping the ball.'"

# "Pro basketball has ganged up on me"

### By Wilt Chamberlain
### *as told to Tim Cohane, sports editor of Look*

The National Basketball Association has two standards of officiating: one for the league as a whole, another for me, Wilt Chamberlain of the Philadelphia Warriors. Until they start calling fouls committed against me on the same basis as for everybody else, I'm not going to develop my full scoring potential and team value. And the Warriors are not going to beat out the Boston Celtics for the Eastern divisional championship of the N.B.A.

One reason I left the University of Kansas after my junior year in 1958 was that I couldn't play basketball in any true sense. I couldn't improve. I was scoring only on jump shots and rebounds. Such other assets as my hook shot, dunk shot, speed, dribbling and passing were all tied up in the little mob scenes around my pivot position. Two, three, sometimes even four men were guarding me. By guarding, I mean they were climbing up and down my 7 feet 1/16th of an inch and shoving me around like people crowding into a subway train.

I was sure it would be different in the professional game. The pros have a rule against the zone defense; there is supposed to be only one-on-one guarding. The idea is to sustain movement and scoring-speed up the game-to please the crowd.

Clever pros always can simulate man-for-man guarding, yet in effect drop off and team up on another player -"collapsing," we call it. But when "collapsing" is obvious and increases the already violent body contact of this game, a foul is called almost invariably. For the rest of the league, that is, not for Wilton Norman Chamberlain. I wouldn't mind battling two men so much, but I shouldn't have to battle three and even four.

The only team in the league that plays me with one man is the Boston Celtics with Bill Russell. They can do this because Russell is the game's supreme defensive ace. Bill is 6 feet 9 1/2, with long arms and beautiful timing. He seems to hang suspended in the air almost half the night. He makes me shoot higher than I usually do, and his tremendous reach leaves my hook shot useless.

Every other team plays me with at least two men; not

necessarily their best men either, but their "hatchet men." Pro basketball is the most physically taxing sport. Pro "hatchet men" make the roughest collegians look as if they're playing tag. These are fellows 6 feet 6 and over, with proportionate weight, strength and aggressiveness. They give you a real beating. The body contact is rising in intensity, and I'm in the middle of it. There are some great shovers in this league. I start a play in the pivot, end up in the corner and never know how I got there.

As a mild hint of what was to come, this season wasn't a week old before somebody's elbow busted open my mouth. In a game with the St. Louis Hawks, one of the mob went for a walkover my right ankle. It was just a sprain, and I missed only one game. But suppose it had been a fracture, and I had been put out of action for the season?

After a game with the New York Knickerbockers, Neil Johnston, our coach, told me I would have to start retaliating. I had been exposed to the same thing at K.U., but I always had been able to control myself. I surely prefer to avoid trouble and play basketball. But a taste of the pros quickly showed me that self-control beyond a point is, in more ways than one, pointless.

Not long after that scramble with the Knicks, Bob Petit of the Hawks happened to run into one of my elbows and had to leave for minor surgical repair - one or two stitches, I believe. I wasn't disturbed. I intended to trade shove for shove. If I have to blast somebody into a balcony one of these nights, I'll do it.

This is no complaint, just a statement of facts. I'm not the first, and won't be the last, touted newcomer to be roughed up. It's part of the pro game, and there is no personal malice in it.

# Chamberlain Duels Baylor at Arena

## By Bud Furillo

### Expect 10,000 for Pro Cage Tilt

Wilt (The Big Dipper) Chamberlain, an entire constellation of stars wrapped up in one player and the finest rookie in the history of pro basketball, performs in the Sports Arena tonight before an expected crowd of 10,000.

The game will be televised starting at 8 over KCOP, Channel 13.

The Stilt's Philadelphia Warriors meet the Minneapolis Lakers at 8 p.m. in a benefit league game for the Salesian Fathers' youth work in East Los Angeles.

The good fathers had better provide asbestos nets for the baskets because two of the hottest pairs of hands in basketball (Chamberlain's and Elgin Baylor's) will be firing away.

The Warriors beat the Lakers, 114-104, yesterday in San Francisco, as Chamberlain scored 41.

This morning, Wilt denied a report out of Philadelphia that he is planning to quit basketball for pro track. He couldn't understand where the story could have come from.

### Double Leader

Wilt leads the NBA in scoring and rebounding and has personally accounted for a big attendance rise around the circuit. Last week he scored 58 points, barely missing Baylor's all-time record of 64. It seems only a matter of games until the ex-Overbrook High School, Kansas U. ace dips his way past Baylor's mark.

The sinewy sensation (a roof-straining 7-2) hit 45 against the New York Knickerbokers Saturday, breaking the all-time Warrior one-season scoring mark...

# Chamberlain Scores 43 In Debut

### New Era Begins in NBA
### ONLY (BUT WHAT A) HUMAN
### BY JACK KISER

The houselights dimmed and a spotlight picked up the huge flag hanging limply from Madison Square Garden's cluttered, scarred ceiling. The teams stood ramrod straight in lines across the foul circles and the assembled 15,000 muffled their vocal chords. Gladys Gooding's organ rolled out the notes of "Oh, say can you see..."

The Age of The Wilt was at hand.

Wilt Chamberlain clasped his hands behind his back and gazed solemnly at the flag for a minute. Then a smile played on his lips.

**WAS HE THINKING** about the havoc he was going to create in the next two hours? Of the six times he had appeared at the Garden before, playing sensationally but still leaving some doubt as to whether he was THE greatest. Or about the few critics who had picked out his minor flaws and used them to stab holes in the Wilt Chamberlain myth?

Neither. The keen Mr. Chamberlain had just discovered that the flag had only 48 stars. Even Madison Square Garden, the sports capitol of the world, has its flaws.

The Knicks knew Wilt's weaknesses and did their darndest to exploit them. He refuses to use his great body to the utmost on offense, being content to pop away with his fadeaway jump shot. So they collapsed on him in droves, trying to rough him up and kept him from getting the ball. He is hesitant about crashing the boards on rebounds, so the hulking forms of Charlie Tyra and Willie Naulls tried to block him out. He isn't the greatest foul shooter in the world, so they clobbered him when he had a decent crack at the basket.

**HE IS ONLY** human. But what a human!

The statistics will show he scored 43 points, grabbed 28 rebounds in the Warriors' 118-109 Saturday night victory. But statistics can't begin to tell the entire story. The story of how he completely halted the Knicks' strong driving, pick-and-go game with his last-second lunges,

142

allowing his man to take pot shots from far out but stuffing leather down the throat of anyone brash enough to drive for the basket. Or the story of his grabbing rebounds, twisting in midair and firing down-court to Guy Rodgers or Tom Gola or Paul Arizin on the fast break. Or the psychological curtain he draped over the Knicks, making them commit offensive blunders they usually don't make.

This was his real strength.

"He was a one-man wrecking crew," said Carl Braun who has watched the greats and would-be greats come and go during his 11 years of backcourt toil. "I've never seen anything like it, and I hope I never will see it again. But I know I will."

**CHAMBERLAIN SEEMED** completely unaffected by his smashing debut. He was as cool, calm and collected as if he'd been a spectator and not a participant. "I've still got a lot to learn," he said later, after he'd finished the formalities of shaking hands with the well-wishers and answering questions fired at him by the usually hard-bitten but now visibly awed New York press. "But all in all, I was satisfied. It was very important to me to get a good start.

"Sure, I've thought a lot about starting my first NBA game in the Garden," he continued. "I wasn't exactly what you call nervous. Anxious is the better word.

I wanted to go out there and start off right. If I'd missed, say my first five or six shots - well, then the other team would be saying that maybe I'm not a shooter. I wanted to show them I was. If I'd missed those shots, then I'd be forcing and they would be relaxed.

Later a huge crowd blocked traffic on the corner of W. 49th St. and 8th Ave., gazing up in awe at Wilt Chamberlain. He chatted with them, shook hands, laughed with them and signed autographs for a half hour..

The Age of The Wilt had arrived.

The NBA will never be the same.

# The Battle of the Giants: Russell vs. Chamberlain

**Associated Press Sports Writer**

Boston, Nov 6 (AP) - comes now the most widely heralded personal duel in professional basketball history - the clash of Bill Russell and Wilt Chamberlain.

Those two, who rank as Giants both in size and professional stature, collide tomorrow night when the NBA champion Celtics take on the rejuvinated Philadelphia Warriors in the first of their 13 scheduled meetings this season.

Each team is unbeaten this season, Boston in five games and Philadelphia in three, and the Eastern division lead rides on the match. That, however, is almost incidental to the Russell-Chamberlain affair.

Russell, the San Francisco product who provided the defense and rebounding needed to bring Boston two world championships in three seasons, is generally regarded as the greatest defensive player in the game, possibly in history. He is 6-10.

Chamberlain, who played last season with the touring Harlem Globetrotters, is in his rookie year in professional basketball's big league, but he's made the biggest splash ever for a first year man.

He has averaged 39.6 points a game in three starts, and coaches and players throughout the league have forecast that he'll rewrite the scoring records. One coach recently predicted Chamberlain someday will score 90 in a single game.

He owns a height advantage of about three inches over Russell and outweighs big Bill by about 40 pounds.

"He's a good basketball player," Russell said, and declined further comment, a sharp departure for the usually talkative athlete.

Russell is off to his greatest start yet as a pro. He has averaged 22.2 points so far this season, far over his usual figure, and has a 25.3 average on rebounds, higher than his previous league-leading marks.

Many critics, including Russell's own teammates, feel that the Chamberlain challenge will push Russell to performances better than any he has yet shown.

It comes to a battle of Russell's experience and defensive ability against the height and scoring punch of Chamberlain.

144

Celtics' coach Red Auerbach says he isn't worried.

"He (Russell) will be up so high for this game that he'll never come down," Auerbach said.

"Look, Chamberlain gets all the write-ups and he's got that big 30-point average, but my guy played him to a standstill at Minneapolis in that exhibition game. My guy can play with the pressure on, and he's got a shot from the corner now that he never had before. Oh, it will be a heck of a thing to see, but my guy is going to come out O.K."

# Wilt Hailed as Top Star

Joe Lapchick, the nation's foremost authority on basketball players, says that Wilt (The Stilt) Chamberlain will soon become the greatest player of all-time.

Southland fans will get a chance Monday night at the sports Arena to see the brilliant 7-2 rookie in action when he leads the Philadelphia Warriors against the Minneapolis Lakers.

Lapchick, coach of St. Johns, was a member of the Original Celtics, basketball's first great team, and later coached the New York Knicks of the NBA.

Lapchick named Chamberlain to his all-time best team and also chose Elgin Baylor, the star of the Lakers, who is set to wage a hot scoring duel with the former Kansas star.

With two of the all-time greatest facing each other in a regular league game for the benefit of the Salesian fathers in their efforts to combat juvenile deliquency, it shapes up as one of the Southland's top sports attractions.

# Warriors Sign Wilt at $30,000; Top Pay in the NBA

## By Fred Byrod

The Philadelphia Warriors finally consummated their long courtship of Wilt (The Stilt) Chamberlain yesterday when owner Eddie Gottlieb signed him for one season at the biggest salary ever paid to a player in the National Basketball Association."

Gottlieb first declined to reveal the amount, then coyly submitted to a series of questions which developed these points:
**MORE THAN** $30,000

(1) Chamberlain will get in excess of $30,000. (The previous high for the NBA is generally assumed to be Bob Cousy's pay from the champion Boston Celtics, somewhere around $27,000).

(2) Including several "future fringe benefits" - which Gotty didn't explain but said did not pertain to a bonus based on attendance - Wilt cost Eddie more than it did when he took over the Warriors' franchise (league charter, players and equipment truck) seven years ago.

### OKAYED PREVIOUS DAY

The announcement was made at a press conference at the Hotel Sheraton. Gottlieb said that, contrary to gossip that an agreement had been reached some time ago, Chamberlain had okayed his offer the previous day, in a telephone conversation while Eddie was in New York working on the NBA schedule for next season.

Gottlieb will leave tomorrow for Europe with the Harlem Globetrotters, for whom Chamberlain played last season and reportedly received $65,000 for 205 games. Originally, Wilt was supposed to make the tour with the Globies, but he said that if he goes at all, he will join them later and play no longer than a month.

Chamberlain said that Abe Saperstein, owner of the Globetrotters, had made him an even higher offer than last year for the coming season, but had not tried to talk him out of his decision to join the Warriors.

### DIDN'T HURT PLAY

Wilt, dapper in a dark blue suit and narrow brim straw hat, explained three factors had influenced him to join the Warriors: (a) it has always been his ambition to play in the NBA (b) he wanted to spend more time here with his family (father, mother six sisters and three brothers) and (c) the counsel of Isaac Richman, legal adviser for both the Warriors and Chamberlain.

# Wilt: The NBA's Tower of Power
## By Bill Lyon

Almost every night now, it seems, Air Jordan will swoop down to earth, snatch up another chunk of a record, and carry it off to whatever mountain it is that he calls home.

A week ago, he incinerated Phoenix for 53 points. It was the 19th time in his career he has hit for 50 or more. It moved him into second place, all-time, NBA.

On Wednesday at the Spectrum, he scored point No. 10,000 in game No. 303. Only one player in history ever got to that plateau faster.

The same player who holds the point record. The same player Michael Jordan will spend the rest of his marvelous career chasing.

And never catching.

Wilt.

"I find myself finishing second to him a lot," said Jordan, smiling. "It's an honor."

When he was playing, Wilton Norman Chamberlain was larger than life. Now that he isn't playing, he is larger than imagination.

He retired in 1973. He was 36 years old his last season, and you know what he shot from the floor for that year? Only .727,

that's all. It is a record that still stands, that probably will always stand.

A curious writer called the NBA offices with this research request: How many records does Wilt Chamberlain still hold?

The answer came later that day: 83. Eighty-three! The man has been out of the game 16 years, and he still holds 83 NBA records.

You may debate who is the best all-round player in the game. (The choice here is Magic Johnson, because he can play all five positions.)

You may argue who is the most exciting player in the game, Air Jordan or Dunkin' Dominique.

You may debate who is the best defender, the best sixth man, the best power forward, the best point guard.

But there is one area for no debate whatsoever: most dominant player ever.

It may even be argued that Wilt Chamberlain was the most dominant athlete who ever lived, though it is admittedly difficult to compare sports.

But he led the sport in scoring. In rebounding. In assists.

In shooting accuracy. Had they kept track of blocked shots, he would have led that, too. What is comparable? Leading the NFL in touchdowns? Leading baseball in homers, batting average, RBIs and ERA?

Air Jordan has now been past 50 points in 19 games. Elgin Baylor had 18 games, Rick Barry 15, Kareem Abdul-Jabbar 10. Add all of them together and you'd barely be *halfway* to Wilt, who did it in 122 games.

The single game he is best known for, of course, is that 100-point towering inferno against the Knicks. That could be as untouchable as DiMaggio's hitting streak, for the simple reason that no team now will allow such an embarrassment, even to the extremes of repeatedly letting the shot clock expire and purposely fouling other players.

In one game, Wilt Chamberlain gathered up 55 rebounds.

In one game, he parceled out 21 assists.

Seven times, he led the league in scoring. One season, he *averaged* 50.4 points a game. The second-highest season average on record is 44.8. By Wilt Chamberlain. The fourth-highest is 37.6. By you-know-who.

Eleven times, he led the league in rebounding. The highest retrieve average on record for one season is 27.2, by Wilt Chamberlain. The second-highest is 27.0 by uh-huh, and the third-highest belongs to him, too.

Weary of the criticism that he was one-dimensional, that his size gave him an unfair advantage, that, after all, a man 7 feet tall ought to be able to score and rebound without even getting up on his tippy-toes, he resolved to show them that he could play the little man's game, too.

So he announced before the 1967-68 season that he would lead the league in assists.

And he did.

He had 702, an average of 8.6. He remains the only non-guard ever to do that. At the time, he beat out such distributors as Oscar Robertson and Guy Rodgers, who didn't exactly double-dribble and stumble over their shoelaces. "With Wilt," said Billy Cunningham, who played with him, "you always had the feeling that he could do anything he wanted."

And that was the catch.

That was what they were always throwing in his face, that it was too easy for him, that he was some glandular goon who ought to be handicapped. Play on his knees, maybe.

Maybe that is why he would shoot that delicate little finger-roll, such a dainty little shot, really, the ball rolling so gently out of those massive mitts. Or the fadeaway, a push delivered while he was backing away from the basket rather than attacking it. It was as though he didn't want to do it just on brute strength, that he had a need to show that he had touch, that he was athletic and aesthetic, not just some lumbering Frankenstein creation who clanked down the court and oafishly jammed the ball.

"When I came along," he said, "there had never been a man my size who could do the things I could do. There still isn't."

Immodest? Yes. His ego approximately matches his wingspan. But is what he says accurate? You bet.

He always stirred deep emotions. Many of them ugly.

Still does. They called him lazy and selfish, and cackled at his helplessness at the free throw line. Mostly, they feared him. They rejoiced that Bill Russell's teams won most of the championships.

Those critics live still. They try to detract from his records. They say there was less talent then, smaller players, no leapers like Air Jordan, that rebounds were more plentiful because shooting accuracy was worse.

Yet no one denigrates what Babe Ruth did. Or Ty Cobb. Or Gordie Howe. Or Red Grange.

Wilt Chamberlain once explained it all in one simple sentence: "Nobody loves Goliath."

# WARRIORS, WILT WHIP PACKERS

## BY JERRY HOLTZMAN

Wilt (The Stilt) Chamberlain stuffed 51 points into the basketball and almost threw in Walt Belamy , too, Sunday night as the Philadelphia Warriors defeated the Packers 122-114 in the feature game of Chicago's first National Basketball Assn. doubleheader.

A crowd of 6,482, largest of the season here, saw the Cincinnati Royals beat the Detroit Pistons 128-112, in the opener and then sat, fascinated, as the 7-foot-1-inch Chamberlain pumped in 24 field goals and three free throws for a single-game International Amphitheatre record.

However, 51 points for Wilt the Stilt is merely his average. It was his incredible defensive play which stole the show.

He held Bellamy, the Packers' rookie center, to 14 points but even this statistic doesn't begin to tell his defensive effectiveness.

In all, Chamberlain blocked 11 of Bellamy's shots, the first five in succession and only fouled him twice during the entire evening.

### Long Distance

Bellamy didn't get a clean shot off until 56 seconds were left in the first quarter and in order to do so had to go deep into the right corner.

During the early minutes of the second period when Chamberlain had already blocked nine shots, Bellamy simply stopped and started looking for his teammates. The shot chart credited Bellamy with 20 field goal attempts but about eight of them were tip-in swipes.

Bellamy finished with six field goals but most of these were scored when Chamberlain was not set in the pivot. Even somewhat tainted and was given to him by the officials who charged Chamberlain with goaltending.

Chamberlain's performance was such that it overshadowed the game itself.

### Excitement Plus

It was probably the most exciting game of the season here and was made so by the Packers, who though outmatched, didn't buckle until the last six minutes when they simply had nothing left.

The Packers, despite Chamberlain, led early, once by as much as six points at 18-12. The score was tied at 21, 25, 27 and 29 before the Warriors pulled out to a 33-30 quarter lead and a 60- 56 halftime ledge.

Sparked by Horace Walker, Bobby Leonard and Ralph Davis, the Chicagoans went ahead again midway in the third period and actually had a one-point lead at 93-92 in the opening seconds of the fourth quarter.

Chamberlain, the only player to play the full 48 minutes, scored 19 points in the final period.

150

trying to convey. Are they afraid that if we don't hear some audio every second of a broadcast, we'll turn off the TV, figuring that there must be a technical problem? Well, here is a clue as to what I do. I turn down the sound, and hear no more from these clowns.

Vin Scully, the announcer for the Dodgers and exception to the general rule, is absolutely marvelous. He reminds me of some of the older sports announcers, men who seemed to have much more class than announcers do today. In years gone by, announcers didn't feel the need to make profound statements in order to sound as if they had a total grasp of all they were talking about, and to convince us that their every word was the gospel truth. Wouldn't it be great if those older announcers could give lessons to today's loud-mouthed models—guys who play games with their words and use cute little lines and ditties that need a detailed explanation before they make sense to the listener.

An outstanding example of this latter breed (most of whose names I can't even think of) is Dick Vitale. Unless you aspire to be a stand-up comic (or to appear an idiot) do not mimic Dick Vitale. He is loud and full of corny remarks that he must explain immediately after he uses them, but he must be doing *something* right: he has almost as many commercials as Jordan. My fear, though, is that kids will choose him as their hero and try to emulate him in the same way they try to copy MJ on a basketball court.

Many announcers are, essentially, only hucksters who will say anything to protect their jobs while kissing ass and telling half-truths to promote the sports industry. On the air they might express one opinion, but in private conversation, you would hear quite a different expression of feelings about games, teams, athletes and the situations they get themselves into. One-on-one, boy, would you get an earful! If you knew that this kind of honesty was going to be forthcoming during the broadcast of a game, you would probably listen instead of turning down the sound.

As I write, I am listening to Cheryl Miller, who does the color for several networks, as she is being questioned at half-time about Magic Johnson's apparent frustration. She is showing a lot of spirit and strength, speaking up about subjects that other announcers tend to back away from. One of the announcers says about Magic, "No, he's really not frustrated, he's . . ." (and the announcer ventures some other guesses about Magic's mental and emotional state). Cheryl disagrees wholeheartedly, as I do: Magic *was* frustrated, and his actions showed it. She offers a good reason for her opinion, and is willing to put herself on the line, which for me is just fine. She says, "Magic just wants that ball in his hands so he can control his own fate."

The concept of controlling one's fate sounds like a great idea, but it reeks of individualism as opposed to team effort. Magic is showing by his actions that he wants the ball more, and that the team comes second, and Cheryl is trying to point out that, for him, the game is an "I" and "me" situation rather than a "we" and "us" situation. Give her credit: most network people are afraid to speak out with that degree of honesty.

A word that is used much too often by media people, one which annoys me every time I hear it, is "unselfish." An announcer might say, for example, "What an unselfish play by Pippen! He is a really unselfish player, and that is the characteristic that has made him so great." I have never, however, heard any announcer use the word "selfish" to describe Michael, the player who takes Pippen's pass and puts it in. Michael doesn't give the ball back to Pippen; he keeps the ball and scores the basket and—yet he isn't considered to be selfish.

This is just another illustration of announcers' inconsistency and their tendency to make important-sounding pronouncements without completely understanding what they are saying. In reality, Pippen's passing the ball to Michael is not a purely unselfish move. It gets him an assist which, as I have mentioned before, is a valuable commodity in today's game of basketball. And Michael shouldn't be considered selfish just because he took the shot. Media people should get their jargon straight.

Whenever a basketball player gives up a ball, allowing someone else to shoot a basket, he is considered to be an unselfish player. Does this mean that when you *do* shoot the ball you are selfish?

Passing the ball to another player does not automatically qualify you to be called "unselfish," especially if you are a guard. That is what guards are supposed to do: move the ball around, get the other guys involved, and help their teammates create movement. There are only two ways to play the game; the right way or the other way. To call passing the ball "unselfishness" is a serious misuse of the term. I call it "good and proper play."

Announcers hop and skip around the things they *should* be saying, and seldom have the guts to come right out and say what they really believe to be the truth. Though they are quick to use the word "unselfish," I have never heard them call a player "selfish." Today's media types don't have that kind of courage—or possibly they recognize the real truth about who should shoot the ball. They use the word, "unselfish" easily, because it implies a compliment, but they use it for a guy who is doing only what he is supposed to do.

Please, announcers, learn what unselfishness is all about as it relates to team play. When Jason Kidd passes the ball as he drives to the basket, even though he could have shot it himself, this is not an unselfish play, in spite of the announcer's enthusiastic pronouncement; it is just a good play. Announcers, do try to remember that for some players, assists are more valuable than points. Although Kidd should perhaps have shot the ball himself, there could have been a hint of a selfish motive in his passing it to a teammate. Have you given that possibility a moment's thought?

Let me give you an example of what I think of as true unselfishness. When I gave up using my natural gift—my ability to score a great many points—I was acting unselfishly. I did this in order to blend into a series of different team systems (none of which were probably any better than the ones we were already employing). The asking may have been done very subtly, but I did what was expected of me. At the time all this transpired, I was the best scorer in the history of the game, and was shooting the highest percentage. However, when I was told to give the ball to someone else, even though he couldn't do the job one-tenth as well, I did so in the spirit of team unity. *That*, I believe, is the meaning of "unselfishness."

I am sensitive about people calling players "unselfish" when they pass off the ball for assists, for a good reason. In Terry Pluto's book, *Tall Tales*, I read on page 351 that, because of my concern about getting assists, I took only two shots during the seventh game of the Celtics vs. 76ers playoff in the '68 season. Pluto added that my selfishness caused the 76ers to lose the game. His implication was that I was more concerned with getting assists than with winning the championship. How ridiculous! Pluto, himself, noted that I was guarded by four Celtics players, leaving four 76ers free to shoot, unmolested. Unfortunately, my teammates picked the wrong time not to be able to hit the broad side of a barn. (Chet Walker, for instance, had only 8 out of 22, and Wali Jones, only 8 out of 25.) *Wiltie, you're selfish if you do and selfish if you don't! Oh, well!* The way assists are regarded today, you are unselfish *whenever* you pass the ball, even though you should have taken the shot.

Too many announcers are kissie-assie and show a shortage of backbone. They like to employ flattering descriptions, but rarely use truthful ones. They blatantly (and incorrectly) use the word "unselfish" to describe what appears to me as just another good play. In all my years of playing basketball and observing the game, I've come across only one truly unselfish basketball player: *me*. I gave up being the leading scorer in the history of the game in order to cater to my teams' whims by passing the ball to the likes of Keith Erickson, Happy Hairston or Pat Riley; guys who could not shoot a lick. At the time, I was the greatest scorer in the history of the world, as is proven by points scored and the fact that I led my team, as well as the league, in percentage shooting for twelve of the fourteen years I played. (I include the year I got hurt, as I was leading the league when I was injured.) In one of those fourteen years, I was second in percentage and in my first year, I was third. I never hear those figures mentioned.

No one has ever actually called me "selfish," but that has certainly been inferred from time to time. Whenever my game seemed to change, it would be said that "he's really playing an unselfish game now, giving the ball to everyone." This comment refers to my being thought selfish when I was scoring—but what is a player called when he gets twenty-seven or twenty-nine rebounds a game, sometimes in addition to ten or fifteen blocks? Is that unselfish, or is that just working your ass off, as Rodman does? (He amasses a lot fewer than I did, by the way.) Why are you considered selfish when you're scoring points, and doing so more than anybody else, but *not* considered selfish if you are getting rebounds? Is Rodman selfish because all he wants to do is rebound? My answer to that question is, "Yes!"

I consistently did whatever the team wanted and whatever the managers asked for. I did all the other things *plus* rebounding. If scoring points was what my team asked me to do, I don't understand how that makes me selfish. That's why they came to me with the ball when they wanted it done. Owners, of course, were concerned about making money, and they knew people would love to come out and watch someone make fifty points a game. People come out nowadays to watch Jordan score points, after all, and believe me, if he didn't score, they wouldn't feel the same about him. That concept was part of the master plan in my time just as it is today.

Redundant though announcers may be, whenever they talk about records being broken—records for steals, for blocked shots, rebounds, etc.—they should never forget to mention, and to repeat often, that records for some of these categories were not kept until recently. They should let their audiences know that the achievements of many of the greats were never included in the record books. That being known, fans can draw their own conclusions as to where they might have ranked.

Remember, announcers are salesmen, here to sell *today's* game—not yesterday's—and they tend to flower over situations as a means of protecting their jobs. When a game is terrible, their strategy is to bring out the good parts, trying to persuade you that something positive is going on. All too often, though, they fall into the same trap; in acting as salesmen for today's game, they step on the old guys in order to show you how wonderful the new guys are.

You constantly hear it said of a guy who is six-foot-one, two, or three, that he "plays much bigger," but you

157

never seem to hear that about a seven-footer. Apparently it is assumed that he is already big enough and, therefore, he can't play any bigger. Well, I am here to tell you that I played bigger, and that is why I was always accused of having incredibly long arms.

Proportionately speaking, I don't actually have long arms. (Jerry West is six-foot-three, and his arms are almost as long as mine.) I could jump very high whenever I got a ball, but they never gave me credit because I was so tall. I was never physically as big as I played. I was so very, very skinny that, at times, I looked almost anemic. The reason for my doing so much weight lifting was to build myself up.

One further item concerning arms. Sam Perkins, a Seattle player, and I had the same tailor. On one occasion when we both happened to be there for fittings, I tried on one of his jackets. The sleeves were so long that, as far as the arms were concerned, I looked a midget inside of it. But no one ever talks about *Perkins* as if he is some big seven or eight-foot guy.

I recently watched Gheorghe Muresan, the seven-foot-seven center from Eastern Europe, make a great move to the middle and shoot a hook shot over seven-foot-seven Shawn Bradley, a center for the New Jersey Nets. I think I know a little about great pivot moves and, believe me, Muresan made one. The announcer, Dick Vitale (whom I, personally, find boring) said, "Well, he scored, but I don't know whether it was really pretty: he looked a bit like he was stuck in the mud—but he got the job done."

Hours later I watched the very same move made by Jordan, who also scored, and a different announcer remarked on the great athletic move that Jordan had just made. Now, why does the smaller guy get so much credit for what he does, while the bigger player, doing the same thing, gets almost no credit at all?

Seems to me it ought to be the other way around: when you are seven-seven, those kinds of moves are very hard to make. Our stature and higher center of gravity tend to work against taller athletes when agility is called for. Small people have much more control over their bodies. Look at a gymnast today, and you'll realize that they can do things that people over six feet would have a very hard time doing. Many of the things that big people do are considered by the layman to be easy, but they are not. So wise up announcers, and start giving big men a little credit for what they do.

Near the end of the third quarter of a recent Indiana game, Rik Smits grabbed a rebound and I heard the announcer say, "That's his first rebound tonight." Smits is seven-foot-four, ladies and gentlemen, and that was his first rebound. This all of which adds credence to my words when I tell you that being tall doesn't necessarily help you to get the ball. Rebounding is a high-level skill and a form of game participation that only a few can do exceptionally well. Success in rebounding has little to do with how tall *you* are, but a lot to do with how tall your *heart* is.

In that same game, I watched Rik Smits turn into the pivot and shoot a little soft eight or nine-foot hook shot. The color guy explained to us that, "You can't let a guy that size get that close to the basket; he'll kill you with a shot like that because, for a guy as tall as he is, that's a very easy basket." Ignoring Rik's poise and his ability to shoot the ball well, and instead of mentioning Rik's talent and great touch, the announcer alludes only to Rik's height. But if Michael Jordan, on the other hand, were to drive in and shoot a lay-up, the announcer would not say, "You mustn't let Michael come that close to the basket and dunk the ball, because that would make things too easy for him."

Whatever Michael has done is assumed to be the result of talent alone.

There is a real difference in the way the feats of small and large players are reported. I recall watching Bradley in another game in which he was two rebounds short of a triple-double. He was given credit for the triple-double, even though he didn't actually get it, and the announcer made a point of commenting that he never saw Bradley get the two missing rebounds. On the other hand, I have watched many games in which Utah Jazz guard John Stockton, needing one more assist for a triple-double, has phantomed an assist that gave him his triple-double. No one could ever say where those assists came from (actually, no one seemed to care), and the announcers never questioned the stats. Seems a big guy's shortcomings are usually called to our attention; but no one seems to question the announced feats of a smaller player—even though he may not actually have done them.

Height may be a God-given gift to a basketball player, but it is not a great player's only asset. What I am trying to say is that announcers seem to have a very hard time giving tall guys credit for being talented. They seem always to be more interested in how big and tall they are, implying that with that kind of size, they should to be able to do almost anything.

If I seem somewhat sensitive about this, it's because I am. You can't listen all your life to people say, "Oh, yeah, if I were seven feet tall, I could do that too," without taking *some* offense. I would like to see us tall people get a bit more credit for the things we are able to do because of our talent, not because of our size.

Everyone assumes that if you are a certain size, every aspect of your game should be better: you should be able to score easier, get more rebounds, run faster, walk longer—all of it. Here is an example of a typical comment: That silly coach from Detroit, Chuck Daly, said I was a good rebounder because I was bigger and stronger than everybody else.

I think it's a David and Goliath syndrome thing. Everybody rooted for David, you know, just because he was smaller than Goliath. They would have been for David even if he had been a general and a great tactician, and Goliath was just a poor weak (but tall) guy who couldn't see very well, couldn't hear at all, and had a bad ankle, a trick knee, maybe even had a cold that day, and couldn't have licked a fly. They would still have rooted for David, I don't know why. If Goliath had come to the fighting field in a wheelchair, do you think they would have had just a little bit of sympathy for him?

Think about how Goliath was beaten. It was supposed to be a match with swords and hand-to-hand combat, but Goliath never had a chance. David used a slingshot from a distance, hit Goliath in the head, and knocked him dead. The little sucker cheated. Those weren't the rules of the fight. But no one seems to care that the fight wasn't fair.

Alas, poor Goliath; no one shed a tear for him. *But Wiltie wonders: how did Goliath feel about it?*

This may be an appropriate spot, before we leave the subject of size, to insert three items from *Wiltie's Myth-Debunking File.* The first relates to reach, the second deals with hands, and the third is about feet. This information is offered as a helping hand for both media people and fans.

We all recognize by now that when basketball players' vital statistics are given by the media, fictional numbers are apt to fly fast and loose (guys who weigh 300 pounds are described as weighing 280 to 290; some who are six-foot-ten are listed as seven feet tall). Let me point out, for the information of all concerned, that head-to-toe height makes no difference—but *reach* does. Some six-foot-nine guys have the reach of someone who is seven foot one—and vice versa. So why don't you people in the media get smart and measure what really counts? Reach has far more impact than height on what a player is capable of doing on a basketball court. And if you want to get really creative, hand span should be measured as well. Believe me, hands along with that all-important reach, do make a difference.

Somehow, a consensus has developed to the effect that, "The bigger you are, the worse your hands are!" and "The bigger you are, the worse you handle the ball!" Everyone accepts these sentiments to be true, but how did *big* hands come to be equated with *bad* hands? Where I come from, big hands have been known to be *great* hands. I recall watching Goose Tatum handle the ball for the Harlem Globetrotters, and Showboat Hall (of many moons ago) as well. They had huge, really humongus hands—and they were great hands! No one could handle the ball as they did.

When a big player has a good way of catching a ball, announcers like to say that he has great hands *for a guy his size.* Even my friend, Bill Walton (a big guy, himself), has made that mistake. I'm here to tell you that size alone has nothing to do with having good or bad hands, or with the use thereof. Little guys should logically be more adroit at using their hands, simply because they handle the ball much more than the big boys. For this reason, and this reason alone, they may, at times, appear to be more capable players. But, if the big players were allowed the same opportunities to handle the ball, you would not see much difference between the tall and shorter players. It is only a myth that, because of their size, big guys don't have good hands.

Elgin Baylor and Connie Hawkins, former NBA player and New York schoolyard great, also had huge, great hands. Their hands were much bigger than mine, even though I am almost a foot taller. Whether a player has "good hands" or "bad hands" depends mainly on how often he has had an opportunity to use those hands. Get the picture? *I get it, Wiltie.*

Writers and announcers seem to like to tell us how big a guy's foot is. They'll point out that a player wears a size 22 shoe, but in truth, that doesn't mean boo. People continually allude to the size of Shaq's feet, but they never mention how big Michael's hands are—and, as I just explained, hands matter. Lest we forget, we are not talking football here, this is basketball. And in basketball, most of the crucial operations involve using your hands, *not your feet,* dummy! (Sorry about the "dummy" bit; sometimes I get carried away.)

I would like to know what the qualifications are for getting a job as a sports announcer or a color commentator. Those who get the jobs seem to be picked because they are either ex-basketball players or ex-football players, or maybe they hold some other kind of celebrity status. Network management doesn't seem to care whether prospective announcers are able to communicate what they want to say, or whether they know very much about the sport in question. God knows, the people who have actual radio or television broadcasting qualifications seem to be the last to be considered for announcing jobs.

What reason do we have for believing an announcer if the people who do the hiring don't care what kind of background he or she has? Media execs assume that because someone has been a coach, he knows all he needs to know about his sport even though he may have been only a football line coach who knows nothing about the other facets of the game.

What management really needs to find out is how well the prospective announcer can communicate pertinent information about the game to the fans. Announcers do not have to teach people how to block or throw a football, or how to call a play; all they have to do is to deliver some well-chosen insights to fans who don't plan to play the game. Do the ex-coach announcers know that? Maybe they should go through some kind of training before they start to announce the NBA games. Since almost anyone can be chosen to deliver us this mess, shouldn't they at least have to pass a test?

Where can you find a sportscaster as biased as Johnny "Red" Kerr, the radio announcer for the Chicago Bulls? Johnny was a great player for Syracuse, and played for the Philadelphia 76ers as well. Johnny was a splendid basketball player and a great competitor, but as an announcer he sucks. He spends most of his time ballyhooing the Chicago Bulls, telling the world how great they are, rooting for every move they make, and crying over every call made against them. Johnny approves of all calls made in the Bulls' favor, naturally. Kerr was one of the smarter men in basketball, and should be knowledgeable about it; but it is obvious that he has shortcomings in objectivity and honesty when reporting the game.

I just heard announcer Hubie Brown, the ex-coach of the Knicks, say once again that Kenny Anderson is doing very well as a Hornet and, averaging fourteen or fifteen points a game, he's racking up a good percentage for himself. Anderson is normally a 39 percent field goal shooter, a percentage so bad that I hesitate even to mention it. *Nobody* in this era shoots 38 percent or 39 percent from the field, unless they are blind, crippled, and lazy to boot. The announcer applauds Anderson's record, but he should be doing just the opposite. Here is a guy who is making $40 million but is shooting less than 40 percent from the field. How in God's name can Kenny form the words necessary to ask for the salary he's getting?

Someone should ask guys like Anderson, "What makes you think that you are worth this kind of money? Are you pulling people into the stands? Are you helping your team to win your conference or to qualify for the playoffs? I would give a lot to know what makes you think that you are worth so much." Has the press asked these questions? Has *anyone* asked these questions? If they have, and if any of the players in question have answered, I'd sure like to know about it. It would be worth the price of a ticket to me, not to see them play, but to hear what they have to say.

I watched the Bulls play the Charlotte Hornets when Charlotte was tied with the Miami Heat for the last play-off spot. Chicago had everything sewn up as far as their own position was concerned, but, with eight games to go, Charlotte needed every win they could get just to stay in the hunt. The score at the end of the first quarter was the Bulls 44, Charlotte 17. You might have thought that Charlotte would be hustling; but a glance at the score would tell you how hard the Charlotte players were really working.

The sportscaster who was calling the game stated that Kenny Anderson (the guard who turned down the $40 million) had two fouls in the first quarter and, two or three different times, did not come back on defense at all. He turned up his nose at $40 million or more, but thought it unimportant to come up and down the floor. Think about it. Charlotte was fighting for a playoff spot, and their multi-million dollar point guard wouldn't come down the court on defense in the first quarter. At the beginning of the second quarter, the coach took Kenny out. The announcer, however, remarked only that Anderson would be a free agent at the end of this season. There's an astute commentary.

I do not understand the mentality of a player like Anderson or, for that matter, of owners who would want such a player on their team. I guarantee you that, by the time this book is published, Kenny Anderson will be on another team. Unfortunately, Anderson is not unique. This is the level of effort that we are getting from far too many players today.

This entire game was puzzling, to say the least. The half-time stats were unbelievably ridiculous. Just check this: the score was *76 to 32* in favor of the Bulls. Try as I may, I cannot understand how, playing at home and supposedly fighting hard for the last playoff spot, a team can get out-rebounded in the first half 32 to 15. If you cannot make your shot, you just try much harder on the boards. You run harder, you work harder, you foul more, you fill the lanes, you try everything and anything. You scratch and claw your way back into the game any way you can. But Charlotte did *nothing* in any department. Their stats were so far below Chicago that the figures were hard to believe. Now, this does not happen by accident. When a team that is supposedly fighting for a playoff spot is not even willing to get in there and fight, the message is very clear.

At half time the color commentator said "Chicago, amazingly, is leading in every stat department. The Bulls are playing incredible ball." Why didn't he say, "Charlotte's stats are amazingly bad in all nine categories in which statistics are kept. The Hornets are playing incredibly poor

166

ball." I thought that Charlotte's failure to work hard at anything was more worthy of comment than the fact that Chicago was playing well. A situation which I believe was greatly aided by the ineptness of Charlotte. The commentator never really addressed the fact that Charlotte was playing so poorly; in fact, they covered it up by saying the Bulls were playing well.

Game announcer, ex-New York Knick coach Hubie Brown, is surely knowledgeable about the game of basketball, but Hubie is so busy covering up the downside of the game that he fails to give the viewers any real information or insight about it. Because he wants to keep us viewing, he uses a positive approach, applauding the great way the Bulls are playing, but refusing to mention how bad Charlotte is. The Bulls *are* playing well, but "well" and "badly" are relative, after all, and depend largely on what the other team is doing.

There is so much cover-up stuff going on here, you'd think it was politics. Compared to this, Watergate was nothing!

I am tired of hearing the same old platitudes and outrageous descriptive adjectives used to describe what is just an ordinary play. A wide receiver, for example, may catch a simple, ordinary ten-yard pass for a touchdown, and the announcer tells us how incredible the play was. Listening to his superlatives, you would almost believe that this receiver had just made a Hall of Fame type or Super Bowl-winning catch, and that among all the football players on this planet, only this receiver and this quarterback could have made such a play. This is hard enough to swallow, but it also creates another problem. When a truly exceptional play does come along, the announcer has no way to give it credit, because all the superlative adjectives have already been used.

167

Do these announcers, a great many of whom have never played professional sports of any kind, think that most sports fans are idiots? We're watching the same game they are, after all. I wish they would do us a favor by giving us credit for having some smarts. Remember, we *are* able to see that's why we're watching TV.

*Nowadays it is hip to hype. Instead of selling us something that's right, the media prefers to pour on the hype, feeding us tripe. It takes hours of watching a TV show to catch two short minutes of horses running slow. (Oh, the thrill of the Kentucky Derby!) Though Super Bowl hype is out of control, the game often reeks like another kind of bowl. Then there's heavy weight boxing: The championship fight for hype takes the cake. Four or five months' build up—but is it a fake? When fight night arrives, thousands act like they care, and are willing to pay, whatever the fare.*

*As people, have we become such a manipulated type, that we all act like addicts and can't kick this hype? The problem is not that we don't really care; most of us seem to be unaware, not knowing they have us by the short hair.*

## WILTISM

IF YOU NEED TO KNOW THE TRUTH ABOUT SOMETHING, WOULD YOU RATHER LISTEN TO A CAR SALESMAN OR A PREACHER? BOTH OF THEM ARE TRYING TO SELL YOU SOMETHING, BUT I'D SURE PICK THE SALESMAN. YOU KNOW RIGHT FROM THE BEGINNING THAT THE CAR SALESMAN CAN'T BE TRUSTED.

## AN OPEN LETTER TO MY FRIEND BILL WALTON

*In my opinion, one of the greatest basketball players of all time, and on his way to becoming one of the better color announcers, if he keeps to a truthful line.*

In your effort to get the audience to stay tuned for the upcoming Bulls game, Bill, you tell us that "we are about to watch the greatest player of all time." In the first place, Bill, you should have said, ". . . the best player *I have seen.*" You never saw me when I was doing my real thing. You *did* have the privilege, if you want to call it that, of watching me play during my last five years with the Los Angeles Lakers, but during those years my game was entirely different from the game I played with the Philadelphia 76ers or the Warriors. The Lakers had asked me to play a different role on the team and to be an entirely different type of basketball player, a request which I happily acceded to. So . . . case rests there, Bill; *you have not seen them all.*

Bill, when you try to critique, making us think you know every basketball player who ever came down the pike, you should remember that you are a fairly young man yourself, and never saw some of the great players when they were doing their best work. One of them, Bill Russell, played in the fifties through the early sixties—35 years ago. Bill, you could not have seen Bill Russell play during that time, as you were on the west coast and television did not carry the games as it now does. You would have been lucky, in fact, to have seen Russell play even once or twice. So, my advice to you and to other young announcers and media folk is: stay away from areas where you have no true expertise. Your opinion is, of course, your own to express, but qualify it so that it is recognizable *as an opinion* and let us know that you are not an authority who has seen it all.

*Secondly, I must ask you Bill:* When you think about the changes we have seen in basketball—walking, ball carrying or defensive changes such as zone defense, which opens up the middle to the benefit of the superstars of the league who now can drive for a basket unmolested—would you not say that many of these changes have aided the likes of Michael Jordan? You bet they have! Yet, have any rules been legislated to curb any of his abilities? I don't think so. To the contrary, the new rules have been added for the purpose of promoting and spotlighting his particular talents. Such was not the case for yours truly, however.

Let me name some of the rules that, unbelievably, were enacted to curb my abilities and lessen my chances for showing the qualities of agility, speed, strength, jumping ability and finesse that were well documented during my early days in basketball. The one thing they never could suppress, though, was my power; therefore, people always think of me as the basketball player who was larger and stronger than the others.

Bill, we both know that basketball, at its best, is not played with sheer power, and power alone. (Other more important qualities create great basketball players.) But, Bill, you should have seen my body type in earlier days: it was more like Pippen than Shaq. I had a special ability, however. Take Jordan's power to explode—to get in the air—and I had that tenfold. This was a God-given talent, of course. I had nothing to do with creating my jumping ability or my seven feet of height; genes must be given credit here. I did, however, hone my skills and use all of my assets to the best of my ability.

*(End of letter.)*

170

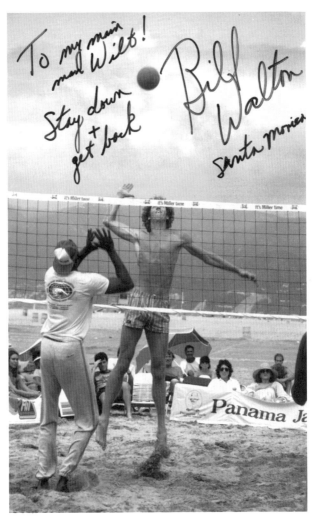

Bill, just as in this attempt to spike...

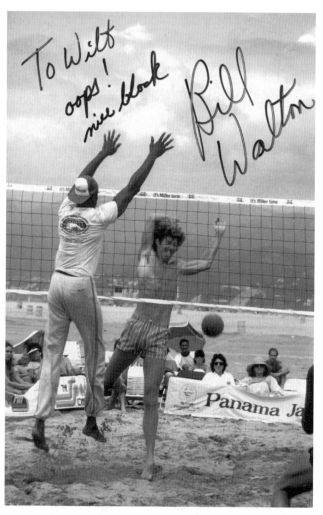

You're missing the point.

Many of you who watch basketball today are not even aware of some of the changes that have been made in the game, much less why and for whom the rule changes came about. It may seem to many a sign of egotism that I bring all this to light, but, as my mother taught me long ago, "Right is right, and speaking about right wrongs nobody." Just for your information, here are some of the rule changes that have been aimed directly at yours truly: widening of the lanes, no passing the ball over the backboard to prevent offensive goal tending, no dunking the ball from the foul line, the waive foul rule, and (actually a non-rule) the no-clock rule. I'll have more to say about rules later on.

We must constantly remind ourselves that these announcers and media men are very now-oriented. They are here to sell today's game, because it is today's game that pays their salaries. They have good reason, therefore, to try to convince us of the greatness of today's players. The current players *are* great, but that does not make them the *all-time* best. For example, I never heard Walton mention Walt Bellamy's name, yet Bellamy, a center, was second only to myself. As a rookie, he averaged more points than anyone else who ever played basketball, including the great MJ—*with the one noted exception, need I add*. Oscar Robertson also scored way up there as a rookie during that time, and his record was established playing against the likes of myself and Bill Russell ten or eleven times a year.

I shake my head as I hear the announcer say that last year the Lakers gave up 105 points, and this year they have given up (would you believe it) just 99. The emphasis is all wrong here. The issue is not the number of points given up by the Lakers; it's the pitifully small number of points scored by the other teams. Talk about misleading stats! The figures make it appear that every team in the NBA—not just a team or two, but *all* of them—became, virtually overnight, great defensive teams. I see a different picture, however. This is not about defense; it's about a remarkable lack of *offense.*

The worst of the announcers are the various color guys who work for the stations that cover home games, the home game announcers for Houston, San Antonio, the Bulls, or whatever other team. One possible exception is Chick Hearn of the Los Angeles Lakers, the elder statesman of these announcers and a true original who has no apparent fear of losing his job or of anything else. Chick is in no way like the rest of them who kiss-ass in a manner that is beyond belief. The others applaud, they cheer, and, when calls go against their team, they get on the referees in a most undignified way.

Honest reporting goes out of the window when these guys go into action. The day one of them concedes that an official made a good call against their team would truly be a day to remember. Chick, on the other hand, can often be heard telling his audience how poorly the Lakers are playing, and frequently makes remarks such as, "They are standing around waiting for Magic to do it all." When praise is in order, he is generous, even in extolling the skill of the opposing team, and he provides listeners with a balanced insight into what is really going on—and lets the chips fall where they may!

Then there are announcers like the one who does the games for San Antonio, a guy who is *always* in favor of the home team. And even though I love Calvin Murphy, the color guy for Houston who does an admirable job and is normally a fairly strong candidate for an honesty award, the associate he works with leaves a lot to be desired. As a matter of fact, the majority of them leave a lot to be desired. I cannot fathom how most of them get hired, unless all they have to do is pass a loyalty exam—plus, of course, the all-important screening test that measures flunky potential. If you think I am lying, take a trip to one of these cities, and listen to the home game announcers. It won't take you long to realize just how one-sided the game looks through their eyes.

How can it be that Dick Vitale can receive so much money in appearance fees and spend so much time on our television screens when he represents so many of the wrong things? How he managed to reach such a position is beyond my understanding. His use of the English language and the thoughts he chooses to express are borderline idiotic. He makes a great deal of money and, unfortunately, he creates a role model for kids that says that success comes from a willingness to clown around and make a fool of yourself. Those who hire him should be aware that people watch him only because he acts like a clown. Not only are his commercials horrendous, but we have enough clowns in the world, already. The circuses are full of them—and that's where he belongs.

I'd like to believe that a personality like Vitale's is not needed to sell today's sports. (Give me Vin Scully any day!) Why his kind get the jobs when there are so many others more qualified, I haven't a clue. There must be dozens of people who have diligently studied radio, television and communications, and have spent long hours learning how to get their point across through correct use of the English language. Unfortunately, these people don't get the jobs. Some ex-coach, a guy with a loud mouth and a strange way of expressing himself, is hired instead.

## WILTISM

**MY ADVICE TO TV COLOR COMMENTATORS: THOU SHALT REMEMBER THAT IT IS BETTER TO SAY NOTHING AND THOUGHT A FOOL THAN TO OPEN YOUR MOUTH AND LEAVE NO DOUBT.**

I met last summer with Matt Guokas, one of my ex-teammates and currently one of the color guys for NBC. In the course of our conversation, I asked him about a remark he had made about me during a recent telecast. Guokas had been asked by his co-worker, "Who would be your choice? You played with Wilt and you coached Shaquille. Both are among the worst foul shooters I have ever seen, but which one of the two would you rather have shooting foul shots for *your* team?" Matt replied, "Sorry, Big Fella (meaning me); I've got to take Shaquille."

Now, Shaq is actually bigger than I am, but I am the one with the "Big Fella" image. Matt had been to practice a number of times and had watched me shoot 90 to 95% in practice everyday. He had also watched me shoot the ball around the perimeter, and knew that I could shoot the basketball. I admit that my foul shooting was lame, but Guokas knew that in critical situations I made a lot of foul shots. He should have answered the question in a more diplomatic way, as any good announcer would, by replying, "You are not going to get me in the middle of those two big guys. Do I look stupid, or what?" (My answer to *that* question would have been easy: an emphatic, "Yes!")

Looking back, I think there were a couple of reasons for Matt's answering his co-worker's question as he did. Matt was living and working in Orlando, and he knew damn well that Shaquille is very sensitive about his foul shooting. Matt, being no fool, knew there would be repercussions if he chose me as the winner of the "Best Of The Worst Foul Shooters" competition.

I said to Goukas, "Come on, Matt, you'd really choose him over me?" He thought a moment, and replied, "You've got to understand that Shaquille is very sensitive about things of that kind. That's why I said what I did." All I could think to say to that was, "But, *I* don't have any sensitivity?"

Then I asked him, "Why don't you say these things on the air?" He looked at me with a crazy stare, and said, "Wiltie, only you would dare."

*That little anecdote contains a lesson, Wiltie:* Announcers will say anything on TV, but when you talk to them in private you'd be surprised at what they have to say about contemporary players. It's a black and white story: white on television, and black in person-to-person conversation.

Not only has Matt Guokas become a terrible announcer, he can't see any more, and has shown himself to be not only partial, but one-sided as well. Case in point: For what might have been the first time in history, a technical foul was called on Jordan for pushing off on a play. Jordan questioned the call, prompting the referee to give him a technical. Then, would you believe it, MJ questioned *that* call. Despite the fact that Jordan should have had even *more* technicals, Guokas said, "I can see why he was mad: he didn't really push off, you know."

Sure, there were a lot of bad calls being made on both ends that day but that doesn't give anyone license to lambaste the referee. When other players get technicals, they are expected to control themselves even though the call was a bad one—but not in Michael's case. When Jordan fouls and reacts badly to the call, Matt's response is, "I can see why Michael is mad; he didn't push off." I have news for you, Mr. Guokas: he *did* push off—in the referee's eyes, even if not in yours—and we all know whose eyesight counts in a situation like this. Every player, right or wrong, must learn to swallow that bitter pill.

Jordan is two for six at the foul line. Guokas states that the foul shooting of both teams has been awful, and he goes on to give his own analysis of why this has happened. He says that foul shooting has been so awful because defensive play has been so strong, going on to explain that when you play defense really hard, you break the rhythm needed to shoot easily at the foul line. Now, I shot awful fouls for 14 years ladies and gentlemen, but they never said it was because of my defensive play or the fact that I was grabbing twenty-five to thirty rebounds a game and blocking another fifteen shots, as well. Not at all. They said I was a lousy, terrible, awful, ridiculous, unbelievably poor foul shooter—no mention of hard defensive play or of anything else that may have had a negative effect on my foul shooting. They never gave me that kind of consideration. I wonder why?

My purpose here is not to soften the blows that were repeatedly laid on me many years ago; that's history. (I *was* a terrible foul shooter in the pros.) What I am getting at is the media's tendency to make excuses for Jordan. If he misses four out of six foul shots, they don't merely comment that he is human, after all, and he just missed; they explain that the tough defense he has been playing has destroyed his fluidness at the foul line.

That may well be true, folks, but don't assume that the same reasoning will used when other players blow a shot. It applies only to the great Michael Jordan's misses. That amounts to a double standard, and is not fair to the rest of the guys whose play is less than perfect from time to time.

Matt Guokas said they didn't double team me as much as they do Shaq. Take a look Matt. This was the kind of defense I encountered from high school until I retired.

I am not quite sure how Guokas reached the number one position in announcing the big games. As a pro player he left a lot to be desired, and as a coach, he left even more. Now, as an announcer, he comes off sounding knowledgeable about almost everything. *Does* he know all the answers? If he did, he would probably still be coaching, or maybe even playing.

I think that Guokas' selection was one the worst hiring decisions that could that could have been made, and why he occupies the main seat, I am not at all sure. On second thought, I really do know the answer. These guys are chosen, not for what they are capable of doing, but for how far they are willing to go along with what the TV and NBA want the listeners to hear. Matt straddles the fence often, and skillfully says the right things (virtually nothing) at all the right times.

Yes, I *am* down on Guokas, and I know him well enough to be justified in holding this opinion. I have often heard him announce, yet I have never heard him say anything notable or positive about the skills or performance of yesteryear's players. He is one of the guys whose major concern is selling today's game (today's game pays their salaries, after all).

It could be that I'm too hard on Guokas; maybe we'll all sell out somewhere down the line. I hope I'm wrong.

I recognize that personal power gives a person a lot more freedom in broadcasting. The voice of the Lakers, Chick Hearn, appears to occupy this enviable position. He says whatever seems right to him at the moment. Maybe I should give Guokas another twenty of thirty years to establish that kind of power base.

My purpose in bringing attention to Matt Guokas is not to demean him in particular. I know Guokas, and he is not a spiteful guy. I like him, but he falls short when it comes to being a good, straightforward announcer. Guokas does not stand alone in this respect, however; he only typifies what most announcers are like. They gloss over the ineptness of certain athletes, and are afraid to point truthfully at what is really occurring. In this respect, they are like the coaches who, afraid of finger pointing, never chastise their players or tell them bluntly that some of the stuff they are doing is totally ridiculous.

If I hear one more announcer describe Magic Johnson's making another "no-look" pass, I may just get sick. First of all, a truly no-look pass would be incredibly stupid. He has most definitely looked to see where *someone* is, but whenever he turns his head one way, he plans to pass the ball the other way. That's where we get the "no-look" part. One would think that by now surely the players would be wise to ploys of that nature (that's just how dumb many of the players are) but the announcers don't point those out, either. We do not hear them say, "You should know by now that Magic is passing the opposite way he seems to be looking."

Here is another illustration of what I mean when I talk about the media's tendency to put a slant on certain situations. The third game being over, announcers Bill Walton and Matt Guokas were comparing notes. Seattle was 20 points down before the end of the first quarter, and lost by 24 points. The announcers seemed to feel that in this particular game, Seattle more or less lay down and died. Then Matt spoke up, "No, they didn't lie down," he said, "Michael Jordan played so tremendously well in the first half, they were just hit by a buzz saw." He neatly removed the onus of the loss from a team that played badly by pointing out the great performance of someone else.

The facts reveal that Michael shot less than 50 percent in the first half, and before he made the last four (uncontested) shots in a row, he was shooting closer to 30 percent. He finished the game with about 34 points and, over all, his shooting was only in the 40 percent range—

not a tremendous percentile when you are shooting the ball as often as he did. Seattle's loss really could not be attributed to *this* great performance. (Most opposing teams, in fact, would welcome that kind of shooting from the great MJ.) The plain truth was that the Seattle team was just plain awful, and the real credit—or discredit—for their loss belongs only to them.

So, why not tell the truth about the game, Matt? If you don't know why, I can tell you. It's all about selling the fans more bullshit instead of criticizing the ineptness of Seattle. You have to be a salesman, Matt: promote the old game, hang on to your audience, and keep that J-O-B.


Another media story concerns Bill Walton's response to the technical foul that Michael Jordan did *not* get in the fourth game against Seattle. A foul was called on him, and Michael responded with outrage. He had been given a technical foul earlier in the game, and things were not going his way). He charged the referee, expressing his feelings in no uncertain terms. Virtually everyone there thought he should have been given a technical foul— but he wasn't.

The referee had just called a technical foul on the other team for a much lesser cause and Michael was the object of the Seattle player's foul. The guy who had committed the foul then walked in a huff, but his manner when walking away so offended the official that he was given a technical foul.

What do you suppose was going through that referee's mind when Michael confronted him? Was he concerned about being the one to throw Michael Jordan out for the first time in the history of basketball? Or was he afraid he'd go to hell if he stepped on God's toes by committing such a deed? We'll never know for sure.

Bill Walton's response to this incident showed that he is, at long last, losing it. My friend (and he *is* my friend)

182

said that he didn't think a technical was in order because "Michael really isn't that kind of a guy." Walton continued by saying, "It isn't the real Michael who is doing this; he really isn't the type of guy to act this way." Walton contended that inasmuch as MJ normally doesn't do that sort of thing, he should not be penalized by being ejected for doing a no-no that would have had any other player suspended. That creative line of reasoning implies that it's okay if you happen to shoot someone dead, just as long as you haven't been accustomed to going around killing people. Wow! Where are you coming from, Bill? Please let's get back to fruits and nuts and the truth.

*P.S. to anyone who happens to agree with Bill Walton about this:* We get what we deserve in this life—or at least we should. If a player punches another player in the mouth, the offending player should be thrown out of the game, not excused because he had never thrown a punch before. I, personally, can't believe that Bill truly meant what he said, but there are a number of people who agree with him. On the other hand, a lot of people, including the Seattle Supersonics, were outraged. I am not surprised; they should have been even *more* outraged than they were.

So it comes down to the age-old question: Is there special treatment? Do all the superstars get special treatment when they play?

I have to say that, to some degree, there *is* special treatment. I have mentioned before that if the superstars are put out of the game or on the bench, fans will be disappointed, hurting revenues. But on the other hand, one player cannot be allowed to control the show.

*Wiltie, did you get special treatment when you played?* People point to the fact that I never fouled out of a game, almost insinuating that I was given special treatment. But that was not how I played the game of basketball. I attacked the ball, not the person, and I used my bodily skills to

183

keep myself out of foul trouble on defense. And now I get looked upon as if I had been getting special treatment.

Yes, I got a certain kind of special treatment, as you will hear if you ask any official who ever refereed my games. The special treatment I got was their doing me the favor of *not* putting me on the line as many times as they could have, because they thought it was embarrassing for me to miss all those shots. That was the only special treatment *I* got.

The officials often used to say to me, "Wilt, if we called all the fouls that were actually made against you, the game would consist only of you going to the foul line—and we all know what a boring game that would be, watching you go one-for-two. I agree.

Let it be known here that the actions of the referees in relation to Michael Jordan are not his fault; the people who allow them to happen are to blame. If, because he is a star, he is allowed to carry the ball over and walk as much as he deems necessary, who could blame *him*? And if the referees are intimidated by Michael, they shouldn't be out there on the court.

## WILTISM

REMEMBER, OUR BED IS MADE FROM THE WORDS WE HAVE SAID. SINCE WE MUST SLEEP IN IT UNTIL WE ARE DEAD, WE SHOULD WATCH OUR MOUTHS AND USE OUR HEAD *(AND THAT GOES FOR YOU, TOO, WILTIE.)*

# FIVE

# FANS

The game of basketball has undergone some big changes in the past few years. As fans, you have accepted those changes—whether you know it or not.

The game was played much differently in my day. Our game was technically more correct, and our style of play involved less of what I call "showboating." Today, showboating is accepted as just a part of the game. In fact, many of you come to games chiefly to see a showboating-style player do something outrageous.

If the kind of antics we see on the court today had occurred during the time I was playing (doing a 360-degree dunk when your team is down by ten points, for example) those stunts would not only have been looked upon by the fans as incredibly silly, but the players, themselves, would have asked, "What the hell is that guy doing?" And furthermore, the showboater would have been benched immediately. Nowadays, if MJ doesn't give you at least one fantastic shot of that sort during the course of a Chicago game, you go away disappointed, whether Chicago has won or not.

I have talked to fans all across the country, from New York City to the beaches of Southern California, and I have been surprised to find that all of them—people from different places and from all walks of life—concur with my opinions about professional sports. *Can you imagine Wiltie? You're with the majority here!*

Most fans don't seem to be happy with what has been going on in basketball. They sense that the pro game is on a slide, and they're only going along for the ride, hoping and praying it will rebound to the right side. Most people want to see a change, and I tell them, quite honestly, that *they* are the only ones who can make that happen—and it will happen only if they change their habits of game attendance. Instead of continuing to support the present system, they will have to stop attending games altogether, and shift their support to something else. They agree that this makes sense; but more than talk will be required.

I haven't come across anyone recently who doesn't see a lot wrong with basketball and with the attitude of many of today's professional athletes. Talk is cheap, though, and change is not easy to come by. Come to think of it, I probably should be grateful that *something* is cheap, because those damn game tickets are *not*—and they are not about to get any cheaper.

How, you may ask, did the cost of tickets reach such astronomical heights? I'll tell you how: we let it happen by doing *nothing*, by accepting *anything*, and overlooking *everything*. We should have expected that this would get us *nothing*—and that's exactly what we got. If you are happy with the status quo, you're welcome to it; but if you are interested in changing things, stayed tuned.

*Big-mouthed Wiltie, trying not to be absurd, thinks
that, in this case, he deserves to be heard. Allow me to tell
you what's on my mind, for players and owners whose
insensitivity borders on crime. It's simple; fans can make
them pay, by not showing up at games—night or day. How
many of those spoiled people will then get their way? The
financial impact of an empty seat, will show that a team of
fans can't be beat. Unless players and owners get on the
ball, they may have to play to an empty hall. From fans
united, just a small peep could help make ticket prices a
lot more cheap.*

### INFLATION AT THE ARENA

When ticket prices go sky high, only the very wealthy
can afford to buy seats in the first, second, or third row—
or even in the fifteenth row, for that matter. There was a
time when you could take your kid or someone else you
cared about to a game and, as a special treat, you might
get tickets down in the very front rows. Instead of the usual
$6.50 or so, your tickets may have cost a few dollars more,
of course; but do you know what you might pay for a front
row seat in Madison Square Garden today?

When I was there just a couple of years ago, those
seats cost $450, and last year they were in the $1,000 range.
But hold on to your hats: this year they are going for $1,500.
*$1,500, ladies and gentlemen—$1,500!*

I don't mind their charging whatever amount they can
get for the luxury boxes—six figures if they can find people
who want to pay that much to get above and beyond the
rest of us—but $1,500 for regular down front seats? Who
can afford to buy tickets at those prices? Only a very select
group, I assure you. That, from my point of view,
constitutes prejudice, pure and simple. The little guys no
longer have even the most remote chance of being able to
enjoy the game they love from a closer perspective just by
paying just a little more for their tickets.

187

What are the owners and the NBA thinking of when they allow prices to go to $1,000 a ticket? It's obvious. They have made a deliberate choice to market their product to a different kind of person, putting it beyond the reach of the people who have long supported the game and helped make it what it is. As an average fan, I would tell them to shove it. I'd say, "Take your middle-of-the-road seats and your seats up in the boondocks, and you know what you can do with them. If you make it impossible for me to afford the better seats, I will not come to watch a game at *any* time."

*What are the owners and NBA really saying here Wiltie?* They are saying to all of us, "If you ain't got the money, honey, forget about coming to this game, Sonny." How dare they! In almost any other sport, whether at the amateur level (which I love) or whatever, most of us can afford a ticket. At a water polo or swimming match at Pepperdine University or a volleyball game at UCLA, we pay our few bucks admission and we can sit anywhere we want. Those who are first to get there can even get a front row seat. There is no discrimination here. Having money makes no difference in where we are allowed to sit.

It's a shame, and ridiculous, too, that the people who are real fans have been priced out of the ballpark—literally and figuratively. But basketball and football are not the only sports that have been affected. Take the Olympics, for example: $650 to $750 for an opening ticket! Who can afford those numbers? Only the well-off, unfortunately; the little guy is out of luck.

I repeat, if this isn't a case of discrimination, there has never been one.

Let's talk a little more about this. Basketball is a sport that was never intended for the blue bloods. From the very beginning it was a game that common everyday people could play and everyone could view. I remember the days, not too long ago, when celebrities and other VIP's sat up in the middle of the stands with the rest of us and were treated like everyone else. The earlier you got your ticket, the better chance you had for the best seating. Now these folks are pampered and catered to; they have the money, and that is all that seems to count today.

Of course, there's a PR advantage for the franchise in having the celebrities visible to the TV cameras, a fact which hasn't escaped the attention of the owners. So, once again, we have a sellout to power and money, and less-important people—the real fans—are left circling the bowl, headed down the drain.

## Wiltism

**A JUG WILL HOLD ONLY SO MUCH WINE BEFORE IT BEGINS TO OVERFLOW.**

**How MUCH MORE WILL WE BE ASKED TO PAY BEFORE WE SAY AN EMPHATIC, "No!"**

As I said in the first part of this book, sports can be seen as a metaphor for life, and in many ways life and sports mirror each other. There is a similarity, for example, in the way we make our opinions known in civil life and how we can do so in the sports world. Our most powerful and important liberty involves the right to vote, and we can use this right as a statement of protest in the sports world as well as in our political life.

Our ability to protest against what goes on in politics is limited, unfortunately, by the choices we are presented with when we step into the voting booth on election day.

In most places, we can choose one of the candidates who are on the ballot, indicating that we really approve of that person (which we may not) or choose not to vote at all. I believe that we should always have an additional option: "None of the above." Then, instead of being forced to choose the lesser of evils, we will be able to make a clear statement that we do not like *any* of the candidates.

Richard Nixon was the last President I voted for. Since then I have voted for, "None of the above."

In the world of professional sports, when we attend a game, our attendance is actually a vote, and is interpreted by the team owners and others as a vote of approval for the game—as a statement that we like it. On the other hand, if we *don't* approve—if we *don't* like the game—we can register the same kind of protest in sports as when we cast a ballot for "None of the above" on election day. We can use the "no show" technique to register our vote. A "no show" vote is cast by our absence.

A vacant seat will indicate to even the biggest of fools that you are unhappy with what you have been paying for, and that this is your way of protesting. An empty arena will quickly get your point across, and demonstrate to owners, management, and players alike, that it is time for a change—a change in their attitude, in the players' performance, in the prices they charge, and in their respect for the ticket-buying public. Their new-found respect can be demonstrated by allowing *all* fans— not just certain rich and famous ones—the right to seating anywhere in the arena, and at reasonable prices.

*The "no show" thing may be hard to do, but believe me, it's best for me and you.*

This country of ours was founded on an important idea about the value of each person's individual spirit and the right of each of us to do our own thing. These are the ideas that brought people with a pioneering spirit to our shores. They came here from all over the world, and they forged this nation of ours into something that other countries around the world could look upon as a haven for all, no matter what their belief might be.

The spirit of these pioneers made us the strong nation that we are—their individualism, their unwillingness to be subject to someone else's control, and their desire do their best for themselves and their families. So why are we now letting ourselves be led like a group of sheep— by unhealthy ideas, pushed here, and told to go there, while society tells us what is right and what is wrong. We have become robots without minds of our own, forgetting that we have the power to make most things change if we sincerely want to do so.

*Let's stop being the jackass who pays the bill; it is time to start using our individual will.*

I spoke not long ago with a basketball fan who believed, as I do, that the no-show approach is the only effective way a fan can express how he feels about professional sports. This man is very wealthy, but he, like the rest of us, is appalled that only people like him can afford a seat in certain areas of the arena. He agreed that sports fans, thousands of them, must be willing to say, "I'm not going to take it any more!"

As you basketball fans know, the NBA is currently loaded with former Continental Basketball Association (CBA) players. The CBA seems to have become the farm system for the NBA, though it occurs too me that perhaps the flow should go in the other direction. You fans should give serious thought to seeing some of these CBA games; you might be more apt to see real basketball there than when you watch the current best of the lot in the NBA.

It looks to me as though the CBA guys "try harder," just as second-place Avis claimed to do in their commercials of a few years ago. I may be unfair to Hertz in comparing them to the NBA, however. Hertz is number one, to be sure, because they *deserve* first place.

## WILTISM

**LOWLY TICKET BUYER OR WEALTHY CORPORATE FAN, IT'S TIME TO GET TOGETHER TO TAKE A FIRM STAND; ALL OF US, UNITED, CAN CHANGE THINGS, MY MAN.**

## THE SEE-SAW SYNDROME

One of my special dislikes relates to fans who are afflicted by the "see-saw syndrome." These are fans who come to the arena to *see,* but not to see the game. They come so they can *say* they *saw.* You know who those see-sawers are; they can be spotted with no trouble. They don't really care about who's winning or even who's playing. You can hear them talking constantly while they're looking around, interested only in making sure they see who they are supposed to see, and that they, themselves, are seen.

For some see-sawers, it may not even be about who is at the game. Some of them just want to say, " I was there the day Magic came back," or, "I saw MJ when he scored 50 points." Any momentous event will do. Now, no one can deny that this is their right; they're paying a hefty dollar for that sight. But how often can you say you saw a truly memorable game?

## THE MISINFORMED FAN

Please don't regard this as a put-down, but fans, as a group, could use a bit of an education in certain aspects of sports. For this reason, therefore, in the next few pages I have included some information that may help to correct some sports myths that become widely accepted. I'll also ask some questions that may cause you to do some thinking.

As I've said before, no one ever roots for Goliath, but in today's world the fans are not always sure who Goliath is. It was very easy in days past: you always assumed that the biggest and the strongest athlete had an unfair advantage. But today, it's often unclear as to who actually has that kind of advantage.

In world gymnastic competitions, the general rule is: the smaller the better. There are exceptions, of course, but you rarely see a girl over five feet tall or a man over six feet. The real Goliath in this sport is that little seventy-five pound, four-foot-six girl with the low center of gravity.

*She's* the real Goliath in this sport—but you fans root for her with gusto. So, I'll have to change my mind. We do root for Goliath, but Goliath is no longer always the biggest and the strongest.

It follows that, if being small is an advantage in gymnastics, size must create a disadvantage. So, when you see someone big out there participating in gymnastics, give him or her a hand—maybe even a *helping* hand. These people are to gymnastics as five-foot-three or -four Muggsy Bogues is to professional basketball. They need that extra help or encouragement because they are doing something truly special.

Would you be at all surprised to learn that Ernie Abercombie of Oklahoma, who led the Big Eight Conference in rebounding a couple of years ago, is only six-foot-four? If you were to check the listings of all the great rebounders, both college players and the pros, you might be even more surprised to find out that most of the best are between six-foot-four and six-foot-eight—no taller.

In rebounding, as in almost every sporting event, there is a prototype athlete, a supposedly "ideal" physique for that event or skill. Most people think that the taller a rebounder is, the better. But if you check out the teams that have the seven-foot-five to seven-foot seven centers, you will find that their centers rarely lead the league in rebounding. In fact, they don't lead even their own respective teams in rebounding.

Because of the agility required for proficiency in rebounding, tall players actually have a tougher time. Seventy-five percent of all rebounds are taken below the rim of the basket, so a smaller player with his greater speed and quickness actually has an advantage in getting the ball.

During the Cavaliers-Hawks game the other night, the announcer remarked that Cleveland probably leads the league in getting rebounds that have hit the floor. This statement should give you a clue as to how low you must go to get a rebound—not how high you must fly—and it leads to one unavoidable conclusion: being seven-foot-seven is not a help when it comes to getting floor balls; it's a hindrance.

When you hear that Charles Barkley, at only six feet four and one-half inches, led the league in rebounding one year, and has always been among the top rebounders, that feat should strike you as outstanding. And it is. But I can remember the great Elgin Baylor. He was only six-foot-four, but used to get 17 or 18 rebounds a game. He would have led the league in rebounding almost every year if it hadn't been for Bill Russell and Wiltie. *Rebounding's not about being tall; it takes much more to rebound a ball.*

Most fans do not know what to look for in a player. As a matter of fact, many players do not know what to look for in their own bodies. A large number of them spend far too much time building a sleek muscular body instead of honing their skills, often forgetting that skill is the factor that will ultimately lead them to their goal.

*Sports, to my way of thinking, have always been the ultimate test. They give each of us, through competition, a chance to show our best. Sports that began in the arenas of Greece and Rome, have come a long way and now can be viewed at home. Creature comforts were missing way back then, but you may be certain they played to win! Athletes gave of their very best, because death hung in the balance if they gave any less.*

## FYI

Have you ever wondered how a coach develops his game plan and strategic plays? I certainly have! As a knowledgeable basketball fan, I would like to ask some of the league's coaches:

> How come, when you're down to one last shot to either win the game, tie it, or whatever, we seem to see nothing but helter-skelter on the court? Instead of having one or two great plays you can go to automatically when you are two or three points down with three seconds to go, why does it look as if you just let your players go for it, hoping that one of them will get lucky when they throw the ball up? You seem to have no really dependable plays, double picks or anything of the kind that can be relied on to free a man to get a shot off. What *do* you teach your guys?

Following that same line of reasoning, when everybody in the world knows that in the last quarter of a game, (and for sure during the last few minutes) MJ is going to get the ball every time, *why* is there still no plan? Since you *know* where the ball is going to go, and you *know* he ain't going to give it up unless the world comes to an end, you have an advantage. Double team him, triple team him, put five guys on him—however you want to go about it— but for Pete's sake, *have a plan*. Even if MJ might be inclined to give up the ball (miracles could happen), wouldn't you rather take that scoring opportunity away from the one player who has proven that he lives for it and produces when given a chance?

Questionnaires are definitely a good way to find out how the fans feel about certain important subjects. It's not too difficult; you just ask some precise questions about matters that fans might have strong feelings about. We don't realistically expect that owners or general managers will ask the fans' advice on every little thing, but since it is supposedly for the public's benefit that the owners are doing business in a particular city, it seems to me that allowing the fans to be a little bit involved would be a good idea. Then later, if things go wrong, the public might not be so quick to put all the blame on management.

Just in case management does *not* knock on your door to ask your opinion about what is going on in your city, here are some suggestions: When you, as sports fans, have something to say, you should make your demands heard— through the press, by petitioning, or by displaying placards at the game. In desperation, you could even streak; that would attract the attention you seek. You could, for example, walk down the aisles of the Forum holding up a placard reading, "How about saving some good tickets for the real fans?"

Make a little fuss about the fact that all the good tickets are held back and sold to big corporations or to movie stars who use their clout to get them—while you, the average Joe and Jane who have been the team's big supporters since you-know-when, are shut out and cannot get a really great season ticket, or even a single great ticket, period. If you speak up, and put some pressure on them, you might find that, in the future, there will be good tickets left in reserve for average ticket-buying fans. *All* fans, after all, deserve to have a good seat once in a while.

## THE MISINFORMED FAN

Media and PR people have always done their best to use numbers to sell us on various athletes and sports. They like to use statistics as a guide in telling us who's doing wrong and who's doing right. But when you reach the point that you can recognize the meaninglessness of most of the numbers they use, you can get past all that stuff really quickly and see it as BS.

Triple-doubles and double-doubles (records that were not kept in my time, by the way) are employed today as a barometer of a basketball player's performance. But when we look at these stats for the top players, it gets a mite confusing. Even though MJ is everybody's favorite, and most media people label him as "best in the business," he probably has fewer double-doubles than any major star in the league. He had no triple-doubles at all last year—at least none I've heard of. Furthermore, I'm not sure if he's *ever* had one. MJ provides living proof that double-doubles don't really enhance one's game; his game needs no enhancement.

When both Jason Kidd, a second year player, and Grant Hill of the Detroit Pistons, also a second year player, lead the league in triple-doubles, it convinced me that those double-doubles and triple-doubles are worthless as indicators of a player's performance. Actually, some of the doubles that are announced to show that certain jocks are to be admired for a good day's work, may have had no relevance at all to their team's winning or losing.

Most of today's double-doubles and even triple-doubles would have been looked upon as a *lousy* day's work for most of us who played in my time. In those days, fans did not have to be told that a player had a triple-double in order to judge his worth. Performance was what mattered, regardless of the number count, and that is why MJ doesn't need pretentious stats to remind us of his greatness and his value to the game.

Did you know that, as a basketball fan, you are paying for more, but getting less? Both points and effort are going down. Therefore, you are getting less; less of a game and less from the players. Game time is going up (almost 30 minutes longer per game than in my era), but do not be misled into thinking that you are getting more for your money. Game time is going up only because there are more time-outs *(translation: "commercial time")*. That, I am sure, is *not* what you thought you were paying to see.

| Year | Length of Game |
|------|----------------|
| 1995-96 | 2:11.08 |
| 1974-75 | 2:00.06 |

| Year | Shots per Game |
|------|----------------|
| 1995-96 | 81.5 |
| 1976 | 103 |

I can't help but think that basketball fans are, at least partly, to blame for our being subjected to horrible performances such as we saw when the Orlando Magic played the Chicago Bulls in the third game of the '96 play-offs.

Let me explain my reasoning here. Orlando had lost the first game by 38 points, but in spite of that, TNT reported that the viewing audience for the second game was the second largest in NBA history. I cannot imagine why anyone (unless they like horror films) would want to see two teams play each other for a *second* time when, in the first game, one of the teams lost by 38 points? It defies belief.

Basketball fans collectively contributed to making those viewing audience numbers what they were. Instead of just turning the TV off and refusing to watch at all after seeing that first disgraceful exhibition, we choose to punish ourselves and to watch again and again.

I tuned in to part of the third game on the radio as I was shaving, and found that, unfortunately, this game was following the same pattern. Both teams were so bad that even the announcers, who had been bending over backwards to make things look good to the viewers, could not find anything positive to say. Orlando, playing at home, scored only four points in the fourth quarter—but droves of fans were still sitting there watching. Why are record-breaking audiences tuning in to games like that? Were *you* watching this fiasco? And, if so, why? Do you tune in only because you are really tuned out? Or are you into masochism? Perhaps horror flicks are your thing?

I may be on the right track here: we're talking about the enjoyment of horror. Horror has always held the attention of American viewers, and watching the Orlando Magic play against the Chicago Bulls was one horrific show. No longer an athletic contest, it was just another Halloween movie—*Halloween 1004* or *Friday the 13th.* (I don't, by the way, approve of this misuse of my Number 13.)

Even though the Chicago Bulls-Orlando game was hardly worth holding one's breath for, fans had to wait three or four days to see it. You see, NBC wanted to avoid showing the games on days when viewing audiences were expected to be small, so everyone was forced to wait to watch the single most horrible game of any importance that has ever been seen in the playoffs (with one bright spot: we *did* get to see Jordan and Pippen and the rest of them in action). Chicago won, hands down, but they cannot feel proud of this particular victory. They played *almost* as poorly as the Orlando team—yet they still won by 20 points. That should give you an idea of just how bad Orlando was.

Orlando was supposed to be the second best team in the NBA. Through '95 on into '96, they played close to .800 ball, and based on percentages, that record should put them into the higher ranks as the fourth or fifth best team of all time. Well, if this is one of the best teams of all time, I'm Ricky Barry on the foul line. (I would have said Calvin Murphy on the line, but we do look a bit alike—in color, if not in foul shooting—and I don't want anyone to make a mistake here.)

Grant, who has always been a warrior, was reported to be injured in the first playoff game. As a result, he had only one rebound and zero points during his 30 minutes of play in that game, and should not have been on the court at all. He could only hurt his team by being out there, and, sure enough, that's just what he did. Not only did he hurt his team, he inflicted more damage on himself, as well. His coach didn't have sense enough to know that by playing Grant, he hurt the entire team's effort. After it was clear that Grant couldn't cut the mustard, what took the coach so long to take the poor guy out? Who knows? The trainer finally had to go out and get Grant off the court. Who needs a coach like that?

What do coaches tell their teams when they are getting out-rebounded by thousands? They *should* be saying, "I want all five guys on the boards." I'm curious to know what the coach of Orlando told his team at half-time. Did he say, "You know, fellows, they are out-rebounding us, they are out-hustling us, they are out-doing us in every way possible. We've got to do something, so let's not keep on doing the same old thing—nothing." Or maybe he turned the TV on and listened to what the color analyst had to say (which you can be sure was designed to con the viewers into staying tuned for the second half). Why not go to the bench? If he had been playing his bench earlier during the season instead of worrying about Shaq and the others getting their average, he might have had some guys ready to play when it counted. Unfortunately, that was not the case, and I fault the whole organization, starting with the coach.

## WILTISM

**MANY OF TODAY'S PLAYERS ARE TRULY ABYSMAL ATHLETES WHO ARE OUT THERE ON THE PLAYING FIELD DOING ABSOLUTELY NOTHING. THERE IS A PROBLEM, HOWEVER, IN DOING NOTHING: YOU NEVER KNOW WHEN YOU ARE THROUGH. THAT IS WHY CONTINUING TO DO NOTHING IS SO EASY.**

There is no doubt about it: self preservation is the first law of nature. I am reassured that it is still operating when someone like center Alonzo Mourning, who plays for the Miami Heat, was traded by the Charlotte Hornets because his demands convinced them they could no longer afford him. I had the pleasure of meeting Mourning for the first time some months ago. He came up to me in a restaurant, said, "Hello," and proved to be quite a gentleman. I already knew him to be a great basketball player and someone who shouldn't be looked upon as out of order for demanding the best contract possible. But salary decisions are up to the owners, after all; and the sport will go under if they pay everybody what they demand. Players have every right to make demands, but they do not have the right to think that their every demand will be met.

I'm here to tell you, folks, that most of these guys would (if they had to) play for $100,000 a year. In fact, almost *all* of them would, especially if they don't have a college degree. But we are paying some of them $100,000 a day! *They could have been bought for so much less, but blame the owners for most of this mess.*

I seem to hear from players a constant cry of, "Trade me!" And, of course, they all want to go to a team with championship possibilities and/or where they can get the most money. What I don't hear is how very much they enjoy and appreciate the city they are in. Fan support no longer means anything at all to them. That's why I say to you fans that the power to change all this is in *your* hands. You *can* change the status quo, simply by refusing to show. Your actions will say very clearly, "Until things change, count me out. This is my way of showing you that you cannot continue to make whatever demands you feel like making, do anything you want to do, and play the game the way you want to play it. *I am the one who makes it happen for you, my man, but you've shown no consideration for me, your fan.*"

## WILTISM

**PLAYERS TODAY SEEM TO PREFER BEING TRADED TO A CHAMPIONSHIP CALIBER TEAM RATHER THAN STAYING WHERE THEY ARE AND CREATING THEIR *OWN* CHAMPIONSHIP CALIBER TEAM.**

All this is about knowing your sport. I believe that the more you know about it, the more you will appreciate and enjoy it. I also believe strongly that right is right, and right don't wrong nobody! So, if you are going to make judgments and argue about who are the best players and which are the best teams (and who among us doesn't love to do this?) you should have all the facts in front of you.

In baseball, they measure a player by the number of hits he gets in relation to his times at the plate. That's why they say he has a .330 average, for example. His actual number of hits may be immaterial; what really matters is his *average*. Likewise, in basketball, you need to know the percentage that a guy is shooting from the field, because that figure is often more important than the actual number of points he gets. A player may score 30 points, but if he takes 90 shots to get there (a typical pattern for a lot of stars), why should we be impressed? But watch the guy who is making the high percentage; *he's* the one who should be feared the most.

If a player is shooting 60 percent from the field, *he's* the one who should be shooting most of the field goals. And whoever is shooting the highest from the foul line should, in my opinion, be taking most of the technical foul shots.

There is another thing to consider, however, when you look at scoring percentages. In football, if you give a player the ball every time you're down on the half-yard line, he is apt to score a lot of points. Even though almost anyone else could have done the same thing, he gets the credit: his scoring percentage goes up, and so does his contract.

Guys like Marcus Allen of Kansas City are repeatedly given the ball at the one and half yard line, and each time this happens, the announcers tell us how great he is. Sure, he's great. He is, after all, able to score those touchdowns. But no one was measuring his greatness earlier on, when he was *really* running. Even now, they talk about his greatness only in terms of the points he scores—most of which were made because he was given the ball within spitting distance of the end zone.

It's all about points, and Michael Jordan probably knows this better than anyone. Because he knows that his scoring adds credence to his being considered basketball's number one player, he wants to be the leading scorer whenever he's out there. He knows that if he were tenth in scoring, a lot of people would not look at him in the same way they do now. Their perception of MJ is contingent on his being such a great scorer. He could do every one of the many other things he does so well, but without his scoring, he would be just another basketball player.

Then consider Dennis Rodman. He is a great player, for sure, but no one has called him the greatest player ever—and for one reason: points are not the outstanding part of his game. All of the players who have at any time been mentioned as "the greatest"—Kareem Abdul Jabbar, Julius Erving and others— are guys who have scored a lot of points. And, believe me, Michael is aware of that fact.


This evening, for the first time since I started to write this book, I went out for some relaxation, and ended the evening in a conversation that reminded me very clearly why I talk so often about the men I played against during my era.

I was standing at the entrance of a popular night club in Los Angeles, talking to a doorman who was probably about 29 years old. In his conversation with me, he was very respectful, but curious. His partner joined us, and we started talking about basketball (which they were reluctant to do because they were afraid I would find it boring). One of the young men said, "I don't want to be rude, Mr. Chamberlain, and I know that you were one of the best, but during your time there weren't very many good, big men. But in today's game," he continued, "because there are so many guys who are big *and* good, you know that basketball has to be a lot different." I realized, as he spoke, that he was being sincere, and that he, like so many others, truly believed that the big guys of today are much better than those of yesteryear.

Then his cohort spoke up and said, "Wilt, I don't know what this guy is talking about. I've been telling him for a long time that if he would just check out the big men who have made the Hall of Fame, he'd find all the great ones of yesteryear listed—but there are almost none today who could possibly make it." I enjoyed talking with these gentlemen, and it should come as no surprise that I didn't miss the opportunity to explain how I felt about the matter.

## CAMERAS

The camera has become a huge part of what's happening in sports, and, for the most part, its role has been a negative one. This camera is basically the same old device that has made a fool out of so many of us over the years. You have undoubtedly noticed that just focusing a camera on most people affects how they act.

Years ago a photographer would say, "Watch the camera and smile." Today, people don't need that kind of encouragement. Just the opposite, in fact: nowadays they look into the camera and do all kinds of idiotic things to cause the person at the *other* end—the one who sees the picture—to smile.

Gaining media attention has become the end goal. If you are a player, you do whatever you can to get on camera because you know the more camera time you manage to grab, the more attention you will get. Time on camera leads to a larger number of people who know who you are and who recognize your face. And recognition ultimately translates into money, via commercials and other means. End result: you and I have to watch people—fans and players alike—act like idiots.

I am writing as I am watching my usual two games at a time, one of which is the Los Angeles Lakers playing the Vancouver Grizzlies. It is no secret that cameramen do not make a point of panning the stands when there are a lot of empty seats. This is an attempt, for the benefit of TV audiences, to maintain an illusion that all NBA games are sellouts. Strange though it may seem, a game might have been a sellout, technically speaking, even though there are unfilled seats. Often, the tickets have been sold, but the seats remain empty because the purchasers can't give them away. They can't find a friend, enemy, or anyone else who is willing to come and watch some of these terrible teams.

That appears to have been the case for the game between the Lakers and the Grizzlies. The seats around the floor where the prestigious people and celebrity types usually sit are mostly vacant. There are more empty chairs than full ones, and somebody paid for each of those empty seats. Paid for or not, though, people would rather throw those hundred-dollar tickets away than come and watch the Grizzlies play.

# A Page To Ponder

### Item #1:

A.C. Green, only a young journeyman Suns player, negotiated a $6,743,000 contract. That's $80,000 per game, folks. What, then, should Charles Barkley be making?

### Item #2:

Patrick Ewing's salary is $18,724,000—$230,000 a game. So, what should Michael Jordan ask for? My suggestion: five percent of the NBA's gross plus ten percent of each player's contract.

### Item #3:

Big Dog Robinson, as a rookie player with the Bucks, wanted $100 million (he got $80 million). Since his teammate, Vin Baker, is the star, what will *he* demand? Two hundred million? Well, why not?

### Item #4:

Pat Riley coached four championship teams during the '80s, but hasn't had one since. Now, Pat is the last person in the world to need *my* help; he owns a healthy percentage of the Miami Heat, earns millions for coaching, and has complete control to do as he pleases with his team. (He traded virtually his entire team away in a matter of just a few months.) But the question at hand has to do with the Chicago coach, Phil Jackson. If Jackson wins his fifth title (one more than Riley's total), what will he ask for next year? God only knows—but that's all right. God plays for him, and Phil will get a good deal.

# SIX

---

# OWNERS AND EXPANSION

## MAD MEN AT THE HELM: AN AFFLUENT CLAN, BUT THEY DON'T HAVE A PLAN

---

Y ou may have sensed by now that team owners place very close to the bottom of my personal list. If there were laws against cheating the fans or against aiding and abetting childish pranks on the part of jocks (and maybe there *should* be), owners would be subject to arrest.

Reduced to its simplest form, here is the basic business plan of the pro basketball team owner. Phase I: Cheat basketball fans by first making ridiculous promises they know cannot be kept. Phase II: Use those promises as a reason for raising ticket prices. And, can you imagine? These team owners, the people who are paying big money to young basketball players and ripping off the fans, are the CEOs' and leaders of major companies—respected pillars of society whom we look to for guidance. Oh, boy!

Owners in general are not doing what they should (and could) to make professional sports a respected institution—one we all could be proud to be a part of, even if only as fans. Instead, they give us expansion.

If you are a proponent of expansion, and not convinced that we need parity, think again, ladies and gentlemen. With the kind of "parity" we have today, a team that is playing only in the .200s could conceivably reach the playoffs, offering you, in the first round, the rare opportunity to watch that unfortunate team play an opponent with a .900 record. What a treat to look forward to at the end of an already too-long season—too long because it has been filled with games between teams of unbelievable disparity.

Let me assure you that such an event can happen. As of the date of this writing, we have completed one-sixth of the '96-'97 season, and if the playoffs were to begin on the basis of the present standings, Denver, a team that is currently playing a whopping .308 and needs just one more loss to arrive at the .200 level) would face the number one team, Houston, currently playing well over .900 ball. How is that for a great playoff match?

P.S. I've just noticed that Denver has had a stroke of luck. Their next game is with the Phoenix Suns, who have a win percentage of .000 ( 0-12). This is the kind of match you'd jump off bridges to watch!

Do you realize that in the last two seasons there have been literally *hundreds* of games in which teams' final scores were only in the sixties and seventies? College teams score a lot more—and in less time. When I played, a player might have played only one game in his entire career in which his team scored less than eighty points; now many teams in the NBA (most notably the Knicks & Cavaliers) are holding their opponents to point totals in the sixties and seventies. I find this situation almost impossible to understand.

Too many pro players are shooting the ball far worse than the college kids, and investing less effort in getting the shot attempt. What does this tell us? It says that the talent pool has become so diluted that we have too few professionals who know enough about basketball to score a respectable number of points during any given game. There just aren't enough quality players to go around any more. *That's* what expansion has done.

*I want to ask you a question, Wiltie.* Suppose someone who was opening a new restaurant were to announce to his potential patrons, "Folks, give me about three or four years to get my food and service down pat; then boy, we are going to have the most dynamite French restaurant in town! In the meantime, however, I expect your patience *and* your patronage." You would waste no time in telling him he was out of his mind. But it gets worse.

Suppose our hypothetical restaurant owner were to continue by saying, "Please understand that we are not going to be giving you any discount in prices during the two or three years (and probably a whole lot longer) that our food and service will be sub-par, but when our service gets halfway decent, we plan to raise our prices a whole lot, probably to double or triple what they now are." Now, wouldn't you know for *sure* he was crazy? *Yes, Wiltie, I damn sure would!*

That is exactly what is happening in the NBA expansion clubs. What our restaurant owner is asking of his patrons is, in a nutshell, precisely what the NBA owners are demanding that their fans put up with. Team owners are offering a weaker and weaker product to hyped up fans who have been led to believe that, because there are more teams, they are getting more talent and higher quality basketball.

These (greedy?) owners are not about to forego the $5 million—or whatever the amount—that each team receives when a new franchise comes into being. Running a team does cost an arm and a leg, of course, and that could be their excuse for the dilution of the league; but the end result is that there is no real chance for parity in the league, and millions of fans across the country are offered a never-ending series of mismatched games.

Instead of giving the fans in their respective cities the strongest teams possible, the owners seem to be interested only in getting more and more money for their new franchises. No matter how many weak teams there are already, "Dumb" and "Dumber" continue to make decisions that dilute the league.

Expansion teams are formed from residue donated by each of the existing teams. Every existing team throws into a "grab bag" the crap that warms the end of their benches (usually holding back seven or eight of their better players). The new team is allowed to pick one player from each team's grab bag, then is additionally blessed with some goodies from the upcoming draft. These are the ingredients that go into the making of an expansion team. (The ingredients make one hell of a cake—one I would never want to eat!)

It is very apparent that there *are* many below-par teams. A person can easily verify that fact by going to a few games or by looking at the standings and the percentages in the paper. The weak teams are playing in the .100, .200, and .300 range; the only wins they get are in games when they play each other. We are being forced to tolerate, now and probably for years and years to come, the consequences of injecting additional sub-par teams into an already weak system. This practice *will* bring about parity in ten years or so: all *weak teams*.

Is there a way to change this deplorable situation? If the owners cared a lick about the fans and the players instead of just caring about making another dollar (or instead of not thinking—period), they could easily remedy this BS. The solution doesn't require a great deal of brain power—only a willingness to give us a better product. A simple rule change is all it would take.

If the established teams were allowed to protect only four men instead of seven or eight, the expansion team could be sure of getting a player of the highest quality from each existing team. With that kind of player material to work with, the new team would require only enough time to pull that team together, and, assuming good coaching, they could iron out the wrinkles quickly. I guarantee that under these conditions an expansion team would be competitive from day one. And established owners, knowing that they would be losing a quality player and weakening themselves, might think twice before agreeing to more expansion.

One of the few advantages an expansion team enjoys today is the assurance that they will not only be in the lottery for one of the (supposedly) best players to come out of college, but that they will be in the lottery for the next five to ten years. This is almost inevitable because they will, for an indefinite period of time, undoubtedly be among the worst teams in the league. I'll tell you, though: five or ten years is a long time to wait for anything or anyone.

*They say good things come to those who wait; but for an expansion team, good things may come too late.*

The era of Commissioner O'Brien has brought many positive developments in basketball; unfortunately, parity is not among them. Here is an illustration that will show you, in case you are still in doubt, just how far from parity we are: It is entirely possible, by studying the schedule for

213

the upcoming year, to pick your team's wins and losses in advance. You know the weak teams and the strong teams, and you can forecast the outcome of almost any given contest before the season starts. Basketball, more than any other major sport, is utterly predictable.

My request to Commissioner O'Brien: *No more expansion for at least fifty years, unless we use my new system.*

---

## WILTISM

**GROWING TOO FAST CAN BE A DETRIMENT FOR A BODY OR AN ORGANIZATION. A SMART ENTITY KNOWS WHEN TO SLOW DOWN AND CORRECT COURSE.**

---

One of the saddest aspects of the expansion team situation is one you might not be aware of. Each potential owner, before reaching status as a viable NBA expansion team candidate, must sell, or commit to, a certain number of tickets for a specified number of years. If they do not presell the required season tickets, they don't become eligible for NBA consideration. Of course, the league makes them sell an exorbitant number of tickets so they will appear to be doing well at the gate. Attendance figures of only 4,000 or 5,000 people would not look good, but that is the number of people who would come to the games if they had not bought their tickets in advance, unaware of what they were getting themselves into—or in *for.*

Large numbers of these tickets are sold to corporations, to companies that are willing to buy them out of pride in their city or out of a sense of civic duty. These companies undoubtedly anticipate that having a local NBA team will bring them definite economic benefits. I do not know all the tax implications, but I do know that companies like to give complimentary tickets to their clients and their big-wig friends. The rest of us—the common people—get no chance at the good tickets; they are already gone. The best most of us can manage is a seat out in the boondocks or up in nosebleed country.

The people who occupy the prime seats are not often really big basketball fans. They are people whose companies can afford to buy blocks of choice tickets, and people whose vanity is fed by sitting in the seats where they can see and be seen. The point here is that, while the stands may be full for a time, they are not full of true basketball fans. Many of these fair-weather season ticket holders even give their tickets away when some of the lesser teams come to town. So, although the stands may be full, this kind of attendance is not a good indicator of how well the home team is really doing as far as the fans are concerned.

You will find out if you talk to people that the game is not as popular as it used to be. Nor does it have the appeal it once commanded, especially in playoff time (always the icing on the NBA cake). It may appear that ticket sale revenues are stable, but believe me, that is only an illusion. The truth is that there are not as many fans buying tickets as you may think.


Most owners will do whatever it takes to have a winning team. When they own an above-average player, they appear willing to overlook anything and everything to make it possible for him to continue playing for them. Roy Tarpley of the Dallas Mavericks is a classic example. Tarpley had a drug problem, and the owner sent him to rehabilitation clinics—not once, not twice, but three times. After returning to the team, he continued to have trouble, so he went to Europe to play, then came back to the Dallas team, repeating this cycle over and over again.

The Mavericks keep bringing him back because they own him, and they want to get their money's worth. They consider him a valuable commodity, and they care not at all how many drug tests he fails or how many times he has to be sent to rehab centers. They are going to stick with him, no matter how addicted he is, as long as they believe he can help the team. Hence, the classic yo-yo routine.

Steve Howe, who was once a brilliant pitcher for the Los Angeles Dodgers, provides another example of owners in their yo-yo mode. I'll bet there is not a baseball fan in America who could give you an accurate count of how many times Howe has been sent away to rehab clinics, then brought back to pitch in the big leagues again. The Dodgers went through this cycle six or seven times before they decided to do away with Howe. (He now pitches for the Yankees.)

When will these owners realize that the game is bigger than any one person? If a player fails a drug test, he should be banned from the league. *Forever*. Let him go, and move on; that should be the policy. It is straightforward, easily understood, and would serve as a deterrent, as well.


Wisconsin's senior senator, Herb Kohl, owns the Milwaukee Bucks. I'm not sure whether or not he is a smart businessman, but I do know he is very, very rich. Like most owners, he will lay a bunch on just a hunch, and needs no good reason to pay a player millions for a season. He was able, in fact, to give Mike Dunleavy $10 million to be coach and general manager of the Bucks. I have frequently wondered why he would give so much power to an unproved man like Dunleavy, a guy who had just been let go by the Lakers, and who had never shown himself to be a good coach or to have the ability to take a team that has been as bad as the Bucks have been for years and move them upward in the Central Division .

The owner, Senator Kohl, may ask, "Well, what business is that of yours, Mr. Chamberlain?" I would answer that I have no quarrel with Dunleavy's making $10 million for whatever he does, but I do believe that the players, coaches, and various other people in the business use Dunleavy's case as the basis for their reasoning in asking more, and more, and ever more—and the resulting escalation of salaries will hurt *all* of us. In order to pay these ever-higher salaries, the owners will simply raise the prices they'll charge the long suffering fans. *I* am one of those fans, so Dunleavy's salary can and does hurt me, whether he is worth his pay or not. Maybe someone of the caliber of Red Auerbach or Johnny Wooden might be worthy of that kind of compensation—but Dunleavy? What has Dunleavy "dun"—lately or ever?

Even if you had the money and seats were available, you would still be standing in line behind certain celebrities if they happened to want those seats. It is definitely a plus for owners to have their most visible seats filled by note-worthy people who, they hope, of course, will help to draw fans who come to the games just to see celebrities. Celebrities have now become a part of the show, in fact, and, for many fans, are a bigger attraction than the game itself.

I remember when anyone could buy whatever type of seats they wanted, predicated on how much they could afford, plus how big of a fan they were and how early they were willing to get there to get the best seats in the house. To some extent this system should be put back into operation. Owners should always make sure that there are some good seats available for the everyday fans on a first come, first served basis. This arrangement would not hurt the organizations' ability to sell season tickets, but fans would have a chance to purchase good seats for every game if they were willing to be among the first in line.

Thank goodness there are still some sports, even though they may be the amateur variety, where sports fans can still get a ticket for $4.50 or $7.50 (and I don't mean *$750*) on a first come, first served basis. The promoters of these events understand the needs and financial limits of average fans, and do not trample on their wallets. Professional auto racing, too, provides for hundreds of millions of fans in all parts of the country the opportunity to watch events at extremely reasonable prices. The Dodgers, too, are sticking in there, holding the line on ticket prices, and I am sure there must be other organizations as well. For the most part, however, big business has ruined the small man's chance to feel that he's really a part of the sport he dearly loves.

I don't want to hear the owners complaining about player's salaries and whining, "How can we pay our players these exorbitant salaries if we don't raise ticket prices?" It seems obvious that if they can't make the payroll, they must be doing more than one thing wrong; but what most fans probably don't know is that players' salaries are *not* actually paid out of ticket sale proceeds. Salaries are normally paid from revenue derived from television contracts and from sales of new franchises—sales that put millions upon millions of dollars into each owner's pocket. Then, of course, there are the ancillary fees and licensing rights which allow owners to make "boo-koo" money from the products they sell—ash trays, hats, tee shirts, jock straps, etc. You name it—they sell it!

So, it should be clear that owners do not need your little old extra dollars to cover their players' salaries. Furthermore, most owners are not really concerned about the money they make from their ownership of the franchise. They have income enough from their other enterprises—

the kind of big bucks that made it possible for them to spend $150 to $200 million for a team in the first place. So, we can all relax. There is nothing for us to worry about: the owners and their families will always have enough to eat whether they charge you $5.00 for your ticket or $500.

How about it, owners? Couldn't you give the little guy a break and a chance to enjoy a piece of this cake? Letting some tickets go on a first come basis would show that you are trying to do your best for all of us, not just for the chosen few who are blessed by being the people who have most of the money in the world, or who are the most famous.

I am not the one who can change all this, sports fans; it is really up to you to do the job. So, here is a hint. If I were you, I wouldn't buy those lousy tickets until they started to give you some respect and a chance to get seating on a fair and impartial basis.

Have you ever flown the supersonic Concorde? My guess is that most of you have not. Tickets prices are so damn high that only a sheik or corporate executive can afford the luxury of a Concorde flight. What were the builders thinking when they designed this aircraft? They must have known from the beginning (and should have said so) that only the rich would be able to afford to fly in this plane. And NBA owners have become just as callous.

---

## WILTISM

**"FIRST CLASS" DOESN'T MEAN THAT YOU ARE THE BEST, OR EVEN THAT YOU'RE GOING TO GET THERE BEFORE ALL THE REST. ALL IT PROMISES IS THAT YOU'RE GOING TO GET THERE WITH A LOT LESS CASH.**

---

Though they're in this business for the dough-re-mi, basketball owners should have more respect for the game's his-to-ry. If they were to take time to learn about the game's past, they would realize that basketball, unlike some other sports, had its beginnings among the common everyday people. It is no accident that many of today's most skilled players are from the other side of the tracks. Why, then, are the common people being priced out of a chance to view the players that they nurtured, supported and watched develop?

Basketball owners loudly claim that they are civic minded, and that they brought their franchises to their cities because these wonderful cities deserve the best. They make statements such as, "We are going to do all in our power to give the good people of Miami (or Orlando, or the other cities) the opportunity to be a part of it all." They forget to mention that the "good people" they have in mind are the "good people" who can afford supersonic sky-high ticket prices.

Fortunately, basketball is a game that the poor can afford to play. It was never intended as a game for the elite, and its origins were not like those of tennis, polo, yachting, dressage, or even of the re-created Olympics of 1896. All of those were exclusive games which furnished a setting where members of the leisure class could hob-nob and compete. When Dr. James Naismith invented basketball, it was for the masses. But now, viewing basketball at the professional level is no longer an option for the very people the game was created for: they cannot afford a ticket.

I wonder if we will ever return to the closeness and spirit of concern that characterized the earlier owners and founders of the NBA. That spirit was once the most integral part of the NBA, but now that we have so many franchises and varied ownerships, I doubt that management can any longer focus their full attention and concern on what is right for the organization. *Yes, Wiltie, I do miss the old neighborhood-store closeness. Why must everything today be of multi-mega dimensions?*

Back when I started to play pro ball, there were only eight teams in the NBA, and we all knew each other so well that even today I can name, offhand, the owners or representatives of each of those franchises. (I may be a little off on one or two, but you will get my drift.) They were:

**Ned Irish** (New York Knicks): President of the corporation.

**Ben Kerner** (St. Louis Hawks): Basically the sole owner.

**Walter Brown** (Boston Celtics): One of my favorites, and the person to actually break the color barrier in professional basketball when he allowed five men of color, wearing the Celtics' green, to start at the same time. What the Celtics did from that point on, for themselves and for the entire league, is history—world championships following world championships, then more world championships.

**Danny Biasone** (Syracuse Nationals): The primary owner of the team, and inventor of the 24-second clock; a wonderful visionary of a man.

**Fred Zollner** (Once owner of the Fort Wayne Zollner Pistons, the team that later became the Detroit Pistons.) He had more money than all the others put together, but was smart enough to know that you couldn't buy a league. Zollner realized that solidarity had to come from working together, so he never used his money as a hammer in dealing with the rest.

**Les Harrison** ( Rochester Royals): Owner. Later that team was moved to Cincinnati and became the

221

Cincinnati Royals. Today's fans now know them as the Sacramento Royals.

**Bob Short** (Lakers): Short was one of the Laker owners, but whether he goes back to the time when they were the Minneapolis Lakers, I am not sure. He gave way to Jack Kent Cooke, who became the owner in Los Angeles and the last team owner I signed with and played for.

**Eddie Gottlieb**: This man, probably the cleverest of all the owners, pulled one of his most famous coups when he gave up a 1954-55 number-one draft to make me, while I was still in high school in Philadelphia, his number-one draft choice. Here's how it happened.

For those of you who may not be aware, back in those days a territorial draft was used. Under that system, each franchise had the option of drafting players from the colleges within their own geographic area before any team outside that area could do so. For example, if I had gone to Harvard I would have belonged to the Boston Celtics in the territorial draft; or if I had gone to NYU, the New York Knicks would have had first shot at me, and so forth.

At that time, the whole sports world knew that I was being pursued by over 200 universities, and Eddie, not knowing where I was going to college, did not want to lose me to some other team. Recognizing my talent and potential draw, he wanted to make sure I remained his property. Hence, he was willing to give up his 1954-55 number-one draft for the promise of getting me four to five years later.

Each of these eight owners was an outstanding human beings, and each was to me like a knight of the round table. They sincerely cared for each other, and all shared a common goal: to make professional basketball the best it could be.

One of the important ways the early-day owners differed from those of today was that many of them had to rely on the sale of tickets to survive (that's right, ladies and gentlemen, *to survive*). They were, in this respect, very unlike many of today's owners who are millionaire executives of multi-mega corporations, men who almost couldn't care less whether their teams make millions or just break even.

Another difference between the owners of today and yesterday is a major factor in the NBA's current problems. Not only do the owners of today's teams have very little loyalty to the others, they don't even *know* each other. *If, standing in the men's room, one pissed on another's shoe, he'd neither know or care if the other's name was Mike, Bob or Lou. So, why should they care about cutting another guy some slack, when they don't even know his first name? (It could even be Jack.) We could help to eliminate the things that now seem such a disgrace, by turning back to the old days, when owners dealt face to face.*

Here is a question for those who go to the ball park and cheer for the likes of Darryl Strawberry (not too long ago under house arrest for beating his wife with a bat or whatever, and behind in his alimony and child support—despite making three million a year). Tell me, please: Who among us condones that type of behavior? Obviously, some do. Even though Strawberry's unsavory deeds are common knowledge, you—yes, *you* New York fans—are out there cheering him on when he's at bat, just as if he had done no wrong. It doesn't seem to matter a great deal to some of you whether he hits his wife or hits a baseball.

What kind of man is this that we would want to make him a hero? Or an even better question: what have *we* become that we need this man to worship? We should be so giving to those who are more deserving!

I often wonder why an owner would want to have a player with such low morals on his team. And you fans are just as hard to understand. Strawberry's very presence in Yankee Stadium profanes the names of the great men who have played there; yet he is your hero. How our values have eroded!

I can picture it now, and I fear it won't be long in coming: A player who is still the property of one of the contending teams is on death row. The owner calls the governor, saying, "Look, I know he is scheduled to get the electric chair on Friday at midnight, but we have big games on Saturday and Sunday, and we sure could use him this weekend. So please, will you give him a short stay of execution—say until Monday? After that, he's all yours."

That's typical of the attitude of some of the owners and a lot of the fans. They don't care what their players represent, just as long as they help the team win—even if only for a short while. So, when you hear about an owner making a call to the state governor to say, "Give him a weekend stay—we need him here to play," don't be surprised. Remember: *you heard it here first!*

Here is a bit of advice that I will offer, *gratis*, to owners: One of the very best moves that you could make right now on behalf of professional basketball would be to create an advisory committee, a group of people who would bring to the NBA their views on rule changes, player personnel, disciplinary actions and expansion progress. The primary qualification for membership on this committee should be *integrity*. Committee members must be people who are not susceptible to being led around by the nose by owners; they must be immune to being impressed by money. And, of course, their courage and knowledge of the game must be beyond reproach.

My own personal recommendations for committee membership would include the following people:

**John Wooden**—the Wizard of Westwood.

**Bobby Knight**—an especially viable candidate in that he deals in the right way with college players of today who may in the future be in the NBA. (I doubt, however, that he would be willing to serve, as he has never been a fan of professional basketball.)

**John Chaney**—another great college coach. He is included on my list because we need input from the colleges, since they form the NBA's true foundation.

**Pete Newell**—known as a basketball guru for coaches and players alike.

Various ex-players from the NBA—and who better than **Bill Russell, George Mikan, Dr. J, Earl Monroe, Larry Bird** and **Wes Unseld**, among others?

These are men who have no axes to grind and no hidden agendas. A committee composed of people of this caliber could provide NBA owners with the kind of balanced input and invaluable advice that, if followed, could return integrity and pride to professional basketball.

Untold millions of fans watch their favorite athletes' every move, both on and off the playing field—on television, or video, and often in person. Other millions dream of becoming like their heroes (or even better). These athlete stars have become our tin gods, and, in the eyes of many of us, they can do no wrong. If by some freak circumstance, trouble should befall one of them, we quickly cover our eyes and ears, and turn blind and deaf to their mishaps.

We don't let ourselves think of these players simply as human beings who have shortcomings and frailties, or expect our erring pros to accept responsibility for their

225

actions. Instead, we make all sorts of excuses for their behavior, and continue to treat them with respect, just as though they had a perfect right to behave as they did. Herein lies the underlying problem and the real challenge that faces us today. Until we can place responsibility where it truly belongs, we cannot hope to turn professional sports in a more positive direction.

Who is to blame for the current state of affairs? I am confident that you know the answer to that question. *We* are to blame, of course. We are guilty of setting certain men above others and of allowing them a different standard of conduct, simply because of their exceptional talent.

All of us would probably agree that entertainment has some intrinsic value, but we get into trouble when we try to attach a dollar value to it. Is the value of star athletes higher than that of the people who educate our kids? Is the game that they are a part of more important than ending poverty and homelessness, or finding a cure for AIDS? Is going to a game more fulfilling than eradicating these evils? I think not.

We have become a world of escapees who, like ostriches, bury our heads in the sand while we immerse ourselves in mundane and frivolous endeavors. Nowadays, a gathering of friends and family on a Sunday morning in the fall is more apt to involve watching a pro football game, live or on television, than going to church together. Our values have definitely changed.

The way we regard our jocks as minor gods is not far removed from the other kind of worship. And our superstars, themselves, believe in their exalted position. So why should we be upset when they expect us to condone or even honor whatever they choose to do?

We have created our tin gods; now we must live with them.

# SEVEN

# MEDIA
## THE POWER OF THE HOUR

**TELL ME, WILTIE: HOW DO YOU FEEL ABOUT DEALING WITH THE MEDIA OF TODAY?**

To tell the truth, this is one area where I have to hand it to the contemporary players. These guys have it all over athletes of the past—and definitely over me. I don't think I could cope with the demands that the people in the media place on athletes today. You'd need a graduate course in "Communications and Media Protocol" to know how to handle these media guys.

Win, lose, or draw, jocks have to address a host of media people after every game. No matter if they are tired, injured or dying, they are expected to answer questions in a cordial manner, and even make people think that they enjoy the experience, when all the time they're hating every minute.

And the questions! For the most part they're embarrassingly inane. Most are insulting to the intelligence of players and viewers alike, and so childish that the answers are obvious. You have to wonder why a reporter would ask questions like these: "How do you feel now that for the nineteenth time your team has lost the seventh game of the world championship by two points?" Or, "How does it feel to be beaten by that last-minute ninety-foot shot?"

Interviewers just want to see the poor guy's eyes well up with tears as he speaks, and they hope he'll get caught up in the emotion of the moment and say something stupid. It's absolutely absurd, and I simply could not put up with that BS.

You may have noticed that this kind of exploitive interviewing was done quite often during the Olympics, in interviews with the men gymnasts among too many others. The ultimate in interviewing stupidity was reached when three-time Olympian and multi-gold medal winner Janet Evans was asked how she felt about breaking her toe just prior to her final Olympic competition. Talk about your dumb (not to mention cruel) questions! How would *anyone* feel?

Unfortunately, that incident was by no means unusual. More recently, in an interview with Monica Seles after she had been forced to withdraw from a match at Madison Square Garden because of a shoulder injury that required surgery, an interviewer asked, "How would you rank this misfortune in relation to all the other problems you've had?" In her place, I would have replied, "On a bad-break scale of one to ten, I think I'd give this one about a nine; but in compassion, I'd give *you* a zero."

# WILTISM

THE CONSTITUTION GAVE US THE RIGHT TO FREEDOM OF SPEECH, AND WE HAVE FOUGHT HARD TO HOLD ON TO IT. BUT IN THE MEANTIME WE SEEM TO HAVE FORGOTTEN THAT WE HAVE ANOTHER RIGHT: *THE FREEDOM TO KEEP OUR MOUTHS SHUT.*

Most sports organizations require that their athletes talk to the press. The reason is obvious: the organization depends on the media to promote their players and games. And the owners, because they are paying their players a lot of money, can insist that they be available to talk to the media after each game or match, no matter how they feel, physically or emotionally. I personally do not believe that a league (or federation, or whatever) has the right to demand that a player sit there and, even though the ordeal becomes almost unbearable, answer questions for a designated period of time.

The press representatives that do the post-game interviews with pro-athletes should have to follow the same kinds of rules and show the same kind of respect as the President's press corps does at White House press conferences. If *those* reporters ask a really inappropriate question of the President, they are simply declared *persona non grata*—no longer welcome. A similar fate should await sports reporters who persistently ask questions that stir up animosity and confusion: they should no longer be allowed in the locker room. If they will not follow protocol, they should be barred. *Period.*

Have you noticed how, after a Wimbledon match or any other major tennis event, both the winners and the losers, before they leave the court, have to make a speech before, not only the fans in the stands, but the entire world-wide television audience. The losers always have to go first, graciously thanking everyone present for coming and watching them lose. ("Thanks for sitting there watching me choke," or maybe, "Thanks for coming to see both of us play our worst.")

This charade is nothing short of preposterous. After a hard-fought contest, an exhausted player should be allowed to say a simple "Thank you" and "Good bye." But no, they must make a speech—whether in France (even if they don't speak French), or in Spain, (and they don't speak Spanish), or wherever else in the world they might be.

Asking this of an athlete is way beyond fair. These are tennis players, after all, not orators. Public speaking of *any* kind in any place might make a given player very, very nervous. (Having to make speeches in class might even have been the reason a player left school early to join the tennis circuit.) But if a player doesn't talk after a match, he or she is labeled as not a nice person, and *that* albatross is worn around a player's neck for a lifetime.

Choosing to speak or not to speak should be the absolute right of every athlete, with no penalties attached for either decision. If jocks were allowed the option of speaking only when they truly wanted to instead of when they have to, they might have something to say that's worth listening to.

Reporting the facts can sometimes be difficult for a sports reporter. I can understand that, after seeing a team every day and even riding with them to different venues, a reporter might have a hard time telling a story with brutal honesty. Under these conditions, doing a piece that is negative about the team or comes down hard on a player can be difficult. But honest reporting is the job of those who are in the media, and since a great many people depend on their every word, they should make sure that everything they write reflects what they really believe to be true.

*It takes some heart to be for real, and most reporters are afraid to do the real deal—they end up giving out a phony spiel. We know everyone's not like Detroit's Hill, so why give almost everyone a clean bill. You've got the information; all you need is the will.*

Have you noticed how the various media can take a single situation (always negative, of course) and apply it across the board? From a drug incident involving one youthful tennis player, Jennifer Capriati, they drew the overall conclusion that young stars cannot handle the pressure of playing professional tennis. But how about Steffi Graf, Gabriela Sabatini, Arantxa Sanchez Vicario, Mary Joe Fernandez and a host of others who started at 12 or 13 years of age? These young people are model citizens, and the whole world can be proud of their accomplishments.

I hope the media will come to understand that isolated instances of all kinds are bound to happen, but what is true for one bad apple is not necessarily true of the whole barrel. I hope, also, that the parents of Venus Williams and many more like her have not drawn broad conclusions from a single incident. The larger picture shows that young athletes, with proper supervision and care, have been able to conduct themselves well and handle their careers admirably. And remember, please, that Jennifer Capriati's case cannot be summed up easily. I know her parents to be loving and caring people, but, as we know, the best laid plans of mice and men often go astray.

We have been privileged lately to witness a growing number of public service announcements during televised games. They feature players who, for the most part, do them out of the goodness of their hearts. In trying to get kids to read or to do something else that is positive or beneficial, these guys are doing a fine service, I admit. However, there is no way to measure the effect of these spot announcements, and I am not at all sure that the results are what we expect.

My guess is that preaching of this kind has no real impact on kids. In the first place, the spots are repeated so often that the kids no longer watch them. Furthermore, they know that the players do them only because they are asked—not out of a true conviction. When a player says, "Hey, kids, stay in school," the kids retort, "Easy for *you* to say. You got a $40 million dollar contract after turning down $20 million, and now you're telling me what *I* should do to make some money?"

The moralistic messages are oversold, and they are pitched to the wrong people, at that. The young people who need this rhetoric are *not* the ones who are listening. Those who could use the advice are out somewhere busily getting into mischief, and couldn't care less about hearing some wealthy, pompous athlete tell them how they should behave.

Sure, making these short spots is a fine public-spirited gesture, but if we really care about doing something good for the misguided, why don't we put our money where our mouths are? We should take the money that is now going into ineffective public service announcements, and use it for projects that would give young people jobs and a chance to participate in something worthwhile.

Juwan Howard of the Washington Bullets does a public service spot on how he loves to read. He reads, he says, while he does push-ups and sit-ups and while he's shooting baskets. He is trying to convey to the kids that reading is good, and it *is* good, of course. We all know that. What the viewers *really* need to be aware of is that we are building more and more prisons while we are closing more and more libraries. How are kids ever going to get a chance to read if this is allowed to continue?

If the NBA is sincerely concerned with its public service image, why don't they build some libraries, open them up in the name of the NBA, and let the players who are making millions and millions of dollars put their money where their mouths are by supporting worthwhile places for kids to further their education.

Sports radio shows tend to be a bit more honest than other elements of the media. This has probably happened because the shows thrive on contention, and hosts willingly use the truth when it will stir up controversy. They know that listeners will react strongly to provocative statements about certain teams or athletes. Radio people have access to the same information as the newspapers and TV, but they are more willing than those in the other media to confront their callers and their listeners with the truth.

For a real understanding of what is happening with sports in general and with the teams in your area, I recommend tuning in to the local radio sports stations. I have generally found the hosts of these shows to be a lot more up-front and honest than some of the people who broadcast nationally. Even though the local guys love to incite controversy, they are also looking for the truth. And they know that if you are honest, you are apt to be controversial.

Unfortunately, money is the name of the game; so everyone caters to television, and that's a shame. Virtually everything that goes on in sports is predicated on how television wants it done. Television calls the tune, but you can hardly blame the Sports Federation for that when the

233

networks, after vying against each other for the TV rights, end up paying $300 or $400 million for the NBA contract.

The networks may actually find themselves in a money-losing situation, because many sporting events don't turn out to have the popular appeal that was anticipated. So they must find additional ways (primarily increased advertising) to produce income. To accommodate the larger number of commercials, television broadcasters now call the timeouts for each team. When the announcer says, "It's a TV timeout," action stops—no matter what phase the game is in. Even if a good running action is going on, and the teams need to keep the action going or lose their cohesiveness and momentum—they have to take a timeout, nonetheless. That is the worst kind of BS!

*Do you know why they have to call a timeout at that particular moment and no other, Wiltie?* Because they want to be in sync with all the other stations around the world. *And why is being in sync so important, Wiltie?* That's easy: it's so that you and I won't be tempted to watch something else while their commercials go on forever, and ever, and ever. If we do try to switch channels, all we are going to catch is one commercial after another on each and every network. If you haven't caught on to this, check it out sometime. Go from CBS to NBC, then to ABC and Fox— any of the major channels; you will see nothing but one commercial after another, because they are all on the same schedule. For the networks, this system is great, but it hurts the hell out of you and me—*and* the teams who are forced to call a timeout just when they have momentum going for them.

Television has become so powerful that without it, a sports endeavor is apt to fail. On the other hand, working *with* TV often means being forced to change the format of the original game, perhaps to the point that an entirely different game or scoring system is created (as happened in collegiate and beach volleyball).

Even if the networks are hurting financially because money isn't coming in as they had hoped, we can't just sit back while they take over completely. We must not allow them to make a mockery of the games. Here is where we need another change in order to accommodate the needs of *everyone* who is involved in televised sports.

Since the media has the power to make or break a sport, I was saddened to see how shabbily they treated the Olympic track and field trials. They gave those events extremely poor coverage, on Sunday choosing to show golf, instead. And even on Saturday, they cut away from track and field to show what was going on at the golf tournament. Track and field was shown only when it was most convenient—for TV, that is. It certainly was not convenient for track and field fans.

This kind of treatment by the media does not help to make track and field a bigger sport in America.

What is the reason that most of the major papers in every metropolitan area focus almost their entire attention on the professional side of sports? Every one of them will tell you that they are responsible news organizations and dedicated to the general welfare. And they'll tell you, very seriously, that civic pride drives them to do their very best for the area they serve. But whom do you see on their front pages but Tyson—convicted (not accused, *convicted*)—of unmentionable crimes. And there he is again on the sports page, with a feature article designed to lure us into watching him make his millions of dollars per second ($40 million a year, minimum). What a great example the newspapers set before us!

The Boxing Federation should never allow this man to make as much money as he does while he remains so unappreciative of the opportunities this country has provided him. There are too many others who better deserve the kind of breaks and attention that he has been given—individuals who, through no fault of their own, have never had Tyson's opportunities. But what do we hear from the media? "As servants of the public," they preach, "we are in business to give the majority what they want." They pompously tell us that they are blameless, as they feed us what they think we want to see and hear.

So much for the social conscience of the print media.

*I'll take the Golden Gloves and only three rounds over ten rounds of overpublicized, overpaid pro clowns who just walk around, with no punches to be found. You would agree if you gave it a shot instead of watching those fights that are nothing but rot.*

Executive types who give Rodman air time and offer him as a role model for kids to follow either have no heads at all, or those they have are up their collective asses. When they use in their ads someone like Rodman—a person who will not comply to many of his team's rules and regulations—they say to kids all over the country that this is how you are rewarded when you act as he does. You get to be in commercials and make millions of dollars, while you do just as you please.

Thanks to this group of money-hungry CEOs, we are all going to reap what the advertisers sow. Think about that, you corporate decision-makers who constantly complain about what's happening to the world today. *You* are what's happening to the world today!

Is there truth in advertising? Let's hope so, because there is very little truth in anything else that the NBA and

NBC are doing regarding their commercial output. How is it that we can watch four commercials in what is referred to as a "twenty-second timeout"? Yes, I said *four full commercials.* Could each of those commercials be only five seconds long? Come on, people, let's get real. Those are half-minute to one-minute commercials. So how in God's name can four of them be run during a single twenty-second timeout?

We all have learned to take TV advertisements with a grain of salt, but for a case of unadulterated dishonesty I doubt you can beat this. For nearly a year, ESPN ran an ad promoting a set of video cassettes titled, *Totally Awesome.* The promotion commercial claimed that one of the tapes contained footage said to be ". . . from Wilt Chamberlain's 100-point game."

Talk about blatantly false advertising! NO films were ever taken during that game—not even a camera shot. Take it from me, ladies and gentlemen: I was there, and I know this to be true. Furthermore, everyone at ESPN was sufficiently knowledgeable about sports to have known it, too. They knew the ad was a lie, and that no film footage of that game ever existed (though one still shot was taken *outside* the arena *after* the game). Knowing the ad to be false, they still allowed it to be shown for more than a year (it may, in fact, still be running). This is beyond crazy; it is downright fraudulent! Why did neither the NBA or ESPN take action to get this ad off the air?

I have knowledge, of course, only about the part of the ad that pertained to me, but the ad contained other claims that related to other athletes, as well. I wonder (but I have no way of knowing) how many other falsehoods were contained in the commercial. I'll leave it up to you to guess. The whole set of tapes could be had for $19.95. What a bargain! But what you were getting, who the hell knows?

(ESPN take note: I'd sure like to see that non-existent footage!)

In traveling around the country, I have noticed that newspapers customarily have a major league attendance box that sometimes takes up as much as a fifth of a page. These boxes usually deal with road and home games, and matters such as this year's attendance relative to one thing or another. I often ask myself why information as dull as this, just because it is about the pros, is thought to be worthy of taking up that much space. That part of the page could have been better used for showing, for instance, a picture of a kid training in an amateur sport or accomplishing something of merit. Just having a picture in the paper might inspire her or him to achieve something worthwhile. And seeing that picture in the paper could encourage other young people, as well, to head down a more productive and honorable road.

I'll never forget how proud I felt when, as a young kid just out of junior high school in Philly, I saw my picture for the first time in one of the major Philadelphia newspapers. And, even though I might not have been aware of it at the time, deep down that was truly a time of elation and inspiration. I recall that I was very proud, and my parents were, as well. I remember, too, that everyone in the neighborhood mentioned seeing my picture, and offered congratulations.

*A note to sports editors: You can decide what goes into that space, and what could be better than putting a smile on a kid's face? There's the real power in what the press can do; so don't be just a turnstile, counting attendance as people go through.*

My congratulations to the Los Angeles Times! This newspaper (and there are probably others I am not aware of) has been giving some overdue space to high school athletes. By selecting an "Athlete Of The Week" in both boys' and girls' sports (often featuring track and field) the Times is giving recognition to the amateurs of the world— the young people who will be tomorrow's leaders. In this, they are doing the right thing, as far as I am concerned. (On the other coast, the New York Times, supposedly one of the better papers of the world, gives little or almost no space at all to any but the pros.)

*Other papers, I'm sure, are doing their share. But I wish that many more would care.*

It is no secret that virtually every Super Bowl game in history has been an immense letdown. The endless con that precedes the game is not only ridiculous, it's insulting to every fan with an ounce of intelligence. The media people tell us every year what a great game is in store for us (never mind how bad all the rest of them were). Giving us the benefit of a little doubt, they *should* say, "We *hope* a great game is in store for us." After all, even though both teams are good teams, a good game is never a sure thing. Sometimes two of the best teams in the world produce a lousy game; so if two lousy teams are on the field, what can we expect?

Nothing today seems worthy or right unless bolstered by endless unadulterated hype. We have reached the point where the hype has become a bigger event than the main event it is promoting. Take the "coming attraction" trailers for most films today. They show you every bit of the film footage that has any merit at all. Then later on when you see the film itself, you come out feeling cheated because you had already seen everything that was worth watching.

Do film executives and event promoters fear that their game or event couldn't possibly stand on its own merit?

They must think that, without their using a carnival barker's approach, no one would show up. Back in the good old days, a World Championship—or a championship of any kind, for that matter—was a worthwhile attraction because you could be sure that the best would be going against each other. In boxing, the number one contender always fought the champion. But now, since that is no longer true, they have to hype both the fight *and* the challenger, because if they didn't hype him, you probably wouldn't know who the hell he was. For that matter, considering the current wide variety of champions, you might not even know who the *champion* is. (And when the fight is over, you still might be in doubt.)

The spin doctors of the sports world will use anything at all to make you believe that the game they are promoting is a must-see event. Hours are spent talking about the matchups, how the teams present such a contrast with each other, and how that factor alone can make the game worth watching. The whole approach seems to hint that the game itself probably won't do anything for you, but the matchups could be interesting.

None of this would be needed if the game could be counted on to be what it should be. Hype wasn't needed when we played the Boston Celtics. No one had to urge the fans to "Come watch Wilt Chamberlain, the greatest offensive player, go against Bill Russell, supposedly the greatest defensive player." No; the Boston Celtics were the best team in the world and the fans needed no encouragement to come watch them. We had a chance to beat this team, and people were eager to see just how well we would take advantage of the opportunity.

More recently, when you had Shaq and The Orlando Magics against Olajuwon and the Houston Rockets, the hypesters conjured up a momentous confrontation between

Olajuwon and Shaq, ". . . two of the greatest centers in the universe," blowing it up to be the kind of once-in-a-life-time occurrence that should not be missed. The championship alone is no longer enough; the real drawing card has become the incredible contest between the two basketball giants.

Then, to everyone's disappointment, the battle fails to happen. These two giants don't even play against each other. Most of the game, someone else is guarding Olajuwon because he is too quick for Shaq, and they don't want Shaq in foul trouble. *That's* how much battle is done.

In all that hype, where was the truth, and where the honor? Where is the heart and soul of the game? Clearly, there is no faith on the part of the media that we fans have sense enough to watch something of quality without being told a lie.

Even though the great hyped confrontation between Shaq and Olajuwon never actually materialized, we *were* treated to a commercial featuring the two of them going against each other. As you might have guessed, the commercial *itself* was hyped as a big deal. Stop and think about that for just a minute. They first hype the big confrontation (the game) to you as a fan; then the rivalry (the commercial) is hyped to you in your role as a consumer. Talk about getting mileage out of a single event! And this one never even happened.

The real game and the real commercial did have one thing in common: there was no fear that either one of them would involve any kind of true contest. (And I thought there were laws against false advertising!) The only competition involved probably had to do with who would get the most money for doing the commercial; the actual battle may have been between their agents.

Shucks! We might as well go watch wrestling. There, at least, we'd know we were getting hyped right from the start.

## WILTISM

**HOW DO YOU KNOW WHETHER YOU'RE WATCHING A GAME OR A COMMERCIAL? YOU KNOW IT'S A COMMERCIAL IF THE PLAYERS ARE MAKING ALL THEIR SHOTS.**

The pros get more than their share of attention from the media—more than is given to any other level of sports. And unfortunately, special (and undue) focus falls on the more sensational stories about pro stars. Media folks have a strong preference for sensationalism of a negative nature instead of the positive variety.

I am forced to ask myself why, *why* do publications like the Enquirer and People magazines flourish? Do we have, lurking in the dark recesses of our minds, a lust to hear about things that are truly bad, gross, and even flat-out evil? We can't wait to take it all in, and those publications feed off of our worst impulses. They make us victims of our own weakness by feeding us garbage.

This sensational stuff has no place in our everyday tabloids. Let's leave the bad crap to the magazines that want to print it. *There are so many healthy things to read about and see, so please give us the good stuff in our newspapers and on TV.*

"Only in America," and "It's the American way." We have heard those phrases—and accepted them at face value—for most of our lives. But I am not sure we shouldn't take a closer look at one aspect of our so-called "American way."

I'm all for the "innocent until proven guilty" principle, but how do you feel about a situation where, after being proven guilty, someone gets another chance, and another chance, and yet *another* chance? And how about a person who makes millions and millions of dollars out of his bad-boy image and his pranks, then capitalizes on them so that the more he acts up, the more money he makes?

That is the scenario followed by the Tysons of the world—with, I might add, the active cooperation of the media. As the leading proponent of this program, Tyson gets an incredible bad boy image, then uses it to increase his chances to make tons more moolah. (Could there be an incentive here for him to misbehave?)

The way it works reminds me of the wrestlers who (just in fun, of course) try to sell their mean, bad-boy image. *But Tyson does it for real, and that's a bad deal that should have no fan appeal.*

We have so little appreciation for the opportunities that America gives us for making a buck that we allow athletes to misuse them. We allow individuals like Tyson to repeatedly do things which reflect negatively on *all* athletes—especially on men of color. With the enthusiastic assistance of the media and the (silent) approval of their various federations, they do whatever they want, and profit from their actions.

It is time for the federations to start using banishment or suspension if they want us to believe that they are serious about monitoring the behavior of their wayward jocks. If they sincerely intend that these misbehavers will get no chance to profit by breaking the law, they'll have to show us. Until penalties are imposed, those governing organizations—not to mention all of *us*—will continue to be demeaned. Lawbreakers should, in fact, lose their ranking and chance for any championship fight; but no, that almighty dollar makes everything right.

What about the guys who train hard and walk a straight line? Should they have to give up their position and opportunity so that some guy who just got out of jail has an opportunity, within a matter of months, to fight for the heavyweight championship of the world? The lawbreaker doesn't even have to come up through the ranks! That is *not* my idea of the American way. And if it *is* the American way, it's time for an amendment and a change to a *better* way.

I tend to harp on the media for failing to give the credit that is due to some of the old-timers, but my reasons are valid. Archives for the years prior to about 1976 are virtually nonexistent. Records were not even kept then, at least not in the way they are today. As a result, we oldtimers will not have a chance to be seen by our grandchildren in the same way that the guys who performed during the '70s, '80s, and '90s will be seen by succeeding generations, on tape as well as in print.

Contemporary athletes are focused on their own game, and most are uninterested in the history of the game or in giving credit to the players who helped make basketball what it is today. So, by default, there is only one group we can look to for help—the people of our media. Only they can serve as our chronologists and glorify us if such is deserved. If we don't hear the truth from *them* about how we were and what we went through, our story will be left in limbo and our accomplishments will go unremembered. And I, for one, don't want to see that happen.

Players tend to do a lot of talking about what they are going to do against certain teams. And the media, always looking for a controversy or a quote that will interest us in watching the game, eats it up. When Alonzo Mourning claimed that his team could beat the Bulls, that was his right. Unfortunately for Alonzo, his forecast was flawed. As it turned out, he didn't have a real good series against the Bulls. But people in the media, by making it appear that Alonzo was speaking out of character, was happy to use him as a way to get our attention.

I know Alonzo as a man of integrity, and a person for whom I have a great deal of respect. Furthermore, I know that the press will turn things around if it benefits them, and are perfectly willing to make us all look like fools. In this case, they twisted Alonzo's words, making it appear that he was saying, "Oh man, we are going to *kill* the Bulls." Now, everyone knows that Chicago has the better of the two teams, so I don't think it likely that Alonzo was quoted exactly as he spoke (or as he *intended* to speak)—and that's unfortunate.

My own policy was to let my playing do my talking for me. I have never, at any time, or at any stage of my athletic career, said that I was going to beat the pants off of anybody (or even that I would *barely* beat anyone, as far as that's concerned). And I was not the exception. In our time we were never asked that kind of question, and none of us found it necessary to put down our opponents or forecast the outcomes of games. But today, every sports reporter will try to hype players and steer them into conversations to suit their own purposes. Hence, every player would be well advised to watch his words.

Did you observe the hype of Chavez and De La Hoya, ladies and gentlemen? Another Tyson-style scenario, and they got us again. The fighters were down in weight, but the hype was just as heavy–and the results were, unfortunately, just the same. They don't care how poor you are, how rich you are, whether you speak English, or

Spanish, or whatever else—they are going to hype you, baby. *They'll find a way to get your dough by hyping you out for that big-time show. And what's going to happen? By now you should know: The fight is going to go no more than one, two, three or four.*

Here is a question for which I've never found a satisfactory answer. Maybe the media can help me out here.

Even though "the greatest" was a tag that was seldom attached to my playing, *my* records and *my* performances are the benchmarks against which other centers are inevitably measured. As exceptional centers have come on the scene, they are rarely (if ever) compared with George Mikan, the first great, *big* man ever to play the game, or the great (and also big) Bill Russell, or the number-one scorer of all time, Kareem Abdul-Jabbar. Why am I the measuring rod against which great basketball players are compared? Can you media people explain this? Am I only a yardstick here? I'm confused.

Speaking of the media's fondness for comparisons and their synthetic duels between players, I am reminded of another puzzle. When I was playing, the news headlines and articles consistently pictured me as pitted against the same five or six players. Sports section headlines seemed always to portray me as being in competition with Bill Russell, Walter Dukes, Elgin Baylor, Walt Bellamy, Nate Thurmond, or Kareem Abdul-Jabbar—all men of color. I have always thought, however, that the most logical players for me to have been measured against—those who were actually most comparable to me—were Bob Pettit (the league leader in scoring when I entered the NBA and the rebounder who was second only to Bill Russell) or Dolph Schayes (the six-foot-nine-and-a-half perennial star of the Syracuse Nationals—now the 76ers—who was later to be my coach).

246

I have never figured out for sure why I was rarely, if ever, mentioned in relation to the latter two athletes, but so often compared with players in the first group. I have always wondered if this could have had anything to do with color. I hope not, because talent knows no color.

Even since my retirement, the same kinds of inconsistencies have persisted. *Every* great center of color has been compared to yours truly: Kareem Abdul-Jabbar, Ralph Sampson, and, more recently, Patrick Ewing and Shaquille O'Neal. But oddly enough, Bill Walton (the greatest college center of his time who was *not* of color) failed to inspire such comparisons, even though he played more like me than did any of the other centers. Can some media wizard tell me why?

Too many media people are wimps and wussies who are afraid to tell the truth. Today's game, either directly or indirectly, pays their salaries, their bonuses, and their perks. If there is no game, there is no job and no income. So they are out to sell today's game, and to do that they think they must highlight only today's players. What angers me about this is that they often step on the players of yesteryear just to point out that today's players (and today's game) are much better.

Johnny "Red" Kerr, a color commentator for the Chicago Bulls, is a good example of how this works. He has nothing but magical and positive things to say about Jordan, but he has never to date said a word about Wilt Chamberlain, a guy he played both with and against. When he sees Jordan do something he applauds it, but never adds, "Yeah, but *Wilt* did that about thirty or forty times." You'll never hear that from him, because if he says anything positive about Wilt it will be looked upon as negative to Jordan. This strategy may serve to keep Jordan in the limelight, but when a knowledgeable and supposedly informative interviewer makes such an omission, the result is a distortion of the truth.

Sports Illustrated ran an article a while ago that described Rodman as "the best rebounder in the history of the world." They had talked to Chuck Daly, who was Rodman's coach when Dennis played with the Detroit Pistons, and who currently does some work on television in addition to coaching. Chuck was of the opinion that Rodman could move his body certain ways when he was airborne, as though he changed direction in mid-air. *Sounded like hot air to me, Wiltie.*

The interviewer asked, "What about Wilt? Doesn't he hold all the records?" Chuck, a very decent coach (and, I thought, an intelligent man) passed it off, saying, "Oh, Wilt. He was just bigger and stronger than everyone else." We all know, of course, that none of the big guys have led even their own teams in rebounding—not Eaton at seven-foot-four, Bol at seven-foot-seven or Smits at seven-four.

The only true seven-footers (referring here to actual height as opposed to the figures quoted by the media) to lead the league in rebounds during the NBA's 50-year history were Kareem Abdul-Jabbar (once) and David Robinson (also once). These two have played a combined total of thirty seasons, and everyone knows how talented they were—and are. It's not just height, and it's not only agility, though both players had these qualities. There are other dimensions involved, among which desire and skill are primary.

Not content with disparaging *my* ability, Chuck went on to mention Bill Russell, saying, "Bill was good, too, but he had no one to compete against." Chuck very deliberately put both Bill and me down in order to build Rodman up, even though Rodman, heaven knows, is a tremendous rebounder and can stand on his own. No one needs to put yesterday's players down to make someone like Rodman look good. Yet they do it, just to build up today's game. Just consider the source, however, and remember that Daly is a sports announcer and basketball coach whose job is predicated on a healthy NBA.

Because this kind of distortion happens so often, the history of basketball is being left in the shadows. I don't mind the media's selling today's players and today's game—I can understand the need for that. But I *do* mind their belittling yesterday's pros in doing so. Commentary like this comes from weak announcers who are trying to protect their jobs. Ironically, one of the reasons for their job insecurity could be that they do not know the history of the game, and are unable (or unwilling) to put today's game in its proper perspective.

## WILTISM

**MEDIA MOTTO: AVOID THE TRUTH AT ANY COST, AS LONG AS YOU APPEASE THE BOSS.**

# EIGHT

## OTHER SPORTS

### IT'S NOT ONLY BASKETBALL THAT'S TAKING A FALL

#### HORSE RACING AND RACE CAR DRIVERS

People are always concerned about an athlete's size, and size is almost always equated with strength. But something else is more important than either size or strength: *from the very start, it's always been the heart*. If this is true, and I believe it without reservation, the greatest athletes on earth have to be jockeys and race car drivers.

Watching these men and women—people of ordinary size—control over a half ton of magnificent beast with agility and endurance, is nothing less than awe-inspiring. No one shows more resolve than a race car driver who faces death at every turn. Many people do not think that race car drivers and jockeys are *bona fide* athletes, but I emphatically disagree. Their quickness, reflexes and endurance are put to the ultimate test each time they are in the driver's seat or the saddle, and their lives are literally on the line every second.

251

My choice as the toughest thing to do in sports: racecar driving. J.J. Brandt, Jr. (left) and Mario Andretti (right) and other drivers prove that what matters here is not the size of the man but the size of his heart.

Bet you never knew that I owned and rode trotters and pacers.

Even in my 50's, I was playing with and against athletes of the caliber of the 1996 Silver Medal Volleyball Team. I am proud of my role in bringing volleyball into the limelight.

## VOLLEYBALL

As I watch volleyball on TV and at the Olympics, I marvel at how popular it has become. But do you know who actually gave modern-day volleyball its big start here in America? Uh huh, it was yours truly. My volleyball team (the "Big Dippers") and I toured throughout the Cntinental United States, Hawaii, Puerto Rico and Canada, letting it be known that this game, that almost everyone had forgotten, was a great sport.

You thought it was Karch Kiraly who launched volleyball's return to importance, didn't you? He *was* the greatest volleyball player alive for five or six years, and led America to two gold medals in the Olympics—but this is volleyball history, folks, and it's important that we learn about our past.

I was the first president of the International Volleyball Association and brought professional volleyball to America at the highest level. I was also a team owner and player.

I was named the Most Valuable Player in volleyball's second All-Star game. Paradoxically, the same sportswriters who did not think I was worthy to be on the All-Star team, were the same men who voted me MVP of the game (shown on NBC). My being voted MVP in two different professional sports was probably a first ever.

## BOXING

My beloved father, who was boxing's number-one fan when he was alive, regarded boxing as a true art form. But let me remind all of the boxing fans who share that same belief that dueling was once considered an art form as well. Unfortunately, the end result of a duel was often fairly dire, frequently causing immediate death. Boxing can be lethal, as well, but rather than immediate death boxing deaths causes debilitating injuries often resulting in gradual and premature death.

I am convinced, beyond any doubt, that head gear should be mandatory in professional boxing, just as it is in amateur boxing. Amateurs put their bodies on the line each time they step into the ring, but they are smart enough to protect their heads from damage. The number of boxing-related deaths resulting from brain injury is startling. (This, by the way, is the reason I could not go through with my fight against the great Muhammad Ali.) Boxing is a brutal sport, which should, in my opinion, be abolished—at least on the professional level. At the very least, we need a stronger boxing commission—a valid body of caring and concerned men and women—not just a commissioner.

When are they going to get the message here?


I have always believed that greatness is measured not only by what a person does, but also by the caliber of the person they do it against. Knocking a teenager off the throne as a boxer or outdoing a kid running down the street in a race—these feats hardly merit for the "great" label.

For one thing, competing against the best tends to bring out the best in most of us. Only when someone is able to beat those who have proven their capability can they begin to meet the basic requirements for greatness. How can I know how great a fighter Tyson is when I see him fighting no one of stature?

Back in the days of old, especially during the golden era of boxing, people fought real contenders, and the number one guy was the one every boxer wanted to fight. When a fighter beat the top guy, he knew he had beaten someone who had at least a prayer of a chance in the bout.

Boxing used to be a better, more tightly regulated sport. Rankings from one to ten let the boxing fan know who the viable candidate was—the fighter who was next in line to fight for the championship of the world. After a fighter worked his way up the list, the champion had to give him a fight. That does not happen any more. Nowadays, you don't know who the number one contender is—or even who the real champion is—because there are so many belts and so many varieties of champions. And the guys at the top pick their opponents with an eye to making a buck, and to holding on to their title so as to make *more* bucks.

The only position that matters any more is the number one position: the championship. If you are not the champion, you amount to nothing in the minds of many. In boxing, as in all sports, people tend to give credit only to the champ, forgetting that without a worthy adversary, the top position has no real worth. It is fine to be a champion, of course, but as I said, in boxing we have so *many* champions that they have lost their credibility.

As long as Tyson fights virtual nobodies, I haven't a clue as to how great a fighter he is. When a fighter beats guys who are not only less than number one, but whose level is totally undetermined, what does it really mean if he wins? It means only that he has just made another fifteen or twenty million. The defeated fighter was a pretender, not a contender.

*Why should a Tyson take up so much media space? His actions are often a real disgrace. We promote him and make him a millionaire. Many are more deserving, but no one seems to care. Look in the mirror and ask yourself, "Are you impressed only by people of wealth?" It's money that now seems to rule life's game. (Oh, what a pity, oh, what a shame!) Without our support, they all would be through. The outcome is left up to me and you.*

When, as a sports fan, I think of George Foreman as the heavyweight boxing champion of the world, I have to wonder what the other boxers look like and who awarded them their credentials. Furthermore, if George Foreman is the honest, straight-talking preacher of the truth he would like us all to believe he is, he should have leveled with us right after his fight against the German.

Everyone in the world who saw that geriatric slow-motion slugfest, knows that George got beat, and badly, each and every round of the fight. He should have admitted this and said that he didn't want the heavyweight championship given to him under those conditions, and offered his opponent a rematch. He would have earned more respect with a statement like that than he ever will by wearing a tainted championship belt. We know he was beaten. The three guys masquerading as judges knew it as well, even though, for whatever reason, they chose to see it another way—their way (the wrong way).

Boxing managers' up to Cus D'Amoto's era tried to get me into the ring. Here, Howard Johnson, light heavyweight champion, smiles as I explain, "I'm a lover, not a fighter."

## TRACK AND FIELD

It is mid May, 1996, and I am attending the finals of the Pac Ten track and field meet at Drake Stadium. It looks as though they will be fortunate to have 3,000 in attendance at a ticket price of $6.00 for all seats—a real bargain, as every seat is a good one, and many great athletes will be competing. Most of these athletes are of Olympic caliber, and most are hopefully preparing for the upcoming Olympic games. What nicer way could there be to spend four or five hours with your family? For only $6.00, in absolutely perfect Southern California weather, you can watch some of America's finest athletes doing their very best.

The real kick-in-the-ass here is that these unspoiled jocks truly appreciate your being there, and often come up to talk with you. Amy Alcott, America's premier high jumper, came over to greet me and some of the people who were sitting near me, to say, "Thanks for coming and rooting us on." I'd like to ask all of you fans who go to professional events— basketball, football, baseball, or whatever other sport—when was the last time one of *those* athletes thanked you for showing up to support them in their egotistical efforts? I should warn you: don't hold your breath while you wait for it to happen.

Many of us are under the illusion that athletes are getting better year after year. This popular sentiment is, unfortunately, far from the truth. I have been watching the Mount Sac relays, and paying particular attention to a guy in the long jump pit. I couldn't help thinking about how different this pit is from the ones I used to jump into—not to mention the pits that were available when guys like Jesse Owens were jumping. At that time you had to jump into an unkempt pit full of divets and holes, filled with God knows what kind of materials. (None of which you'd ever choose to fall into).

The Mount Sac athlete had just jumped twenty-six feet, eight or nine inches, putting him barely out of first place. He was bouncing up and down and waving his hands as if he had just broken the world's record. Well, sixty years ago, Jesse Owens was jumping about that same distance. Even though these new athletes are blessed with improved equipment and conditions, they aren't jumping much better, on average, than the athletes of sixty years ago. Imagine what Jesse could have done if he had been using today's superior equipment—the boards and new track materials that give you more bounce and help you to move faster. His record would be untouchable.

No, successive generations of athletes *don't* automatically get better as years go by. Just as wine has vintage years, so do athletes. Like the heartbeat pattern on a monitor screen, we go through peaks and valleys in sports (and in all the aspects of our lives). And, as far as I am concerned, these are not peak or vintage years for sports in general.

It has always been a mystery to me why the great Carl Lewis, when he leads in a race, often starts to ease up as he approaches the finish line. Instead of running straight through the tape as you are supposed to do, he makes a visible move to decrease his momentum (a habit that can actually increase a runner's chances of pulling a muscle). Either that is his way of showing off a bit, or perhaps he thinks he is saving needed energy for a later race or a later day or later year. I can't be sure. Many times he might have broken a record if he had run through the tape, but he chose not to do so.

Easing up seems to be a common characteristic among today's athletes. When they choose not to jump that last jump or run as hard as they can run, they not only rob the fans of the chance to see them perform at their best (what the fans pay to see); they also rob themselves of records and successes that they might have earned. What's more, doing less than your best is just not professional.

Here I am with members of my "Wilt's Wonder Women" track team. I am not a happy camper here as I had just been beaten by the little one in a long distance race. (I most definitely have respect for female jocks)

## Football

The Dallas Cowboys—"America's Team." An appropriate slogan for a team that in many ways presents a mirror image of American society. This mirroring seems to happen especially during the off season, a time when they have faced so many problems. We don't need to document the difficulties of Michael Irvin and some of the other players, but isn't it strange that these same problems don't seem to attract much attention *during* the season? *Why is this, Wiltie?* Here is the reason, ladies and gentlemen: *A win covers up every sin.*

When a team is losing, all you hear is an endless series of complaints and excuses. But if that team is winning, it's a different picture—even though they have just as many skeletons in their locker room, *You will not hear a winning team whimper or cry. They'll just heave a relieved sigh, and hold their Stanley Cup Trophy high. Winning has a way of curing all, but when you lose, heads must fall.*

The case of former Ram football player, Darryl Henley is a reminder of what has been going on with many of today's athletes. Darryl was allegedly caught by an under-cover agent trying to work out a deal to knock off the judge who had convicted him on drug charges. Then we heard that he wanted to knock off a L.A. Ram cheerleader who had allegedly finked on him when she was caught with a suitcase full of drugs that she was allegedly transporting for him. Sure seems like Hollywood, but this is *not* the movies, folks—it's real life. Apparently, our athletes are determined to be just as bad as any movie character ever filmed.

## WOMEN IN SPORTS

Women's gymnastics is a sport that seems to have gone completely haywire. Well before the 1996 Olympics, I was watching a televised dual meet between Oregon State and California, and was amazed to see that the young ladies were smiling, apparently happy, healthy and obviously enjoying what they were doing—a joy to watch. All appeared to be about nineteen or twenty—energetic, vivacious, and looking like one would expect young people of their age to look. Watching them, I was reminded (and unhappily so) of the young women who would be going to the Olympics later in the year.

Female gymnasts are quite different from the men in both age and appearance. Female Olympic-level gymnasts are usually extremely small (four-foot-six to four-foot-eight) and generally weigh between sixty-four and ninety pounds. (There have been exceptions, but not many.) These youngsters are not only incredibly small, but to me they look anemic. In contrast to the Oregon State and UC women I'd been watching on TV, they ofeten have a

261

seemingly unhappy look, as if they are not enjoying what they are doing. When the top athletes in gymnastics fit this description, you have to wonder what has happened to the sport that used to be filled with graceful, charming and happy women—gymnasts who were able to combine athletic ability and skill with the poise and grace that come with maturity and wisdom.

The once-graceful sport of women's gymnastics has been turned into a tumbling act for the young and nimble— youngsters whose bones haven't yet hardened. Size makes a tremendous difference in gymnastics, and the top women are your four-foot-six, eighty-pound giants. Physical immaturity is a factor in their small size, of course, but it also gives them the elasticity they need, and aids them in difficult and dangerous tumbling maneuvers. Unfortunately, it also results in many mishaps.

Many a little Olympic hopeful, in order to get the serious training she needs, has had to leave home to live with her coach in some remote spot in Colorado or wherever. (Coaches, of course, are active participants in their small clients' dream of qualifying for the Olympic team by the age of fourteen.) Olympic competition can bring fame and wealth for a young woman—but at what cost? Mothers and fathers have given up their daughters for almost their entire young lives, wanting them to be with the very best, but not understanding that, for a child, being at home is really the very, *very* best.

I am saddened as I observe what has happened to a great sport. I'm not recommending that we legislate against the young kids, but when you have a sport that is made to order for underdeveloped juveniles, something is wrong. What has an Olympic sport come to when a college student is too old to compete? Believe it or not: a college freshman is already over the hill for Olympic-level gymnastics. But as I watch the college girls perform, they clearly appear to be so much happier and healthier than the poor, anemic, non-smiling, undernourished-looking mighty-mites of our Olympic teams.

Obviously, something is wrong with this picture. Perhaps the college gymnasts are the ones who should be in the Olympics.

## WILTISM

**CHANGE IS INEVITABLE AND CAN BE POSITIVE, BUT SOME THINGS NEED TO BE CHANGED BACK.**

You may ask why the topic of women's sports is so important to me. I am concerned because I see here a reflection of what is going on in men's sports as well as in other areas of our lives. We are forever focused on the appearance of a thing, forgetting its substance. We respond to the glitter of fool's gold, and no longer value the real thing.

Basketball, as well as other sports, is becoming purely a show. The game glitters, but technically it is not being played as basketball should be played. To many fans, a sensationally clever dunk or a spectacular basket has far more value than the everyday kind of basket that consistently helps a team win. Are we more concerned with how the shooter looks as he makes a basket, or the fact that the basket is being made? It's nice if the two aspects of a game can be combined from time to time, but I think we have lost sight of which is the most important.

Similarly, in women's sports we too often look for "showtime" instead of perfection of performance. Our attention should be focused on the beauty in the way an athlete plays the game, not on the athlete's physical

263

attractrivenness. Figure skating is the major culprit here, and we wonder if beauty isn't sometimes the first thing to catch a judge's eye. Not that beauty isn't appreciated. Showtime is fine in its place, but it can make the observer lose sight of what a sport is all about.

I am now watching some ladies wrestle—the legit variety of wrestling. In view of the fact that women in wrestling is a relatively new development, one of the announcers asks, "Do you think this will ever become an Olympic sport?" The other sportscaster, apparently a very big fan of wrestling and very knowledgeable about it, replies, "I don't really know, but people have been wrestling since the year one. It's one of the most natural things we do. We've wrestled from the time we were kids—even animals wrestle—so why not women's wrestling in the Olympics?"

He's right, of course. But there are a lot things that we've been doing since the beginning of time (such as fighting wars), and the fact that we've done them forever sure hasn't made them right. I am not quite sure how I feel about women wrestling—but on second thought, why not? As the announcer pointed out, it is a natural part of the animal kingdom, and like it or not, we definitely are animals.

To my knowledge, no one has ever argued that movie audiences should be deprived of watching the talent of a Shirley Temple, Mickey Rooney, Jackie Coogan or of any other young bright star, simply because of their youth. Child stars have not been discriminated against because of their age alone. And the same principle should apply in sports.

The professional demise of my friend, Jennifer Capriati, who had a drug problem, should not be used as a reason for preventing other young people from having an opportunity to do their thing. Some of the older tennis players seem to think it should—that professional tennis should be the exclusive territory of players over a certain age—and they are lobbying for an age restriction.

Is it possible that the embarrassment of being beaten by a thirteen year old could be the real reason for their concern? Maybe they are fearful that the younger ladies might kick their butt.

Any limitations of age that are put on female tennis players may prevent them from playing during the best years of their athletic lives—their younger years. They may never again be able to perform at their peak level or have anything better to contribute, and they should be given a chance to show us their best while they can. Venus Williams, the promising young tennis player of color from northern California, was caught up in the age-group mess, but boy, would I love to see her play! Youthful athletes may not be old enough to smoke, drink, or create the mayhem that the older ones can, but if they are good enough to contest against the best and win, then yes, they are old enough.

Here Jennifer Capriati and I joined forces to play in front of a sold out crowd for a charity event.

265

Twenty-six-year old Michelle Smith from Ireland, 1996 Olympic winner of the 400-meter Individual Medley, had never before won an Olympic event. In fact, no woman from Ireland had ever won an Olympic medal. As someone who has avidly followed the international swimming scene for many years, I had to wonder how she was able, suddenly and unexpectedly, to win so convincingly?

A person is, of course, always considered innocent until proven guilty, but knowing that Michelle's boyfriend was recently banned for using an improper substance, and remembering the old saying that birds of a feather flock together, it seems only natural to think that at some point she might have been exposed to the illegal drug scene. I hope with all my heart that such was not the case; she had tried for so many years and seemed to be worthy of the medal.

Steroids have marred many an athletic endeavor. Even though modern athletes are well aware that their use can cause permanent physical damage (or even death), some are still willing to take their chances, particularly if an Olympic medal hangs in the balance. I blame society for placing so much emphasis on winning and for making the financial rewards to gold medalists (from endorsements, appearances, and commercials) so irresistible.

One of my fears concerning women's participation in male-dominated sports is that they may push their bodies far past their capabilities. (Men also do this, of course.) Females, like all athletes, will always try to be the best they can be. But many women end up in areas where they really don't belong, just to compete at the high levels that were meant only for men. In order to do this, some women are turning their attention to the same types of drugs that have enticed men—performance enhancing drugs that they believe will transform them into super-athletes or give them the bodies of gods. (I am in favor of anything natural that will enhance one's performance, but I sometimes wonder what "natural" is anymore.)

There is no question in my mind: females should be given a better opportunity to show their athletic ability. I know, from personal conversations and through my involvement with women in sports, that some are quite content with the status quo and are willing to accept second-class status. Is this ignorance, or is it the result of brainwashing—or am I just way off base?

I don't think I'm off base. These women, in my opinion, do not understand that they are being given an unfair shake when it comes to a having a chance for equality in sports. I want it to be very clear that I appreciate women's unending campaign for respect. Women are now high jumping, long jumping, and running at almost the same level that I was in my heyday—and I was a world-class track and field athlete. So, I do not speak out of a lack of respect, but just the opposite. I want to see women have a fair chance to demonstrate their athletic talent and to get the recognition they deserve.


I believe we would all acknowledge that men in general are blessed with superior weight and strength in muscle mass, and that men excel where explosive movements, jumping, quickness and speed are required. These are abilities that play an important part in every well-known sport or game, and men possess them in abundance.

Today's games were made *by* men, *for* men, *amen!* And that is why, no matter how a female athlete develops her strength and skill, a first class male high-schooler can normally beat her in disciplines such as high jumping, long jumping, the 100-yard dash, basketball, football, etc. Even though there *are* certain physical qualities in which women have a decided advantage, I believe that in most of the sports that have traditionally belonged to men, the deck is stacked against a woman, and a woman athlete is fighting a losing game that she is never supposed to win.

These statements in no way imply that I believe women are less than men. Quite the opposite, in fact. I have been a supporter of women in athletics for as long as I can remember and am very proud of their accomplishments. I want to see them have a chance to really shine in their sports endeavor. They have already done so in the sport (if the Iditarod can correctly be called a sport) that I believe is the toughest in the world.

The Iditarod is a dog sled race that goes damn near halfway across Alaska. When you look at the number of women who have been in that race in relation to the number of men, and you stop to think that one woman has won that race more than a few times, it is easy to see that women have capabilities that far surpass what we have believed possible.

One of the abilities in which women equal (or surpass) men, is that of *touch*. When I was playing with the Harlem Globetrotters many years ago, a member of the Texas Cowgirls basketball team was doing a half time show with us. She shot foul shots, and she would make 85 or 90 in a row, *blindfolded.* It's all about touch. I only wish she could have taught me the art or that she could have passed her gift on to me somehow.

But I'm afraid that teaching is not the answer. Touch seems to be a gift—one that more women than men are blessed with. Therefore, touch is one of the ingredients that should be considered when the invention of new sports or games for women is contemplated.

Women deserve an opportunity to display their abilities in such a way that they do not have to be compared with men. I want to see them compete in sports and games that are designed especially to utilize their unique abilities. We need to discover where women have an advantage. Then, when we figure this out, perhaps some smart Ph.D's in Physical Education can come up with a sport (or sports) that women can play without being looked upon as second class citizens.

I am hopeful that one day there will be games and sports that will take full advantage of the strengths that women possess: their flexibility, endurance, patience, and high threshold for pain (I've always heard that men could not bear the pain of having a baby), their balance and grace (two things which have been very much a part of gymnastics), and their sensitivity (the "touch" which, in basketball, is almost more useful than sight). Then, perhaps, women will be able to prove themselves to be equal to men as athletes, or even to surpass them.

P.S. I want to amend my earlier thoughts concerning the young female Olympic gymnasts, and extend my congratulations to them on winning the gold medal as a team. Also congratulations are due them for showing so much spirit and courage under duress—the ultimate Olympic test. Watching them do their floor exercise, it was apparent that their grace comes from being a little older and from experience. Of course, there is an exception to every rule—and in this case it's Dominique Moceanu. Her grace under pressure must come from within; it could hardly be the result of her advanced age.

Even before I could get this book out, the gymnastics people have started to honor Wiltie's request. I've noticed that these young ladies are now looking more like normal young women, appearing to be older and more poised. My congratulations to them in winning the gold in the Olympics and showing what real guts and solidarity are all about.

## WILTISM

**EVERYONE IS CONCERNED ABOUT *BEING* THE BEST; BUT WHAT'S REALLY IMPORTANT IS *GIVING* YOUR BEST.**

I had crossed the 50-year mark when my partner Foster Corder and I won the Open Division Championship tournament against some of the best raquetball players in the world. The tournament was held at the Mid-Valley Raquetball Club in Reseda, CA.

I designed the ball for the game "Wally Ball" which combines the skills required for vollyball and raquetball.

# NINE

# MJ AND THE WORM

## THE SECOND COMING

MJ and Dennis Rodman have two things in common: athletic talent and marketing skill. Each instinctively knows which of his qualities—as a personality and as an athlete—make him uniquely attractive to the public. Each uses these qualities with deadly accuracy.

On the court, Michael knows that he must score points, and Dennis knows that he must get rebounds. Off the court, of course, Rodman's self-promotion as Mr. (or Mrs.) Eccentric leads to commercial opportunities galore. Each athlete engages in selling himself in order to increase his marketing clout. And marketing clout, of course, sells product.

In a very real sense, these stars *are* the product. Using basketball as a vehicle, MJ and The Worm have made of themselves media events. They have become intrinsic parts of today's media—hype and all.

For the above reasons, among others, these two superstars seem to merit a chapter of their own. And here are some of my observations, gleaned over a period of years, that led me to that conclusion.

## MICHAEL

I would never say that Michael Jordan thinks of himself as a god, but in his followers' eyes he has become the Exalted One. Commercials that focus on his ability to fly and to walk on water have done nothing to dispel this perception, and the media have played right along. In an interview, MJ was asked to whom he was going to bequeath his mantle when he retired. He calmly replied, "Anfernee Hardaway seems to be the most worthy prospect."

It is taken for granted that MJ has an exclusive patent on greatness. No one questions the assumption that the mantle of superiority belongs to him alone—to keep or to pass on as he sees fit.

Basketball is the only sport in which this kind of assumption would be accepted without question. Michael and others are totally incorrect if they believe that he is the best—but perhaps that is completely beside the point. The primary issue is: Just *what* is so important about who is the best basketball player? We don't see this kind of concern about who is the best hockey player, the best baseball player, or the best in a dozen other assorted team sports.

Why is there no concern about who is the best among players such as Mickey Mantle, Joe DiMaggio, Ted Williams, and Babe Ruth? All of these athletes played a variety of positions and possessed different strengths. Each could be the greatest at what they were doing, for a day, a game, a week, or a year; but *none* of them (and none of their fans, for that matter) talked as if the game revolved around them—as if they were "it." In basketball, however, when you talk about the greatest, Jordan's name automatically comes up. He *is* a fantastic basketball player who adds a great deal of excitement to the game, but as far as being "it," I don't think so.

Why is there room for only *one* of us to be in an elevated position? I wonder if it is because this sport is loaded with so many stars of color. Does race enter the picture in basketball? Is the old "divide and conquer" concept being put into play?

Players in other sports can accept their laurels and enjoy their accomplishments without continually striving to stand out in comparison with some other star. Only in basketball is there such constant badgering of stars and others, asking their opinion as to who is the best.

Team sports, by definition, involve teamwork. Players do different things, but each makes their special contribution to their team. All are working towards one common goal. How anyone decides to value a player's importance to the team is a subjective matter.

Can we agree that Jordan plays a position in a team game? He wouldn't qualify as the greatest center, nor is he the greatest ball handler, or the greatest at many of the other things he does on the court. Going one-on-one against other top players, I don't see him consistently coming out on top.

Jordan is obviously forgetting that he is a guard, and if he had to guard some of the guys who play the center position, he could be in trouble. Think back to what happened to Dr. J, for example. *He* wore the "greatest" laurels in his time just as MJ does today, yet Kareem completely annihilated him in a one-on-one match. (So, what does that make Kareem?) It's my belief that the same thing would happen if MJ were to go one-on-one against certain of today's quality players. He could be destroyed.

273

Every contemporary game is recorded and stored on a master tape in some television studio, and probably on video tape in thousands of homes, as well. Unfortunately, we earlier players were not recorded in this way, and consequently we are not able to show today's young whippersnappers what we were capable of doing.

We have never really had a chance to let people see just how great some of us were during our prime. It could be that the "ooh's" and "aah's" given to Michael each time he makes one of his electrifying plays would pale in comparison if today's fans could see the great Elgin Baylor do his thing, or watch Connie Hawkins in one of his miracle drives (and I could go on, of course).

It's all relative, in any case, and "great" is only a relative term. A player can look different when he is playing with (or against) different teams. Michael, for example, looked far from the greatest when he played on the 1992 Olympic team. At that juncture, everyone thought Charles Barkley was by far the best. Playing with today's Chicago team, MJ may be the greatest, but he might not appear to be so great if he were playing with the Sacramento Kings. And what if he had been drafted by Boston, and had to play in the shadow of the already-established Larry Bird? Under those circumstances, would he still have become the great MJ we know and love?

*Ali said he was "the greatest," but was he toying with us all? Or was that claim really the correct call? MJ seems to really believe his claim. If he does, it would really be a shame. For all of this, I think the media is to blame. Those commercials that show him jumping so high, may have convinced him that he can fly—no longer a mortal such as you or I.*

274

Anyone who follows sports is aware of the advantage of having a superstar on your team. These benefits become increasingly crucial in the later moments of a game when everything is so very important. It's the nature of the game that if the ball is given to your superstar, any calls that are made are apt to go his way. Everybody wants to go to heaven—even the referees (who are well aware of where their interests lie). So, if your superstar is looked upon as the Divine One—almost as a second coming—you have a superstar player who is even *more* intimidating, and harder yet to make a call against.

I recently watched Jordan get away with flagrantly dressing down another official, an offense which everyone—even the chicken-shit announcers—agreed should have resulted in a technical. But *this* technical would have put him out of the game: so, of course, it was not called. This man is *the* man!

My object in talking about Michael's becoming so god-like is not to bring him down. I just want to point out that when someone has that type of power and produces that kind of effect during a game, the result can turn out to be a minus for basketball instead of a plus. Michael's ability to get the better end of every call diminishes team sports in general. This is not Michael's fault; he is doing his thing, and is not responsible for the actions of others—or is he? Has he, or has he not, earned the right to those respectful calls?

We have heard many times that Wayne Gretzky was protected by WHA teams: he was not thrown up against the boards as much, nor did he receive the kind of treatment that Gordie Howe and other big stars had to endure during their careers. Is there a parallel between the way Gretzky's treated and the Michael Jordan Treatment Syndrome?

I don't believe that it is good for any sport if one player is placed above the rest, not in what he is able to do, but in the treatment he receives. Michael has proved that he is able to do almost anything he sets his mind to. *Adding gifts of fire to his already burning flame is not only unnecessary, it's a rotten shame.*

I've met a number of players who think they could be (or are) as talented as Michael Jordan, but believe me, they have neither MJ's fortitude or his commitment. No matter whether it's golf, basketball or talking shit, MJ gives it his all. In all my years, I have never seen an athlete as revered as MJ. He is idolized by everyone, friend and foe alike. As I have said before, this translates into a real problem for the jocks going against him (and maybe for those who are *with* him, too). But let's concentrate for the present on the players who are forced to line up against him. How does a mere mortal guard a deity?

Respect for Michael's awe-inspiring talent (which is hyped by unbelievable media attention) has placed him in an exalted position that produces a kind of fear response in his opponents. You see, even basketball players know that it's improper (even blasphemous) to take the Lord's name in vain; so you, as a player, damn sure don't want to be the one to knock Him on his Royal Ass. And just in case you are not buying what I am preaching, tell me when you last saw anyone take MJ down when he drove the lane?

*So, how would you play the great MJ, Wiltie?* I'd play him like Moses did with our real God: I'd meet him at the summit.

You *have* to meet Michael at the summit. When he comes gliding and sliding through to the basket for one of his famous dunks, you have to put somebody on him. Even my favorite, Sir Charles, who has almost more heart than the real God Himself, lets Michael slide through. As for the other players, I can't account for their reluctance. They surely can't be afraid that they are going to get hurt physically, since Michael weighs far less than most of the players who guard him in the point.

The influence of a fear factor might be understandable if it were Shaq they were meeting head-on, time after time. Shaq weighs 330 pounds, but six-foot-seven Jordan weighs only about 197. He is actually rather skinny compared with some of the big boys who are supposed to be covering the middle. So, why don't they hit him—perhaps even risking a flagrant foul? An occasional confrontation would cause Michael to think before driving to the basket the next time.

I remember Magic Johnson's second game after coming back from his self-imposed retirement. He was playing against the Bulls in the Los Angeles Forum, and in his first drive down the middle, Rodman clothes-lined him, almost taking his head off.

That kind of thing never seems to happen to MJ. There almost seems to be an unwritten hands-off rule for him. We all know, of course, that Rodman is a little bit crazy, but you can't be timid out there on the court! And no one could deny that Rodman plays the game with the right kind of verve.

A defensive player actually has an advantage when guarding Michael, for two reasons: (1) the basket doesn't move, so you know where Michael is going; and (2) you know for certain that the last thing (the *very* last thing) that Michael wants to do is pass the ball. You *know* he's going to shoot it. With those two bits of data tucked away in your memory bank, the advantage is all yours—or at least it should be.

No matter how clever he may be, and no matter how the illusion may appear to those who are watching, once a player is airborne, he cannot move his body from side to side. Therefore, when Michael leaves the floor, he can only follow a straight line to the basket—and that is why you have to meet him at the summit.

In the good old days, I had to carry two and three guys to the basket with me. (They were always looking for a free ride.) But, all kidding aside, my opponents were not going to let me go in there unopposed. Even Shaq, big as he is, gets hammered pretty hard as he goes to the basket. That's the price that all the stars have to pay for doing their thing against the opposition.

You can't just let the superstars do it their own way, standing there smiling and waving at them as they go by. MJ gets enough respect and cheers as it is—and from both directions. The way the fans on both sides cheer for him makes every game a home game for Michael, no matter what arena he is in.

For the opposing team to hear more cheers for MJ than *they* get does not help to bring out their best. It is one thing to show respect for athletes you admire, but when they are on the opposing team, and you cheer for them more than you cheer for your own side, that is really hard on the home team, and ego-deflating to say the least.

After the Bulls' seventy-first win of the season, reporters who were surrounding Michael Jordan asked him not to be bashful, but to tell them who he thought was the best basketball player of all time. Quite seriously, he replied, "I think it's me." Now, all of us have a right to at least one vote, and, understandably, he chose to use that vote for himself. But on the other hand, he might have said, "I can speak only about the players I have actually played against, of course, and, of those players, I think I'm the best." That would have been a fairer statement, since there were a number of legendary players he never faced on the court. (And who knows what the outcome would have been in a one-on-one contest between MJ and a non-guard.)

An athlete's stature has always been established by the caliber of the opponents he or she has faced. I learned the truth of this statement as I watched the great boxers who have fought during my lifetime. It holds true in basketball as well as boxing (or in any other sport, for that matter).

I would give a lot to have seen MJ play against Walt Frazier or against K.C. Jones of the Celtics, two of the greatest defensive players of my time—or against Jerry West, a guy who could do it at both ends. And how would MJ have handled Oscar Robertson, the Big O? No one I know could have done it! If we were considering only the players of this era, Michael would fall behind two or three: Magic Johnson, of course, and my favorites, Larry Bird and Charles Barkley. When you keep in mind that basketball is a team game, we'd have to conclude that those three guys have made a larger contribution.

Watching MJ in action, I have the feeling that he is able to cast some kind of spell over his defenders, turning them into matadors who curtsy and wave as he goes by. This is only natural, I guess: he plays with the Bulls, after all.

It is easy to forget that if MJ had not won three championships in a row, he might be seen as just an individualist and a selfish-type of basketball player. If one of his teammates had not made two heroic shots in the closing minutes of the sixth and the seventh games of two different series, Michael would have only one world championship to his name (as of this printing), and the public would surely regard him differently. (Perhaps Michael should think about *that*.) To me, however, he would have been the

279

same great player, even if Paxton had not made those winning three-pointers.

If you have a good memory, you will know that I am not just making up these tales about MJ and the power he possesses. When he came back to play a couple of years ago, his old number had, of course, been retired, as it should have been. But you may recall that things did not go well for MJ, and he started blaming his problems on the new number. He wanted his old number back, and "jumped to the rafters," taking it from where it was hanging, even though this was against NBA rules.

They fined him at first and told him that he would not be allowed to wear the number. But, of course, that didn't stop Michael from doing whatever he pleased—and he pleased to wear his old number. And so he did. They, in turn, threatened to fine him some more, but said they would wait until after the season to decide on the amount. The NBA backed away from the situation, apparently for fear of disturbing Michael and getting unwanted heat from his fans. Would anyone else have been allowed to continue playing under those circumstances? I think not.

The NBA chose to let Michael do whatever he damn well pleased rather than taking a chance of once again losing him to the backwoods of Alabama, or wherever. Yes, the powers that be in the NBA were *afraid*.

I learned about this early in my career when they tried to force me to lose my goatee and mustache. (We were supposed to be clean-shaven in those days.) I told them that my facial adornments had nothing to do with my playing basketball, and that I would not comply: *"No goatee, no Wiltie."* Outcome: I was allowed to wear my beard and mustache, and many others began to follow my lead.

I learned to understand—and to handle—such power moves. But I was, right from the start, the "villain." Villains, of course, are *expected* to do bad things and to be out of step with the rest of the world. Michael, on the other hand, is a minor god—a "good guy" and a leader who is just naturally expected to be in sync with everybody else.

Being a god, MJ actually sets the rules for his faithful followers who must do as he says (though not necessarily as he does). But following Michael's example could lead to some less than desirable results. I can see players all over the country saying, "I don't feel like wearing my usual number today. I think I'll wear number five on Monday, four on Tuesday, and thirteen on Friday because those are my good luck numbers for those particular days."

The puzzle here is why MJ is allowed to flaunt this kind of power before the whole world. Surely the NBA must realize the harm that is done when certain players are allowed to become bigger than the sport itself. This situation leads inevitably to anarchy and rebellion, to temper tantrums and the abandonment of rules and regulations. The rest of the players are bound to ask themselves, "If Michael can do it, why can't we?"

During the number drama, I didn't hear a single person from the media ask Michael, "Don't you think you are being rather childish or unfair by breaking the rules this way?" I wish someone had asked him, "Why do you think *you* had the right to do something that no one else was allowed to do?" They seemed almost afraid to ask these very valid questions, behaving, instead, like members of the press corps at a presidential affair, afraid that if they ask the wrong questions they won't be invited again. Too bad. I would like to have heard Michael's answers.

Let me play devil's advocate once more, and ask you: What do you think Michael's response might have been if he *had* been asked those questions? *Come on, Wiltie, give me an answer. You must have an idea, Wiltie. What do you think?* Well, this is my hunch as to what he would say: *"It's my ball, it's my game and we'll do it my way; otherwise we just aren't going to play."*

A tremendous amount of importance is attached to a player's stats, and because they are so important, the records of present-day athletes are made to appear as impressive as possible, never mind whether their numbers were truly earned. Because stats are manipulated today in ways that make them almost meaningless, they no longer reflect what is really going on in a game.

This assertion was proven during the second half of the 1995-96 season when one of the new New Jersey players demanded that his team and coach give him a chance to make a triple-double. The game was stopped with a few seconds to go, and a play was set up to allow him the assist that would give him his triple-double. When the irate coach of the opposing team discovered what was happening, instead of telling his players to make darn sure the guy did *not* get his triple-double, he told them, in effect, to "just give it to him, and let him do whatever he wants. If he's such an ass that all he's worried about is the triple-double when his team is up by 40 points, and his coach goes along with the big plan, they must really need it." (In his place, *I* would have said, "Let's give him *nothing*.")

There is another reason for my claim that stats—even points—no longer reflect a player's true talent or what actually goes on in the game. I'm talking here about the way that technical foul points are recorded. As it now stands, the points scored as a result of technical fouls are credited to the player who makes the shot. I believe strongly, however, that points received as a result of technical fouls should not be given to anyone special, because no individual on the team truly earned them. Since basketball is a team sport, technical foul shots should be recorded as team points, the same way that rebounds that are knocked out of bounds are recorded as a team rebounds.

Under present rules, if Michael Jordan shoots three or four technical fouls a game, these add to his average.

But, if technical foul points were recorded as team points, those three or four points a game would not be there, and his average, instead of being 31 points a game for his lifetime, would be only 27 or 28 points a game—a big difference. Suddenly, he would not be the number one scorer by average: he'd be down there behind Oscar Robertson, Jerry West and the rest of them—and Karl Malone would win the scoring title.

Let's stop creating illusions with erroneous stats. Basketball is not a Vegas show, even though it *has* become show business. Today's stats are falsifying the real story, making fans think that certain players are doing more than what they are, in fact, doing. Stats are so cleverly used to deceive that basketball games have come to resemble Las Vegas illusion acts such as Siegfried & Roy. With stats, they can turn midgets into giants and mundane players into miraculous athletes—but it is all an illusion.

Although Michael puts the ball through the hoop in a such way that he is given 31 points a game, some of these points are fabricated and, in a way, don't really belong to him. Think what would have happened, for example, if ex-Bull B.J. Armstrong or current Bull Steve Kerr, two very good foul shooters, had been allowed to shoot most of the technical fouls (as should have been their privilege, since the best shooters on the other teams are allowed to do so). They might have added four more points to their totals, and instead of averaging a mere seven or nine points a game, they could have averaged thirteen. Those technical fouls make a difference!

I noticed that Chicago actually allowed Kerr to shoot some technical fouls during one of the playoff games when he and Michael were on the floor together. I'm not quite sure why this happened. Either the coaches lacked confidence in Michael at that particular time, or maybe they were (for once) doing the right thing. Whatever the reason, Kerr did shoot the technical fouls—exactly what he should have been doing all along, since he is the best foul shooter on the team.

Technical fouls are reserved for the best foul shooters. But Michael often gets the chance to shoot them, even though he is not the best foul shooter on the floor when the foul is committed. That brings to mind one of the rules that needs to be changed.

As I suggested earlier, just as there are team fouls and team rebounds, there should be team points when technical fouls are shot. In this way, the bonus would always be on the coach to put his best foul shooter to the line. As things are now, if the coach puts Michael up there and Michael misses, the coach doesn't have to answer to anyone, because everyone assumes that Michael is the best. But those of us who know a little about basketball know that he is not, nor has he ever been, the best foul shooter on his team. He is just the chosen one.

I'll admit it. I'm jealous that Michael gets a chance to shoot all the technical fouls while I never got a chance to shoot any. To be perfectly honest, though, it was my own fault: I was never the best foul shooter on any of the teams I played on—except when I was in kindergarten, but who the hell knows or cares about that. (That's not absolutely true; I *did* shoot well many years ago.)

## WILTISM

**PERCEPTION IS FAR MORE IMPORTANT THAN REALITY. UNFORTUNATELY, PERCEPTION IS MAGNIFIED BY MEDIA HYPE.**

Here is a prime example of how perception is far more important than what is really happening. We'll start with some plain facts. At the time I am writing, the latest data for the '94-'95 NBA season shows that, from the 3-point area, the average guy shot 35.9 percent, and the top ten shooters were in the 40 percent to 48 percent range. Here is where perception does its thing. The "impressive" shooting of Michael Jordan turns out to be a lifetime average of around 30.7 percent from the 3-poijnt line. You coaches and astute fans must realize that shooting that poorly is deplorable, and you would no more allow a player with that kind of percentage (or lower) to shoot your three-point shots than you would allow Shaq or Wilt to shoot technical fouls.

You cannot tell me that most of you, including announcers and coaches who should know better, have not thought of Michael as an outstanding exponent of the three-point shot. In reality, he is not. Instead, he ranks almost as low as you can go. It is all a matter of perception.

This may be as good a place as any to remind you that the guys of yesteryear were, in most cases, better percentage shooters from the field than the present day jocks. Most of our shots were from the area that is now the three-point range, and those shooting opportunities were not as freely available as three-point shots are today. And, please remember this: the likes of Bill Russell, Nate Thurmond and yours truly almost never got the chance, except for an occasional fast break, to shoot unmolested lay-ups; and the space around the basket was our own— not to be ventured into without our permission.

My hat is off to Michael Jordan, not just for his accomplishments, but for the manner in which he has pursued excellence through hard work and perseverance.

*Never hanging his head when things go wrong, he keeps problems in perspective, where they belong. He shows us the difference between good and great; when his team needs a lift, he's never too late. Playing any sport, he always gives his best. That's the true road to ultimate success, and what sets him apart from most of the rest. His defense and dunking are a pleasure to see, though his commitment to excellence is the real deal to me. His talent inspires young athletes to start. He would tell them, "All is possible, but you must have heart."*

Doubt my mobility? Check out this photo. My ballhandling skills were polished during my days with the Harlem Globetrotters. (How often do you see three players guarding M.J.?)

## RODMAN

When I talk in negative terms about certain sports figures and situations, I do so only in the hope that the end result will be constructive. And it may be that my telling you a few tidbits about my own past badness will convince you that I have no intention of putting myself on a pedestal with a halo around my head. Those of us who have, ourselves, been down some questionable paths are, I believe, in a good position to assess today's problems— problems the halo kids know very little about.

Young athletes today are confronted with a dilemma that, quite frankly, would confuse *me* if I were in their place. This is the problem they face: should they be the "baddie" or the "goodie"? Dennis Rodman provides a great case in point.

Dennis is, beyond any doubt, a supremely talented athlete; but if there is one person who best personifies the "baddie" in today's professional sports, it would surely be Rodman.

What does Dennis do? He does just about anything he wants to do, and his transgressions have been well documented. He doesn't come out to warm-up with his team before a game (he says he doesn't need to warm up). The concept of team unity is foreign to him. Before the game is over, he has taken his shoes and socks off, and sits at courtside as if he is at a picnic, appearing unconcerned about what is happening on the floor. While other players are chastised for having their shirt tails out, he takes his own shirt completely off, sometimes shedding nearly all his clothes before the game is over.

Just before this book went to press, I noted that the Utah Jazz had unexpectedly halted the Bulls' start of the season 12-game streak. Dennis, after being ejected from the game, commented that it was, ". . . just one damn loss, that's all." I was disappointed to hear that he accounted for his poor performance by explaining, "I wasn't really interested in the game. I didn't have my game face on." (I had previously assumed that he *always* had his game face on. Shows how wrong I can be!)

Rodman pays no attention to coaches or anyone else in authority, apparently convinced that he can do whatever he damn well pleases. And what's worse, his antics have made him a hot item commercially and, let's face it, a very popular player with the fans.

Somewhere around March 14, 1996, when Rodman was with the Chicago Bulls, he was suspended for twice butting an official in the head. The suspension was for six games plus fines to the tune of $225,000, a penalty that was considered to be the heaviest in NBA history. Was the whole suspension a farce? I think so. Did it hurt the Bulls one iota? I doubt it.

In the first place, a fine of this sort means next to nothing because no one knows who is going to pay it. Secondly, the six-game suspension he was given came at a time when the Bulls did not need him. They'd had a winning season, the Eastern Conference was already locked up, and they had the home-court advantage, as well. Rodman's suspension was, in fact, a blessing in disguise for the Bulls. His absence from the court gave some of his teammates more playing time and helped them get ready for the upcoming playoffs. It also gave Rodman's body a chance to rest and heal—a plus for the Bulls in their run for the championship.

To return to the severity of Rodman's punishment, there are three questions I'd like to ask the Commissioner: Why the suspension was for just six games? How he arrived at a fine amount of $225,000? And just what is the rationale for fines, anyhow? The idea that a monetary penalty is a deterrent is completely ridiculous. In order for penalties to have any impact whatsoever, they must inflict some kind of pain. For a player, the areas most sensitive to pain involve money, visibility and position in the stats column. Those are the areas that the penalty system should target.

If you had been a witness to the blows that Rodman rained on the head of that unfortunate official, you would realize that the man could quite possibly have suffered a brain concussion or some other injury that would have made it impossible for him to work for a long period of time. If Rodman's attack had had *that* kind of result, I'm sure that the powers that be would have looked upon the incident differently. They would have been forced to take more drastic action, and Rodman would undoubtedly have been suspended for the rest of the season. Then further sanctions could have been imposed on him after the incident was fully investigated.

The punishment given Rodman amounted to a mere slap on the wrist, and was a cowardly act on the part of the league office. They appeared to be afraid to detract from the glory of the Chicago Bulls—from the hoopla that surrounds Jordan and that entire team—fearing that the Chicago fans would react negatively. Their concern was for the championship and the records.

What did the other members of the team think and say about Rodman's action? How did Jordan feel about it? Did any one of them confront Rodman? I did not hear one teammate speak in defense of the official. And, as I write, there has been only a weak press release from the Chicago team, headed by Jordan, stating that they frowned on the actions of Rodman. (This statement sounded about as sincere as if I had publicly proclaimed my love for hot beer.) The team obviously had to say *something*, but instead of mouthing prefabricated BS, I would prefer they had said nothing. That is, in fact, what their statement amounted to—*nothing!*

Reaction from the fans was no better. In fact, there are childish individuals out there who, even now, are laughing and saying that the official deserved Rodman's attack because he'd made a bad call. But any fan or player who condones this kind of action ought to look into the mirror and ask, "What am *I* really all about?"

Placing a hand on an official is a definite no-no in any sport, and the reason is easy to understand. The nature of the official's job puts them in a very precarious position to begin with: the action of the players means that referees are at physical risk in every part of the court, field, or arena. (Officials have even been killed in South America.) For these reasons, game officials must be protected from wild and emotional players who could, and often do, lose control. What Rodman did, however, was way beyond "wild and emotional," and in relation to his offense, his punishment was totally absurd—so absurd that it creates a temptation for other players to do the same thing.

I was surprised at the reaction (or lack of it) by the officials and their union to the head-butting incident. These men, earlier in the year, had gone on a strike for more money, claiming that they were not being given their due respect. Without officials, they claimed, the NBA could not function properly. Contrary to their opinion, the league *did* function without them for more than a quarter of the season. However, they eventually got just about everything they wanted and returned to work.

How strange that later, when an official got battered by a crazy-acting player, the officials said nothing. Their union *should* have stated emphatically, "We are not going to work if you let Rodman back into the league without some really severe sanctions. Officials should not be threatened, intimidated, or risk being injured by an apparently mentally disturbed basketball player who goes off at the drop of a hat. We never know what a troubled and possibly psychotic individual like Rodman might do, so you will have to get rid of him or we won't work." That's what they should have said—but I have not heard the officials or their union say one word about the incident.

In view of the fact that in other parts of the world officials have been killed by crazed and irate fans, abuse of officials should be dealt with harshly. My belief is that the officials' best move would be to go directly to the public. They should state flatly that they refuse to work games unless the likes of Rodman are banned from the league, and suggest that in the future, the Rodman types should be subject to review.

It appears likely, however, that we will continue to allow players to batter officials, punished only with a few suspended games (which allow him to rest his body) and a token fine (which probably will be paid by the team or written off as a business expense). The officials' union would be smart to take a long, hard look at this practice before one of their members is seriously hurt.

The message conveyed by recent events is clear: as long as you have talent you can get away with murder, and the league will do nothing about it. The reaction of the fans and sportswriters is puzzling; they always seem able to find some reason or excuse (a bad call, for instance) for the delinquent player's actions. But a bad call doesn't justify taking physical action, no matter what.


I recall another incident that involved a physical attack by a player—not against an official, but against another player. It happened back in the late seventies, and Kermit

Washington was the perpetrator. Following that occurrence, Kermit was suspended for more games than Rodman, but his fine was not nearly as large. (That kind of money wasn't around during those years, even at the mint.)

Kermit's offense involved a free-for-all brawl during which Kermit, caught up in the melee, threw a punch at an opposing player who was approaching him from behind. The punch landed cleanly enough to make any heavyweight boxer envious, and broke the jaw of Rudy Tomjanovich (currently Houston's coach). For this, Washington was severely fined and crucified by the media, despite the fact that he had always been a good guy both on and off the court.

A single offense led to Washington's being virtually blacklisted, and he never recovered the place he had once held in basketball—an undeserved demise, from my perspective. Yet Rodman, who butts referees and causes mayhem with a style of play calculated to lead to conflict and disruption, survives a similar offense and lives on in basketball as if nothing had happened. Attitudes have changed!

Before moving on, I should mention that assaults by players upon officials are not the exclusive property of basketball. Other sports have their share as well, but they often deal with them somewhat differently. Take the case of Roberto Alomar of the Baltimore Orioles. Unhappy with a call, this epitome of refinement spat in the umpire's face. The official and his brethren were understandably upset, and, unlike the basketball officials, they threatened to withhold their services during the playoffs and World Series unless Alomar was suspended—immediately.

The situation was resolved, but not to anyone's complete satisfaction. The important point is, however, that the baseball officials dug in their heels and demanded satisfaction, hopefully setting some kind of precedent.

Rodman, as I have pointed out, has an abundance of talent; that statement is borne out by the win and loss records of the teams he has played for. (He was a major factor in his team's breaking all win-loss records on their way to becoming World Champions.) Rodman is the league's leading rebounder. He leads the league in rebounding by a much greater margin than Jordan's next closest competitor as the league's leading scorer. His place on the first string of the All-Defensive team also confirms that he is a very valuable commodity. But Rodman was not selected for the 1996 All-Star team.

My personal belief is that Rodman was left off the All-Star team because the NBA did not want to risk his spoiling the league's day in the sun. That All-Star weekend is a showcase that demonstrates to the entire world what the NBA is all about, and I believe that to protect their image (and out of fear that Rodman would do something silly) the NBA and/or their All-Star selection committee pretended that he did not qualify for the team.

They would have us believe that Rodman is not worthy of being a part of the 1996 All-Stars, but there is no way in the world that some of the players who were selected could reasonably have been voted in over Rodman. The selection committee is supposedly made up of broadcasters and sportswriters, but we aren't told who is actually on the panel. I don't know where the panel members come from or who they are, but I have a problem believing that they truly know their business. Seems to me their identities should be published so their qualifications could be checked and they could be questioned about their All-Star decisions.

Well, Rodman didn't make the first team. You would think, then, that he'd *surely* make the second team—but you'd be wrong. The second team consists of Shawn Kemp, Grant Hill, Hakeem Olajuwon, Gary Payton and John Stockton. Once again, no space for Rodman.

Now we come to the third team, and here we find Charles Barkley. Considering the numbers he amassed, his high shooting percentage and his top-five rebounding stats, he should have been on the first team. But he made only the third team, along with Juwan Howard, Shaquille O'Neal, Indiana's Reggie Miller, and Mitch Richmond. And once again, *no Rodman.*

I wonder how many more All-Star teams the panel would have had to select (a fourth, fifth, etc.,) before Rodman was picked for one of them. Were they saying that Rodman is not worthy of All-Star selection? How could Rodman *not* have had a place on one of those three teams? A player like Mitch Richmond is better than Rodman? Come on!

As you may have guessed by now, I am not your typical Rodman fan, but I see the NBA's denying him recognition as completely bogus. I will tell you why he wasn't selected: the NBA doesn't want to see him glorified any more than necessary. Amazing, isn't it? We are talking here about the NBA, a reputable, honest organization, but we're finding out that the NBA's need to protect their image is more important than integrity, high principles, or fairness. Sorry, Dennis!

Maybe by omitting him they are making an anti-Rodman statement. (Remember, the Olympic team did not find him worthy either.) If this is the case—if the All-Star snub is just another way to penalize the guy—they would do better to impose their penalty in a way that it would have some value and meaning. I don't believe in penalizing a player for doing something *right*. Penalize him when he does something *wrong*; in this alone, you will be kept very busy.

I wish the media people could have another chance to question the Basketball Commissioner and to ask him (as they did at a game not long ago) whether Rodman is a source of embarrassment to the NBA? The Commissioner (a good man who has performed brilliantly in his job) would probably answer diplomatically, and somewhat as he did before, "Of course not; Rodman is just having fun, and doing nothing to make us believe that he would embarrass the NBA." Then would come the media's opportunity to bore in with their follow-up question: "Why, then, did Rodman not make the All-Star team, and how, based on merit alone, could he be excluded?" I would give a lot to hear the Commissioner's answer to *that* one.

If the NBA is seriously interested in protecting their image, their best course of action is to become stronger, more sensible and more civilized in dealing with a guy like Rodman, and to cease allowing him to run roughshod over the whole league during the course of an entire season. I do not see the smallest sign that this is about to happen, however.

When Rodman declares, on television, "If the team that I am with don't like my actions, they can trade me; I know I'll be welcome somewhere else," he is absolutely right. One of those greedy owners out there would jump at the chance to add a top rebounder like Rodman to their roster. This is the mentality of so many of the present day NBA owners. No matter how bad-acting a guy is, no matter what he does—short of murder (and maybe including that, as well)—he'll be welcomed with open arms, as long as he has talent and can do something for their franchise. Incredible!

And lest you think that basketball is the only culprit here, check out the NFL. Their first round draft choices include a few trouble-makers from the colleges, players who have already shown themselves as candidates for the "undesirable" category.

People regard Rodman in different ways and from a variety of points of view, but it seems as though, however we feel about him, he has the ability to stir strong emotions in most of us. Very *bad* guys and very *good* guys have that quality in common. Adolph Hitler had it, as did Martin Luther King, Jr.

Shortly after the Rodman book-signing extravaganza, a hockey player was asked how he would feel if one of *his* teammates were to show up in drag to sign copies of his book. The hockey player's answer was, "I'm not really sure just how I would feel, but I do know that he would definitely get killed out on the ice in the very next game."

Rodman doesn't seem to grasp (or doesn't care to understand) the idea that he represents both his team and the game of basketball—whether he likes it or not. And the top brass are failing to address the fact that Rodman, as a representative of the NBA, is an embarrassment to everyone in that organization. They know this to be true, and it's time they took action to put Rodman's act in order.

The Commissioner and others in league are not alone in their silence concerning Rodman's antics. The members of his team, too (presumably in the interest of team unity) say absolutely nothing. They always answer, "No," whenever they are asked (and they are asked often), "Does Rodman affect you?" But after Rodman leaves a team, his ex-teammates say, "Now we can go back to having some real unity here without worrying about outside influences (meaning Rodman, though they never said a word about him when he was playing with them.)

A fear syndrome seems to be at work here, which strikes me as somewhat ridiculous. But that's how many of these guys are. They won't stand up for their teammates, or even for themselves), but always stick to a middle-of-the-road position. They apparently prefer to come off as absolute cowards rather than stand up to Rodman by saying, "Hey, man, *I'm* playing on this team, too, and I want some respect. We are all out here trying to win, and you and your exploits are only making it harder for us."

I *do* understand the wisdom of not airing one's dirty laundry in public, but it seems that these guys don't even dare to talk to Rodman in private! I can't comprehend this. Is it really cowardice? Or is it just that they care nothing about anything?

David Robinson is supposed to be an intelligent man, right? He's been in the armed forces, and presumably knows about discipline and such things. But I'd bet you he has never talked to Rodman. (Is he afraid Rodman would punch him in the nose?) I guarantee that if Charles Barkley were playing on the same team as Rodman, and Rodman's actions were causing the team to lose a chance at the championship, Charles would take him out into the back alley and *really* talk to him.

Since I have pen in hand, and as long as everyone else is commenting on Rodman's hair, I will add my remarks to the rest. Now, I'll admit that I like a guy who has some style and is not afraid to be a little different. In this respect, I say, "You're right on, Rodman."

*So, if Dennis wants to color his hair striped with blue, I say that's his perfect right to do. Apparently it's working for him, too; he gets the attention, the ads, and more moolah than me or you. If Rodman has the resolve and dare, and wants to show his special flair by the coloring of his hair, who are we to care? That's his right, and it's only fair.*

The more these great athletes make, the less respect most of them have for the institution that made their immense salaries possible. Anything that doesn't go their way, frustrates them. Like immature children, they are incapable of dealing with any type of adversity, no matter how trivial. Acting like a bunch of kids, they act out, cry, hit, throw things, punch and pout. Imagine the chaos if every player who has not liked an official's call, butted him in the head or kicked him in the ass. That is what we are coming to.

I want you to remember that, in Rodman's case, we have a man who has a history of more than just a few bad acts. How soon will one of his antics turn out to be the straw that breaks the camel's back?

Will there ever come a time when everyone involved in basketball, from players right up to the people who are responsible for running the league, are willing to stand up and say, "Enough is enough! We don't want Rodman on our team or in this league anymore—*period!*" This attitude should start at the team level and go right up to the top of the league. (And for the information of fans who care enough to express their opinion, the National Basketball Association and the Players Association can be contacted at: Olympic Tower, 645 Fifth Avenue, New York, NY 10022.)

People make all sorts of excuses for Rodman, and his teams do, as well. The owners of the San Antonio Spurs wanted him back for a second year, even though his first year with them was filled with an unending series of unfortunate incidents involving Rodman. During a press conference, after the Spurs' management very hesitantly announced that they were giving another one-year contract to their coach, John Lucas, they added that, as far as Rodman is concerned, they didn't think he had ever done anything particularly bad. (Translation: They were willing to condone—or at least overlook—his unbelievable behavior because he brings people into the arena and helps them win games.)

Nowadays we have Rodman tee-shirts plus all kinds of other Rodman paraphernalia. And don't forget all those commercials. There is no doubt about it: Rodman sells. But I wonder about the people who manufacture all that stuff and who put him in all those commercials! Do they give a passing thought to his affect on our society and today's game? Don't they have any qualms about promoting his brand of non-respect for authority?

I wouldn't be surprised if some clever CEO from one of the major corporations were to use the Rodman head-butting incident to advertise his company's brand of headache remedy. The possibilities are endless: A film of the incident, with a voice-over saying "For your really bad headaches, use XX Brand Gelcaps." Or a testimonial showing a referee saying, "I took two XX Gelcaps after Rodman popped me a couple of times, and I was able to finish the game with no problem." Or, they could show a smiling Rodman saying, "XX Gelcaps help me keep my rebounding up to par after head-butting incidents."

There is no limit to how far a negative concept can be carried in the name of making money.

As I was working out on an afternoon in early May, 1996, I noticed that most of the gym's clients were clustered around one of the TV sets, just as they had been during the Super Bowl a few months earlier. The object of their attention was the one and only Dennis. I was struck with the thought that if ever there was a name that suited a person, "Dennis the Menace" fits Rodman.

Watching Dennis, it also occurred to me to wish that his great talent extended to baseball, because if ever two people deserved each other, Marge Schott and Dennis Rodman were born to be that pair. Insensitive, shameful so-and-so's, they've earned the right to get into each other's hair. And, since blond and red are two of Rodman's favorite colors, "Cinci" would be a perfect team for him. I can see him now, stealing bases and hitting umpires over the head with one of Marge's swastika bats.

I find both of these characters offensive to the dignity of mankind, and neither baseball or basketball should have to put up with their embarrassing conduct. Instead, we have clever advertising people pitching Rodman commercials to money-conscious, non-caring corporate CEOs, thus making a bigger hero out of a guy who doesn't deserve it. I want to state for the record that those who exploit players like Rodman for their own financial gain, and who are willing to tolerate the likes of Marge Schott, need a real lesson in the basic values that good people of every race and color have been fighting for since the dawn of history.

I have always believed that no matter what our creed, religion, or belief, we are all one—one race—the human race. If we are to make things better in the world today, we must do it together. As an American of color, I cannot help being appalled when I realize that the actions of a Rodman lend credibility to the stereotypes about people of color that are held by many subversive and racial hate groups. And Rodman, firmly convinced of his right to say and do as he pleases, cares nothing about the picture he portrays to the world.

Enough said—almost. *Get real, you officials of the NBA: stop making guys like Rodman bigger every day. And baseball, take a stand against Marge; the likes of her should never be in charge.*

I admit that I find Rodman quite correct in wanting to be his own man, yet I have strong misgivings . . . *Of course, it's his right to wear pants or a dress, but the Rodman issue is a source of distress. In play, he seems always to do his rebounding best, yet the whole scenario brings me*

300

*nothing but stress. His behavior to many appears bizarre at best; and we wonder if he does these things only in jest.*

*I accept Rodman's wanting to be his own man, and have no fear of how tall he may stand. But it mystifies me how many commercials come his way—he's on TV practically every day! To be a company's spokesman, he's the choice of many; but as their son-in-law? No; I doubt there are any.*

*Why so much attention to this man? Shouldn't there be some kind of a plan? There are many more worthy . . . I don't understand. Barry Sanders' play is brilliant, and likewise Jerry Rice, but for TV commercials, they must be too nice.*

*I say to fans who just go with the flow, "I'm one guy who won't buy the Rodman show. Don't let his likes confuse your minds; for God's sake, read between the lines."*

*I fear for kids who see his antics as right; but what else can they think when adults watch with delight? I fear, too, for people who have fought for dignity—only to have a Rodman play into the hands of those who exploit bigotry. I know Rodman thinks himself to be a most modern man, but he's adding fuel to the fire of groups like the Ku Klux Klan. I say to one and all from the bottom of my heart: The Rodmans' of the world need help, and there's no time like the present to start.*

# TEN

## PRO SPORTS AND KIDS

### PLAYING THE ODDS

Professional sports in America actually involve a fairly limited number of athletes, but do *not* make the mistake of underestimating their scope or their power, especially in the lives of young people. We're talking here about the four major team sports: basketball, football, baseball, and hockey—ice hockey, that is. (In this country, soccer players have not reached the professional stature of athletes in the major team sports.) And, of course, we mustn't forget the individual sports: tennis and golf.

Now, let's look at the numbers. Tennis has a following, as does golf, but in these sports there are probably not more than 3,000 to 4,000 active participants, and of those, probably only 50 or so are household names.

Basketball presents a different picture. With 29 teams, assuming 12 players per team, we have a group of only about 350 people, but the impact of the game far surpasses that of tennis and golf combined. Amazing, isn't it, how such a small number of people can capture so much space on paper and on the air—not to mention space in our minds. America, a country of over 250 or 260 million people, is powerfully impacted by this small, but very influential, group of individuals.

When we consider baseball, we add 700 or so major league players to our total. Then after adding another 1,350 pro football players, we're talking about 2,400 or so professional athletes in the three major sports. However, of that group, there might be as few as 100 or so who are really well-known names—players we can relate to and would actually recognize if we were to pass them on a street in a city other than their own. This number is surprisingly small. It includes about 20 people from the game of basketball, about 15 people from baseball, and another 10 or 15 from football (and even fewer from hockey, because their faces are covered up).

When I actually add up the figures, the entire list of truly well-known athletes probably doesn't total as many as 75 people but, small though it is, this group of people has a tremendous effect on our lives. Tens of millions of us each year watch them perform—via the medium of TV, listening to games on the radio, or watching them in person. In addition, we probably spend an equal amount of time reading about them and listening to sports commentators or talk show hosts discuss them.

Because such a small number of people have the power to create so much grief or pleasure for so many of us, and especially because of their mighty influence on kids, we need a stronger and more intelligent control over our professional sports. Professional athletes have become the idols of our young people. Instead of focusing on realistic, attainable goals, millions of school kids dream only of becoming professional athletes. Sometimes these dreams completely take over their young lives. Parents may also buy into these same false illusions, often believing that the dream is really feasible for their kids.

I don't think it is healthy that these desires are allowed to consume our youth *or* their elders. Sure, it's healthy to dream, but it's not healthy to live in a fantasy world, not fully aware of the odds against you.

To begin with, young kids can hardly be expected to evaluate the percentages or to realize what they have to deal with to overcome the odds against their success. We're talking here about more than just a numbers game; it is an *impossible* game—more impossible than most people probably realize. It's just like the lottery. Even though the odds are a million to one (or even 100 million to one), everyone who buys a ticket wants to believe that they are going to be that lucky one.

Unfortunately, the odds aren't much better in professional sports than they are in a big state lottery. If you figure that there are only 300 slots for professional basketball players out there, and we are a country of 250 million, the odds for success are damn near a million to one. The odds are undeniable, and almost unbeatable. Our kids should be aware of that fact.

## Wiltism

*Lest we forget:*

**In America it can be easy to go from poor to rich.**

**In other parts of the world, just obtaining the necessities can be a bitch.**

## Education vs. Big-Time Sports

Many college kids—and even some high school kids—are leaving school early to join the pros. As long as the money is what it is, they have a right to make the best of every opportunity, with my blessing. They cannot be deprived of an opportunity to earn a living. Isn't that, after all, one of the main reasons for going to college: to better our chance to earn a bigger pay check?

Young athletes should be reminded, however, that not everyone will be able to leave school after their first year and become as successful as Magic Johnson. (I seem to recall that a couple of his teammates left school for the pros about the same time as he did, but can anyone remember their names?) Perhaps we could give more attention to the aspiring young athletes who left school early but *didn't* make it, looking at where *they* are now instead of focusing exclusively on the successful players everyone knows about. There have been hundreds of these guys—players who are no longer there, and who knows where. Talking about this bunch might persuade some of the young dropout "wannabes" to stay in school a little longer.

At the same time, we must be cognizant that just one contract can set a young man up for life financially, *whether or not* he makes it in professional sports.

If we want kids to stay in college instead of leaving school to play pro basketball, we should give them something they can fall back on in life and something they might enjoy studying. Not every young person wants the type of academic course that most kids are forced to take in high school just to get into college. They may not want to be accountants or economics teachers or social workers, so why not let them go to the technical schools where they could learn a trade?

To make this possible, the NCAA would undoubtedly have to make some changes in the accreditation rules; but if such changes could be made, talented young players would be able to learn a marketable skill—something that would enable them to make a living when they graduate—and, at the same time, play ball and gain national recognition at the college level.

Under such a system, when young athletes entered college/technical training with the hope of making it to the pros, they would no longer have to worry about dealing with the required (and dreaded) general education courses. These mandatory classes are the main reason most athletes do so poorly in college and rarely graduate. Given more appealing choices at the college level, they would have a good chance to make a decent living later, even if they weren't able to make it in professional sports.

I am sure that those of you who are followers of college basketball were shocked (and maybe somewhat disappointed) that Marcus Camby chose the NBA route, deciding to forego his senior year. You may also have been taken aback by the willingness of Allen Iverson and Stephon Marbury to give up college. And what about high school seniors such as Kevin Garnett and Kobe Bryant who decided to go directly into the major leagues. There has been all kinds of talk, of course, about the NBA's role in robbing high school students of a chance for further education. But, as I mentioned before, until we can show these kids a better way to make two or three million dollars, maybe we should keep our mouths shut.

Kids might be willing to remain in school a little longer if we could provide some kind of financial inducement for them to do so. If we could figure a way to let aspiring young players make some money while they are playing for a college, or even while they are just attending college, a lot more of them might stay in school. (I am not optimistic about seeing this scenario played out, however.)

I am confident that few people today have a clear idea of what is meant by "getting an education." Most people think that education comes only from what is read in books or heard from teachers in a classroom. But anyone with half a brain who has lived in this world for any length of time knows that, if you open your eyes and listen with your ears, you learn something every day of your life. I can tell you with absolute assurance that playing basketball on a professional level is definitely a learning experience and can teach a young man more than just a little of life— assuming he has a minimal background of basic common sense and is willing to learn.

Why should it be so imperative for young basketball players to have what we call "an education" before playing pro ball, when young athletes in other sports are free at almost any age to command (or demand) all kinds of money? After all, if great athletes in other sports (tennis players, for example) are able to do it at the age of fourteen, why should age make such a difference in basketball? If an opportunity comes at an early age, perhaps all athletes should be free to take advantage of it without feeling guilty.

It seems simple to me: As long as these kids are worthy of attracting an audience and have the qualifications for contributing to a team, they should not be deprived of the chance to do so. This kind of opportunity may never present itself again. And remember, even if they should fail in their first year, with the kind of money professional athletes make, they can afford to go back and get an education on their own (assuming that's what they want to do). Most will be playing ball for four or five years, in any case.

If you are going to go into professional sports, sooner or later you will have to take a chance. You can take it now or you can do it later on. I say, if you're qualified, take it now; if you are not qualified, who knows if you ever will be. If *you* had a chance to make millions, wouldn't you take it? Is there any doubt?

## AGENTS

All novice professional players must accept the fact that, like it or not, they will be faced with a number of things that, at the time, they won't understand. I hope that, when these situations arise, each of them will have someone they can turn to for help. This person could be a parent, or a friend, or even the agent who is making a buck off of them by showing them the right financial path.

Although there are a lot of unsavory characters out there ready to take advantage of young potential millionaire athletes, the number of people who are formally trained and qualified to help them is relatively small. Only careful scrutiny (or blind luck) can help a player avoid the many pitfalls that lie in his path.

Not many young players are as fortunate as Grant Hill, whose father, Calvin, was himself a pro, and was able to pass on first hand information to his son. Like Hill, my friend Ron Cey (an ex-Dodger) was well qualified and able to assist *his* son, who just recently signed a contract in professional baseball. Both of these young athletes were lucky to have the benefit of good advice when they needed it—most do not.

Where can the high school grads and college students who are eager and ambitious to play in the big leagues get the advice they need? There are no easy answers to this question, and for most young jocks, good information is not easy to come by. Help should be made available for them, but from whom? Today's contracts are so complex that even the wisest of businessmen get professional advice before signing anything. To negotiate a sports contract,

309

the pros need an agent, a tax consultant, and a lawyer. How can we expect a nineteen or twenty-year-old to cope without competent help?

Agents are commonly used to fill this need, but determining which one to use is difficult. Athletes must be constantly on guard against being in contact with the wrong people. The NCAA constantly polices young athletes, and can cause problems if a wrong turn is made. And, unfortunately, a single mistake is all that is needed to ruin a career or a life.

Speaking of agents brings up the question (or the problem) of whether agents should be allowed to talk to and influence high school and college kids. In my opinion, agents should be screened more carefully, and their credibility and morals questioned closely. Their character and professional record should be documented before they are turned loose on a bunch of inexperienced kids. We should make it possible for a young person to learn something about these guys before they start plying him with jewelry and buying him with cash.

A reputable agent should say to a young athlete, "I don't want you to talk to me until you check me out. Talk to other people, find out about my work and reputation, and when (or if) you are convinced that I'm okay, we'll talk." If an agent is really straight-arrow about helping a young person, he should not be reluctant to expose his background or to show what kind of person he or she really is. The best way to accomplish this might be for the agent to say, "Here is a list of people. All of them know me well, and some of them I have worked for. Ask any of them to tell you what they know about me, or to give you the name of someone else who can tell you more. You have every right to find out whether I am a good guy or a bad guy before deciding whether or not I am the person who should represent you."

# ELEVEN

## SUNDRIES
### MY THOUGHTS ON A NUMBER OF THINGS

What does it mean to be a sports figure today? In the old days, it wasn't that difficult. But nowadays you not only have to be an ambassador and a source of information about every problem facing the universe, you must, at all times, act in such a way that you are above reproach in everything you do, both on and off the court or playing field.

The pressures are almost too much be imagined, and the demands on athletes are far too great. Remember that freedom-of-speech thing we talked about, the freedom to keep your mouth shut? Well, that principle does not apply here. Instead, players must respond whenever they are asked a question, even though they have no answer. What can be worse than to have to say something when you have nothing to say?

Image has become an all-important consideration for athletes, especially at the professional level. They must think constantly of how the public perceives them. Here's an example of how that works.

I'm all for giving your best shot in any fair contest, even if you knock your opponent on his ass in the process. When you play the game hard, that happens, whether you are on offense or defense. I also believe in extending a hand to aid your opponent in getting up. But most players today think it would offend their dignity or their manhood if they were to help an opposing player to his feet. Their thinking goes something like this: "The bull in me knocked that guy down, and it's up to him to get up on his own." It's as though by showing no compassion, they create for themselves a tougher, more ferocious presence.

You see that same attitude in boxers when they go through their "bad game face" routine before they touch gloves to start the fight. For boxers, this may be acceptable, though it's not lauded. But an attitude that says, "Hey, man, I'm tough and I'm out to do nothing but bad things to you," does not belong in the game of basketball or in *any* legitimate sporting event—pro wrestling excluded, of course. The ruffians of today get away with that kind of thing, however, because that is what their games have come to be all about: acting bad, playing bad—and it's all very sad. Maybe the only recourse available to athletes' nowadays is to become impervious to the bad stuff that surrounds them, and act as the people they truly are—or *should* be.

There is a disturbing similarity between some professional athletes and the kids whose deeds on the streets of our world shock us daily. The careless insensitivity shown by so many of today's jocks to team owners and fans, plus their low regard for rules and regulations—these mirror the disrespect shown by kids for their parents, for law and order, and for the rules of society today.

No matter what his political beliefs, Mahmoud Abdul-Rauf's refusal to stand up for the flag showed an attitude of blatant disrespect for America and Americans. This is the same kind of disrespect that kids show the policemen of their cities and towns. These kids will probably never have a chance to make the dollars that professional jocks make, but players like Abdul-Rauf are able to earn their big salaries because they are privileged to live in a country like ours.

No one makes any more money than our top flight professional athletes, yet they seem to feel that they are being cheated and denied the things they deserve. They have had opportunities and rights that are not afforded in many other countries, and showing contempt for our flag demonstrates a serious lack of awareness of the blessings they enjoy. Clearly, wealth is not the answer to halting the erosion of moral values.

The problems and the hostility of misbehaving kids *and* jocks seem to stem from the teachings they received from their families and the other people who influenced their early lives. If you don't train a puppy to obey commands, he is apt to run into the street and be killed by a car, or he may cause the driver to hit (and perhaps kill) someone else while trying to avoid hitting him—all because he was not trained to heed the command of the master who claimed to love him.

Who is responsible for the dog's death and the possible injury to others? Is the poor puppy to blame? Or is his master at fault for failing to teach him to be a responsible dog? Legally, I am not sure where the blame lies, but I am sure that the poor puppy would have been better off if he had been taught how to behave.

Childish behavior is not defined by age and has no chronological limits. So where does the responsibility lie when the "children" in professional sports don't mind their manners? Do we go back to their mommies and daddies? Seems to me a better plan would be to find responsible people to act as substitute parents. Coaches, owners, and general managers are in a position to play this role.

If those in authority truly want to change things, they must establish *and enforce* rules, even though having to obey them may be a new experience for some team members. Coaches, owners and managers, acting as substitute parents, are capable of pointing out to their players that, as they are no longer children, it's time that they started to act like responsible grown-ups. Even childlike players should be able to grasp the concept that all members of the team are interdependent, and that the negative actions of one of them reflect on all, and eventually impact everyone in the game.

Sadist that I am, I get a lot of pleasure seeing guys play under pressure. As I watched David Robinson play against Charles Barkley in the game with Phoenix, I had to wonder how it was possible for six-foot-four and a half Charles Barkley to out-rebound the awesome seven-foot specimen that is David Robinson? How can a guy be out-rebounded by a player who is almost eight inches shorter, cannot jump as high, and does not have his physical attributes? There is nothing magical about it, ladies and gentlemen; one guy has a much bigger heart than the other, and a greater desire to go after the ball.

With all his intellect and great physical presence, something seems to be missing in David Robinson. He does well in the ordinary games, but when it comes down to nut-cutting time, he suddenly fades away.

I have been getting phone calls from sportswriters who are doing an article on Robinson. They have asked for my comments, but I always decline, not wanting to criticize David Robinson in a phone conversation. I am not criticizing him now, either. I am saying only that the Robinson we see is, as far as I can tell, the real Robinson. He is by nature an easy-going guy who just doesn't have the kind of "inners" going for him that would make him an aggressively strong basketball player. This characteristic becomes clearly evident time after time when he plays against someone—anyone, in fact—who is any good. I wonder what his comment would be if he were asked how a six-foot-four guy got a rebound away from him when they both had an equal chance at the ball.

Robinson was recently picked as the league MVP, and the choice was based on his numbers (points, rebounds and block shots, along with team wins). *Wiltie, if these were the only ingredients considered in picking MVPs', you should have been the league MVP almost every year you played.* I cannot believe that those who do the MVP voting are focused on reality. They should, in my opinion, take a closer look at the guys like Charles Barkley who, at crucial times, always come up with the necessary big plays.

I have been listening to comments by Anfernee Hardaway who has just finished the second game in the playoffs against the Bulls. I hear him tell the media, "I don't know what happened to me, I just (ugh), my legs are flat. I can't jump. I can't really run. I don't have any real feel for doing the things with my legs that I have been used to doing most of the time. Or maybe there's just no desire . . ." This statement might indicate simply that his legs are tired; or maybe *he* is tired. Is it legs or is it his head?

When someone who is twenty-three years old talks about his legs going dead, I have to wonder. The only sports performers I know whose legs go bad at that age are race horses. Their legs go bad because they age six or seven times faster than human being do. Yet horses, even though they lose their legs, are still good for something: they can always be put to stud. Maybe that's what these players with failing legs have in mind and are saving themselves for (just in case basketball breeding comes into vogue).

Michael Jordan was asked at the start of the '96-'97 season how many games the Bulls would win. Ever confident, he replied, "Seventy games or more—and we'll be there in the end." I couldn't help but wonder whether his assurance was based on a belief that his team was that good, or a conviction that the rest of the league was that bad. (Lest we forget: The 11-time championship Celtic team of my era had a tough time winning 60!)

Many of us in the sports world have chosen to march to a different drummer, and we have picked very different kinds of people to be our heroes. I was out with A.C. Cowlings on the Monday that O.J. Simpson was being arraigned. Although I would have figured that A.C., knowing that his best friend was just about to be incarcerated, would be at home feeling somewhat down in spirits, but he was out there with me, perhaps trying to forget the whole thing.

I was amazed at the attention A.C. was given by the people who came up to our table to speak to him and to thank him for being a friend to O.J. Two or three guys kissed him and broke into tears, happy to know that there was still someone around who would choose to be there for a friend.

I have always assumed that guys just naturally stood by their friends, but here were all these people applauding A.C. for doing just that. He helped his friend break the law, yet they didn't seem to worry about that part of it. They just seemed to gravitate toward A.C. since his Bronco tour of the L.A. freeways had made him a celebrity.

SUNDRIES

Once you become a celebrity, no matter what vehicle brought you into the spotlight, you become a target of the autograph seekers of the world. You are someone they can look at, touch, and say, "I was there; I saw him." With A.C., this caught me by surprise. I have always known him to be a good man. But as many times as I have been around A.C. over the years, I have never seen anybody show much interest in him. Then, suddenly, he was as big as O.J. himself.

A.C. signed a number of autographs while I sat there pondering the question of whether these people wanted his autograph because he had driven the Bronco, or because, at possible risk to himself, he had stood by a friend in need. There is no real answer to this question, of course.

Celebrities are what we choose to make of them for ourselves. For some of us, a celebrity might be an actor who does toilet tissue commercials or someone who sells used cars on TV. In a world where everyone presumably has their ten minutes of fame, we are surrounded by celebrities. Anyone, no matter what they are doing, who is seen by more than ten people could conceivably be considered a celebrity. I shudder to think of how we would regard Hitler if he were to be spotted walking down Hollywood Boulevard. I'll bet Marge Schott wouldn't be the only person asking for an autograph. There would be many more elbowing each other for a chance to see him or to get a memento—sad testimony to what our world and times have come to.

Here's a question that keeps cropping up, year after year: Should the basket be raised? And here's my answer: I don't think so. Change is inevitable; that we all know. But should our *games* be changed to suit the era, or should *we* change by learning to better play the game as it is now? Putting it another way, should the game of basketball be

317

adapted to fit the players, or should the players adapt their skills to fit the game?

Raising the basket is not going to help the game of basketball or nullify the big guy's advantage. To begin with, the players who do most of the dunking have always been the six-foot-three to six-foot-eight agile types who have great timing and jumping ability. Until Shaquille came along, Jordan had dunked more balls than anyone I know of, and now almost all Shaq does on offense is dunk. Whether this year, yesteryear, or in the years to come, it has always been and always will be the agile guys who do it best.

Think for a minute: do you see anyone of the size of Shawn Bradley or Ghourghe Muresan dunk a ball consistently? Going back through the history of the game, you'll find, at most, only one or two big guys who could deftly dunk the ball. Even though they can reach the rim, they can hardly get off their feet enough to dunk a ball. There's no need to raise the basket because of only one or two guys, when the vast majority of those who dunk the ball are of normal size—for basketball players.

There is yet another reason for leaving the basket where it is. Technically speaking, raising it would change the trajectory of the ball in a way that would give an even greater advantage to the big guy. The reason involves elementary physics. At the basket's present height, most of the rebounds—at least 75 percent—come from beneath the rim, an advantage for the smaller guy, *not* the bigger guy. This is why most big guys don't lead the league in rebounding. Changing the trajectory of the ball would only make it easier for taller players to get more rebounds.

If an athlete is fortunate enough to have height in addition to exceptional talent, why should he be penalized?

Small guys are not penalized for being small when their short stature gives *them* an advantage. Shorter height and lower center of gravity may help gymnasts, and shorter weightlifters get a break because they don't have to put the weight up so high.

Now, no one claims that shortness gives an unfair advantage to athletes in these sports; but if a big guy is talented as well as tall, you'll hear people say, "Unfair! He has an unfair advantage." Is it unfair that he can jump higher or run faster than other people, or that he is stronger than other people? Hell, no! It's all part of being a great athlete, and he should not be penalized for that.


I would never be so presumptuous as to think that I know what your likes and dislikes are, or how you spend your free time. Those choices are completely up to you. But I do think that there are some things that most of us do as a matter of course without ever looking at them in terms of their real value. Take sporting events for example. Bluntly speaking, a lot of them are a waste of our time and money.

First of all, there is an investment of time in sporting events, just as there is in anything we do. I often hear people say they wish they had more free time. They complain about having to work such long hours, or about their long commute, or about having to do the multitude of other things their lifestyles require, but I wonder what they would do with more free time if they had it.

It's strange that we never think of the time we fill with such things as sporting events, as "free time." We think of basketball games and football games as desirable luxury items, perhaps—things we really want to do. But how many of them have come to be like drugs—not real pleasure, but an addiction?

319

How many of us have ever sat down and thought about how we could better spend the five hours or so that we now use in going to a game? (For a lot of us who are sports junkies, this may happen two or three times a week.) We make fun of the couch potatoes who spend hours on end watching television, but the hours we spend going to our various games can add up to a surprisingly large chunk of time. Even overlooking the absurd financial cost of game tickets; there must be many more rewarding ways to spend those hours.

When we buy necessities such as cars, furniture, and clothing, most of us shop fairly carefully. Because an item serves a purpose and is affordable, we sometimes accept less than what we really want. But when we buy luxury items—and, for most of us, sporting events fall into this category—it's different. Sometimes we pay (probably too much) for something that is a luxury, then, if that item does not bring us full pleasure and satisfaction, we end up feeling like jackasses. How many times have we come back from a sporting event feeling like that?

If you were to look at pro games from the point of view of a smart consumer, would you conclude that you're getting full value for the money you spend? It's possible that we are all spending more time and money on games than they are worth, simply out of habit, or because going to games is the "in" thing to do. From both aspects—time and money—missing a few games might be a good idea. The empty-seat ploy is not only a way to fight back, but it could also be a healthy alternative.

Would you like some suggestions about how you could fill the time you used to spend at the pro games, and still be involved in sports? (If you answered, "No," read the next few paragraphs, anyway. You might find them of interest.)

There is a relatively new concept called the "Master Track and Field Program" that offers older people an opportunity to be active sports participants. ("Older" here refers to folks who have reached the advanced age of 35 or more—not exactly over the hill, by most standards). The program provides a way for folks to stay in shape, have some fun, and be an actual part of a sport instead of being on the outside looking in. It can become an activity for the whole family, in fact. Remember: the family that trains together stays together.

If, on the other hand, being a sports voyeur is your forte, you might take a look at the less-in-vogue sports, and experiment by attending some events on the amateur and college levels. The professionals would have you believe, of course, that when you watch *their* games, you are seeing the very best. I'll grant that, at the pro games, you may be watching the best athletes, but you have no assurance that, at any given time, they will be giving you their best effort or their best team play. Would you prefer to watch so-called amateurs give their best, or watch the so-called best give a lot less?

The "very best" option may be actually participating in a sport, but short of that, there are a number of attractive choices other than professional events. And all of us can become more discriminating about what is worth watching.

Most sports have become more like entertainment spectacles than competitive events, and pro basketball, as I have said before, has become big-time show business. Every big show needs a ringmaster, and in the case of professional sports, the ringmaster role is played by the publicists.

Publicists are the people who concoct stories about athletes and entertain us with fascinating descriptions of the prowess of the mighty warriors they are paid to promote. Their accounts of double-doubles, triple-doubles and other marvels can make us believe that we are witnessing giants at work. But I explained earlier how a double-double can actually be a very ordinary achievement. Believe me, ten points and ten rebounds is *not* a fantastic feat. Even a kid can understand that it doesn't take much to score ten points, yet we are expected to be awestruck when the announcer says, "Grant Hill had a double-double!"

The double-doubles that the guys get nowadays would be looked upon by the likes of Elgin Baylor, Jerry West or me as plain hogwash. We would have been embarrassed to accept applause for anything less than maybe a triple-double, and those numbers wouldn't be in the 10's—they would be in the 20's, 30's, 40's and 50's. Guys like Oscar Robertson averaged, I repeat, *averaged,* not double-doubles, not double-double-doubles, but *triple-doubles* for a whole season.

Can you imagine such a thing? If one man can average a triple-double per game for a whole season, what is the relevance of a double-double? Either this man was superman himself, or those numbers don't mean a hell of a lot. In this case, both statements are correct. The numbers *don't* mean much; and Oscar Robertson *was* a superman.

One of my pet peeves is seeing credit being given to people who don't really deserve it. I'm talking about giving special attention or praise to those who are only doing their job. Take guards getting assists, for instance. Why shouldn't they? These guys control the ball, after all. For this reason, I am not inclined to tout Jordan's ability to get assists. He controls the ball for his team much of the time, and yet, unlike Pippen, he is not even the leading assist player on his own team. Assists become special only when dished out in goodly number during a limited period of time. *That* feat is worthy to be noted.

I have a hard time trying to keep my eye on some of the league's centers, the guys we call "cherry pickers." These are players who get down the court even before their defense assignment is finished, hoping that one of their teammates will get the ball off the boards and throw it to them. Their goal is to be rewarded with an easy basket, usually a dunk shot—a good opportunity to show how high they can go and other feats of that nature.

The player most famous for doing this is Dominique Wilkins, but there are many others—even centers—who like to cherry pick down the court. As I see it, these guys should be out there scoring as hard as they can at both boards as Shaq does, though once in a while even he can be seen down at the other end waiting for someone to pass him the ball for a quick dunk. It could be that these cherry pickers have just misread their job description; or perhaps they are just placing the emphasis on the wrong part of their job.

Do you know the difference between Miller Time and Tyson Time? . . . Okay, time's up! It's Miller Time when Reggie Miller takes over the game with three-pointers and does anything he can to help his team win. Tyson Time is Mike's being in the wrong place at the wrong time all the time—usually about 2:00 or 3:00, morning time.

Anyone can make a mistake now and then, or get a bad break that results in a bad situation. But when you see someone repeatedly make the same mistakes, you know there is a real problem—and the problem usually involves that person's choice of friends and associates.

I have been lucky to have had some fine people as my good friends. *Vince Miller, for one, has known me so long that he knows what I am thinking, right or wrong. And there's my New York friend, Los; when I need a bit of truth, I talk to him the most. And I am blessed with a family— five sisters and two brothers. We don't see each other often, but I would have no others. Then there are the Kutshers, like second family to me. And my Persian friend, Mo-Tar-Jemi, who has been teaching me about life and languages since 1963. I mustn't omit Roz. I have known her for over a quarter of a century, but believe it or not, she's a relatively new entry. I have known most of my friends for a long, long while. Some friendships go back to when I was a very small child. There's my old friend, Ike Richman. Though he's passed this world by, before he left, he introduced me to my good friend Sy. All have had something in common, plain for me to see: Each has done their best to make life easier for me. Love and peace to all.*

*Addendum: A name that must never be omitted from any list of the most valued people in my life is that of Dr. Lorber. Without his help in dealing with physical problems and providing mental assurance, none of what I did in basketball would have been possible.*

Not everyone is blessed with wonderful friends, and for that reason I figure that all of us (including myself) should probably learn to be a little more tolerant of the misadventures of others (and of our own mishaps, as well).

*Are you saying Wiltie, that if Tyson were to replace some of the people that he chooses to spend his off-boxing hours with, he might have a better chance of avoiding some of the pitfalls and problems that he has been plagued with?* Yes, that's exactly what I am saying. When you are popular, it is easy to attract friends—or people who consider themselves to be your friends. When you make a lot of money and can do extravagant things for people, "friends" seem to come out of the woodwork in droves. I am sure that Tyson, like many another sports figure, has as "friends" people who he never would have dreamed would be in his corner. These people turned up at his doorstep along with success, and he would be well advised to be leery of many of them.

P.S. The great and popular ones must pay a price for the multitude of "friends" who surround them. They never know for sure why those buddies are there. One of the keys that has always worked for me came in a phrase I've heard since I was three: "There is no friend like an old friend."

## WILTISM

**IN LIFE, IT'S TRUE: WE ARE WHAT WE DO. THOUGH SOME PEOPLE CLAIM WE ARE WHAT WE EAT, I BELIEVE WE'RE MORE AFFECTED BY THOSE WE MEET.**

One of the best basketball stories I recall from my playing days dates back to the late '60s. It was the end of a quarter, and somebody had taken a shot just as the buzzer went off. A split second after the buzzer, a little guard grabbed the ball as a rebound, but instead of giving it to the official, he held on to it, ran over to the scorer's table, and pleaded with one of the stat guys: "Listen, you've just got to record this as a rebound. It's very important to me because I told my mother before the game that I was going to go in there and mix it up with the big boys today and get me at least one rebound. Wilt seems to be very angry today, and he's not allowing his teammates or anyone else to get any rebounds. So, if I don't get this one, I'll probably never have another chance."

325

They all looked at him and smiled, but I'm not sure whether they gave him the rebound or not.

My favorite movies have always been the ones that have a strong, villainous character, one who brings us to the edge of our seats, hoping the good guy will hand him his just desserts. Every hero needs a real bad guy to make him look better, and if the victory is to really mean something, the villain must be a real contender.

This is how I was perceived throughout my playing career: the BAD GUY! I later became that villain in Conan the Destroyer.

This theme is played out in sports, too. There needs to be a bad guy—a person or a team to hate. The team that is the object of hate could be the Bums from Brooklyn or the Yankees in the pinstripes—any team that continually beats up on your own team. Or maybe it's the Celtics in green, bad guys for everyone but the people in Boston. Whoever they are, you want to do something to them. And the badder they are, the stronger your feelings, and the stronger your reason to want to go to the games.

How much, after all, do you want to go out and cheer for the Chicago Bulls to beat the Dallas Mavericks? C'mon!

---

# WILTISM

**EVERY MOTHER CROW THINKS HER CHILD IS WHITE AS SNOW.**

---

Isn't it amazing how being bad seems to open more doors than being good? Guys of Andre Agassi's type get many more commercials than athletes who more closely resemble Stefan Edberg, the tennis player from Sweden. Edberg has been repeatedly voted the nicest, most congenial player on the pro tour; but how many commercials have you seen *him* in? For years he has been a top-ten player, and he is physically attractive—so why hasn't he been chosen over the crude-looking, rude-acting Agassi, a guy who is considered by many to be the real schmuck of the tour? Agassi has been called a quitter by game officials, and has been known, at times, just not to give a rip. So, *you* tell *me* why the advertising moguls pick him as their spokesperson. It has to be because of his bad-boy image.

Bad as Agassi may be, he *was* able to gain the affection of Brooke Shields. People say opposites attract. Maybe they're right.

I am troubled as to why the sports moguls of today thought they needed to beef up the offensive part of their respective games. They have made a number of changes which have had the effect of boosting the offense's advantage. Here are a few examples.

In baseball: the juiced-up ball—the one that allows so many more home runs. It continues to rear its ugly head, but why is it here? Is its purpose to make it seem that today's jocks can hit the ball farther and more often? Or is it to make the fans happy?

In football: the rule against checking a potential receiver pass, a certain point, or other goodies that have given the offensive guy an edge.

In basketball: the three-point shot, three foul attempts on a shot, and the end of hand checking; all have given a boost to the offense as did the calling of zone violations that allow the middle to be wide open so any good player can drive for an easy lay-up.

Coach Wooden once said to me, "Let them play any kind of defense. The best defense will only bring out the best in the offensive game of truly great players." I agree. This concept worked in my time for me.

Child labor is an issue of the day, and rightly so, I guess. It's a shame, though, that once again celebrities seem to be bearing the brunt of a flood of media fault-finding. They have taken massive criticism of their involvement with companies that use and abuse child labor, even though most of these celebrities had no idea that anything of the sort was going on. Ignorance is not an excuse for wrongdoing, of course, but how many of us would have been caught in the same trap? My sympathy to Michael Jordan, Kathie Lee Gifford and the others who have been under attack.

Nike is apparently not making any shoes in America, and Michael should have been cognizant of that fact. But to be under attack at this point for seeming not to care about how he makes his zillions of dollars, that is an unfair rap. From here on, however, with all the attention that has been focused on the subject, there should be no excuse for anyone to become involved with any enterprise without knowing exactly what that business is all about. No celebrity (or anyone else!) should ever sign a contract with a company or endorse their product without knowing precisely what makes that company tick—even though the financial rewards may be substantial.

From here on—no excuses.


Beauty may be only skin deep, but we live in a shallow society where sex and good looks tend to rule the world. Nancy Kerrigan, winner of a silver medal in the Olympics, had an attacker who thought his own favorite skater would have a better chance at the gold if Nancy was not around. The irony is that, even if Nancy's rival *had* won the gold and Nancy, the silver, Nancy would still have been the one to receive most of the applause and the commercial endorsements. Why? Because sex and beauty have an undeniable impact on scoring in many sports. *Judges respond to the prettiest face; then the winner is seen all over the place.*

Beauty reigns supreme. If you don't believe it, let's compare Nancy Kerrigan, silver medalist with Bonnie Blair, who has won I don't remember how many golds. Even though these two athletes competed in different types of skating events, one woman proved to have a great deal of more talent than the other. Now, try to remember how many times Bonnie Blair has graced your screen in TV commercials? You don't recall very many, I'll bet. Nancy Kerrigan, on the other hand, has been given countless opportunities to show her beautiful face on screens around the world.

Like it or not, people tend to judge us by our appearance. Doors may be opened for us—or not—because we either look the part or we don't. I believe that this reflects an even stronger kind of prejudice than the color line (or maybe any other kind of line). And this "beauty line" has real power, believe it! Have you noticed that in ice skating there are virtually no girls who fall below par in looks? It is simply taken for granted that when the judges evaluate a skater, they are looking at more than skill and ability. Face it: we are watching a beauty contest as well as a skating contest out there on the ice.

Apparently it is not talent that our society values, but beauty. All of which reminds me of my mother's words: *"Beauty is only skin deep, and ugliness is to the bone; when beauty wears away, ugliness will still hold its own."*

We have become worshippers of tin gods in sports, often forgetting the respect and credit we owe to the real contributors in our world—the school teachers who mold our kids minds, the doctors who help us care for our bodies, the lawyers who get us out of jams (if they can) and the scientists who invent serums and medicines that save millions of lives. These are just a few of the individuals who are doing much more for us than the sports figures we admire so blindly.

Our perspective needs a radical change. It's all about attitude, as I learned while talking to a powerfully built, tall, handsome man in the Mid Valley Racquetball Gym where I work out. Thinking he might have been a football player, I asked him, "What do you do?" He replied, "I'm nothing really, just a lowly school teacher." Then, as he began to discuss this athlete and that one, I thought to myself, *Wiltie, this young man obviously admires the athletes he's talking about, but he thinks of himself as only a "lowly school teacher."* That's where the problem starts, folks; it starts right here with every one of us—not only in how we regard our sports heroes, but how we regard *ourselves.*

An Olympic gold medal is no longer only a symbol of outstanding athletic dedication and achievement. A medal has become far more than that—and I am not happy about it. Nowadays an athlete's life-long dream, an Olympic medal, is valued, not for itself, but in terms of the gold it can earn for the recipient. It's still about gold, but a different kind. As the announcers say: "The medal is worth $1.5 million this year."

As I sit here with tears in my eyes, watching the gold medals being presented to our women's gymnastics team, I realize once again what it means to be a part of the Olympics and to have that extraordinary spirit. With the eyes of millions upon them, those amazing young women fought with everything they had and did everything right. Oh, what a sight!

At the same time, I couldn't help but reflect on our Olympic basketball team, so much more superior to all the others, but unable to inspire the same kind of emotion in fans around the world. Tonight's victory proves to me once again that what matters is never how big you are or how much money you have, but how much you are willing to give for the cause that you care most about.

Thank God for the Olympic spirit!

# TWELVE

## CAN YOU HELP ME HERE?
### I WOULD LIKE TO KNOW . . .

I have often been asked by people who appear to be either puzzled or dismayed, "Wiltie, what do you think of the Olympic Dream Team?" My personal belief is that, to begin with, the term, "Dream Team" is a misnomer. The selection committee for the 1996 United States Olympic basketball team actually *destroyed* the dreams of many worthy amateurs, and perhaps of some pros, as well.

I love Sir Charles, but why him again? How unfair! Why not give a talented amateur a chance to fulfill the dream of a lifetime? What could the selection committee's reasoning have been? Has it come to the point that they were afraid we might lose? More likely, it was all about winning, winning and more winning. But what's the point? And how much is enough? Please explain this to me if you can.

I'd give a lot to know who picked our 1996 Olympic basketball team. If I'd known who they were, I might have been able to talk them into choosing me as the designated foul shooter. Why not? I have as much right to be the technical foul shooter as they do to pick the whole damn team.

I am sometimes left in total bewilderment when friends, or even the people I meet casually, ask me whether basketball at the professional level is on the up and up. I guess they have seen too many games where certain players or teams have not seemed to be putting forth an altogether honest effort. And in too many cases, teams are paired at playoff time in a way that does not seem legitimate. The same teams always seem to win in the playoffs, and fans understandably wonder if there might be some hanky-panky going on—dishonesty within the NBA or perhaps special arrangements involving NBC or other television elements.

I always answer these questions with a quick, "Of course not!" I sometimes have a hunch that they might really be asking whether *I* was dishonest, though I hope that is not what is on their minds.

My position has always been that organizations as powerful as television, the National Basketball Association, or any other professional sports organization, cannot truly be dishonest. However, I *do* believe in the power of persuasion (especially the unconscious variety). There is really nothing dishonest about the power of persuasion; we use it often. Fans use it to encourage their team to play harder and more aggressively. Crowd support can persuade players to do things that they would not normally be able to do, especially on an away court. And on home courts, the fans' power of persuasion used to try to "persuade" the referees and influence calls in favor of their home team.

The power of persuasion can be used in other ways. In fact, it probably affects even the game officials. Here's how that scenario might play out.

Referees are undoubtedly affected by the location of games as well as by the cast of characters. Their jobs, obviously, become much more secure if large numbers of fans are willing to pay for tickets to see a game. Officials are well aware that people would rather watch MJ and the Bulls play against Los Angeles and the other MJ, than watch the Atlanta Hawks (admit it: you probably can't name even one player on that damn team) play the Sacramento Kings. Hawks *vs.* Kings would not be a very good final, and would, in fact, hurt the NBA's ratings.

The better rating a game gets, the better it is for the refs in the long run. So, and this is where the power of persuasion comes in, with referees having a natural preference for seeing the stronger teams compete, and knowing the funny games one's mind can play, who should be surprised that a close call just might go in favor of the Chicago Bulls? This is not only possible; it's almost inevitable. As long as human beings are involved, we will surely see the power of persuasion in operation.

I often felt, when I was playing, that I came out on the short end of many crucial calls. Some of these calls resulting in heartbreaking seventh game play-off losses. I can remember thinking that the Boston Celtics always seemed to get the better calls, but that could have happened simply because they were the better team. I would like to think that if I had played long enough, those calls—the good ones and the bad ones—would eventually have evened out. That's what they say goes down— but I don't know. It might have taken 100 years for that to happen.

All of this reminds me of a story I once heard (a story that is in no way to be taken as an expression of my own point of view). It seems that Jesus was arguing with the devil about who knew the most about basketball, and they decided to settle the matter in a game between teams that

335

each would select. The devil said to Jesus, "I'll let you pick your team first, all five of them." Jesus replied, "Okay. I'll start with Michael Jordan and Pippen, then I'll go with Charles Barkley and Larry Bird, and take Kareem Abdul Jabbar at center." The devil said, "Sounds good to me. I already have my team picked out. I don't know their names, but I'm taking the men in the striped shirts. Just give me those guys, and I won't care who else is playing. Any other five players will do."

I do believe, as I said before, that there is no room for hanky-panky in sports. However, television, with its almighty power, can (and does) dictate the days when the games will be played, and at what time. Those decisions may, from time to time, favor one team or another. Certain teams could, for example, get more time to rest than others. But in explanation, the NBA only has to say (or infer), "The choice was dictated by the scheduling requirements of television. TV is where we get our money, after all, so we have to do what the network thinks is best for all concerned."

We who are losers (whether on bets or just in having to watch mediocre games) may be inclined to take a dim view of certain suspicious-looking game situations. I believe, however, that there are only three ways a game can be thrown. The source of the fix would have to be one of these: (1) the players, (2) the referees, or (3) the coaches. But players nowadays make far too much money to be tempted. Referees have too much at stake (and, to make it work, *all* of them would have to be in collusion—an unlikely scenario). And coaches, I am convinced, have too much integrity to give even a passing thought to anything shady.

Bottom line: no matter how bad things may seem when you see questionable calls and watch guys not trying their hardest, I think it's all on the up and up. We just get some bad games from time to time. What do *you* think?

When we hear about players whose behavior is less than refined, we're quick to blame, but seldom surprised. We normally expect somewhat more of their coaches, however. When Pat Riley, normally the epitome of class, and Phil Jackson, the super intellectual, refused to shake hands or even to look at each other during the short period of time that their teams were opponents in the playoffs, I must say I was dismayed. I would have expected that these two professionals, coaches of two of the finest teams in the NBA, and both highly respected leaders in the game of basketball, would have been above that sort of thing. Too bad they had to engage in such unclassy behavior.

I was astonished, once again, when I heard that Pat Riley had submitted his resignation to the New York Knicks office by fax. That's right. This coach who, for the past ten years or so had been the personification of a class act, *faxed* his resignation to a team for which he presumably had enormous respect. Even though no championship was ever won by any of his teams in New York, I think the organization was pleased with him and wanted him back. As far as I know, there was no animosity involved; his reason for leaving to go to Miami was that Miami had offered him a much better deal. (I can definitely understand his decision after hearing what they offered him.)

If all that is true—and I have no reason to think it is not—sending a resignation by fax strikes me as a shabby way to go. Even a phone call would have been preferable, or, better still, an in-person meeting. When you have worked for an organization for as long as he had, and under conditions of such mutual understanding, it seems to me that a more gracious act is called for. When a respected coach ends his relationship with a team in this way, I begin to wonder what "class" consists of any more. Just what is considered right or wrong in sports today?

Mrs. Pat Riley, a friend, will no doubt jump on me for having something negative to say about her husband.

Actually, I have great admiration for Pat. His accomplishments in basketball are so impressive that they fall under the heading of "Only in America." Pat is making a great deal of money, and is more popular than anyone probably thought possible. I should point out, too, that his achievements were won not only through his remarkable will power, strength, and fortitude, but also because his wife stood by his side every mile of the way.

Game announcers like to pick up on all kinds of minor estrangements and differences between players, and generally enjoy elaborating on them with great enthusiasm. But they have not been willing to discuss what has been going on between the Chicago and Miami coaches. Even though the matter has been largely ignored, I say it demands some attention. When the leaders act this way, what does it tell the people who follow the game? Are our kids to think that this is acceptable behavior?

Have you ever wondered why there is so much walking in pro ball? Like many of you, I was curious about this. I got my answer in a conversation with the Wizard of Westwood, John Wooden, who, himself, had been a great guard. Wooden explained that, in order to execute those fantastic dunks and maneuvers in going to the basket, a player has to generate the kind of momentum that can best be attained by running (in basketball, it's called "walking") at the beginning of the play. This is really no different than Carl Lewis' dash down the runway before exploding into the long-jump pit. Carrying the ball only makes it easier for the offense to do their thing. (Giving the offense an additional edge has become a common theme in many sports today.)

Wooden admitted that he could not quite understand why walking was allowed to the degree that it is. He said, "When you watch a guy go to the basket on a fast break, count how many steps he takes before he puts the ball in.

Then let me know any time you see a guy on a fast break who *doesn't* take off with four or five steps before he dunks a ball." This makes for a good show, but technically, it's still walking.

*Note: Apparently the NBA has read this chapter (or read my mind); I've noticed that in '96-'97 walking is being called more often.*

Nobody wants to pay to see a star player sitting on the bench, but in basketball fouling out is an expected part of the game. Basketball, in fact, is the only sport of real importance in which a player *can* foul completely out of a game. And sometimes, if he comes close, a player who is in danger of fouling out may be benched by a coach who wants to preserve him for later use. In either case, the fans lose.

Although anyone can foul out of a game, in actual practice this happens to some players more than to others. We have learned to expect that the stars will, more often than not, get the benefit of close calls. If the rules were applied evenly, fouls would put them out of many a game, but star athletes are, after all, the players people pay their money to see.

A real ethical dilemma, right? Maybe the basketball rules that deal with fouling out need to be revamped.

In my opinion, no one should be allowed to foul out of a game (be thrown out, yes; foul out, no). As it is now, if Jordan fans have come out to see him play, and he creates four or five fouls, any additional fouls may simply not be called. The referees know that if they call any more, Jordan will be on the bench not able to play, and everyone is going to be unhappy. If we were operating under the principle that no one could foul out, the foul would be called on Jordan, the team would be penalized appropriately, and no one would have to suffer unfairly. Under a no-foul-out system fans could always be sure of seeing the best plays and the best players, yet the other team would not be penalized when stars are not whistled for fouls they commit. Offending teams would be penalized, but the player's presence in the game would not be lost.

This seems to me to be a fairer and more sensible approach to foul problems. No one would ever be completely banished from a game on fouls, but an appropriate penalty would be handed to the team that earns the foul. Fouls, when they are committed, would be called evenhandedly against all players, and if any player were to commit more than a certain number of fouls, a technical would be added, or the foul would be shot and possession of the ball retained by the offended team. At the sixth foul (the current mandatory foul-out point) and at any subsequent fouls, there would be an additional penalty shot awarded, giving a further benefit to the fouled-upon team. Or, if an added foul shot is not used, the ball should be returned to the team that was fouled.

I particularly like that last bit—the part that deals with the sixth foul and after. Penalties become much heavier at the point where, under the present system, a player would foul out of the game. It is important that, at the sixth foul point, the penalties truly penalize the fouling team. If they fail to do that—if they have less than real impact—fouling will become rampant. You want players to be forced to play differently when they get into foul trouble. Giving the ball back to the team that was fouled, in addition to giving them an addition technical shot, should persuade the guy in foul trouble to watch his step.

Even though there may be some "cons" to the plan, I think that under this kind of system, all parties can be satisfied.

There are other rule changes, as well, that should be discussed. One, for example, would make the ball free to be taken off the rim by anyone, on offense or defense, as now is acceptable under international rules. I'll be discussing these and other proposals in media interviews around the country, and you will have an opportunity then to call in and talk with me about them.

A note to Shaq:

They are telling you, as they told me, that no one is perfect. Then they turn around and say practice makes perfect. I wish they would make up their minds. We are constantly told to practice and improve so that we can become perfect at the foul line. But if it's true that no one is perfect, how can we expect to achieve perfection? C'mon! Someone make up their mind. That's why I was so confused on the line.

If you've wondered why so many professional basketball players currently sport shaved heads, I might have the answer. This fashion trend could be the result of a story I told on page 187 of my book, *A View From Above*.

The little black boy kneeled down and asked God why his hair was so tight and matted and nappy.

The voice of God spoke, "My son, your hair is that way for protecting you against the strong African Sun."

The little boy replied, "But God, I live in Cleveland."

Thinking fast, God replied, "If you live in Cleveland, Chicago, Detroit, or Philadelphia, you don't need that hair anymore. You can cut it off."

Henceforth, the little black boy did just that, and so did his friends. You have seen the results: one bald head after another.

Never in the entire history of the NBA have there been as many injuries as have been recorded in the last few years.

In every recent year, for example, four or five of the Cleveland Cavaliers' and the Washington Bullets' starting players have been out for 40 to 50 games, or even for the whole season. Why are the players on these teams so prone to injuries? Why so many more injuries now than there were in the sixties and seventies? The game is not as physical now as it was then, so what accounts for the change? Do those teams stress conditioning? Or are today's players bigger babies?

Chris Mullin of the Golden State Warriors has been in the league ten years now, and has been injured almost every year. (You have to wonder how a record like that is possible.) If I were the owner, I would base Mullin's salary on the number of games he was able to play. One of my negotiating points would be: "We can't guarantee to pay you for an entire season when you haven't given us even half a season in any of the last five years."

*What do you think about this Wiltie?* The Los Angeles Lakers are arguing about not getting paid "road per diem." Here is a group of guys, each of whom is making $55,000 a game, and yet they are quibbling about $75 or $100 a day expense money! But here is the unreal part: They want road per diem for playing against the *Los Angeles Clippers!* The Clippers, of course, are in L.A. just as the Lakers are. As a matter of fact, many of the Lakers' homes are closer to where the Clippers play than to their own home arena. But the Lakers are crying for road per diem because they are the "road team."

*This* is the kind of trivial bullshit these multi-millionaire athletes concern themselves with. What do those of you who are taking home $300 to $500 a week think about this? Should we take up a collection for the poor underpaid Laker souls? Maybe we could throw a pre-game dinner for them at the Downtown Mission? The street people might understand, but I sure don't.

*Well, well, Mr. Belle! As I've said, baby, bad news does sell! Now you have the biggest contract in baseball land. (Just more testimony to how crazy things have gotten, my man.)*

The last game of the Buck's '95-'96 season was against Orlando. You might be interested to know that Vin Baker had 27 points, 8 rebounds, and 3 assists while his teammate, Glenn "Big Dog" Robinson had 15 points and a big fat total of 2 rebounds. You read it right: *Two* rebounds, ladies and gentlemen!

Can you imagine? This six-foot-nine guy who gets only 2 rebounds, and who is not even his team's leading scorer, has the audacity to ask for $100 million. Do you think he might be *overpaid*? One thing is for sure: it won't be long before he has *overstayed*.

During one of the playoff games, Sonics coach George Karl took all but one of his starters out and brought in subs. He left just one starter in the game—Detlef Schrempf. Now, Schrempf had 16 points, but had done absolutely nothing except take a few free shots that happened to come his way. He'd made no contribution to the game, hadn't hit the boards hard or shown any real effort in anything but his free shots—but he was still out there on the court, and his team was 25 or 30 points down with a minute to go.

Why he was still in the game, I have no idea, but suddenly he was rebounding and getting a few lay-ups. He did no offensive rebounding when the outcome of the game was still in doubt, but later, during "garbage time," he was getting offensive rebounds. (Unfortunately, the same scenario was to repeat itself during a couple of the later games.)

Why, I ask you, did the coach play Schrempf and not the bench at that juncture? If the coach had given up on winning, why not bench *all* the starters?

Danny Ainge, commenting to his announcing partner on Rodman's book, said that he could only get through four pages of it and would not recommend it to anyone— and definitely not to any children. The other commentator agreed, adding that he'd never seen such big print, and wondered why they had published the book in that way. The gist of Danny's reply was, "Because this man's fans are probably incapable of reading very well." 'Nuff said.

Here is something else you might be able to help me with.

Both Michael Jordan and Magic Johnson, the two greats of the eighties and nineties, retired. Each gave a similar reason for leaving, saying that he had done all he wanted to do in the world of basketball, and now wanted to spend more quality time with his family. I grant that they had won all the major awards and titles their game had to offer, but why couldn't Magic and Michael retire with the kind of dignity that the older players used to show?

Retiring players used to state very simply, "I've had enough. I have enjoyed my career, but now it's time for me to move on." And they really meant what they said. But nowadays, you almost always hear the famous cliché, "I just want to spend more time with my family."

Were Michael and Magic's statements that they wanted to spend more time with their families only a nice gesture on their part? Let's examine the record. What did Michael do approximately a month after retiring from basketball? He became a professional baseball player. Mr. Jordan joined a minor league baseball team in Birmingham and started riding a bus on the back roads of the rural South.

I must, in all honesty, give Michael credit for his willingness to subjugate himself to the horrors of minor league baseball that lay ahead of him. Believe me, I know

344

about riding the bus (I did it with the Globetrotters for 17 years). But, unless I am mistaken, MJ then was farther from his family than he had been when he played for the Chicago Bulls. That "being with the family" bit didn't last long, did it Michael?

The other MJ, Magic Johnson, gave the same reason that Michael did for his retirement: more quality time with his family. So, he immediately took his traveling basketball circus all over the world, even going to places where he was not wanted. Did this career change allow him to spend more time with his son and the rest of the family?

I'm asking here why it was necessary to give us those bogus reasons for retiring when their statements apparently had no basis in truth? Why not be more up front and tell it like it is? Michael probably just wanted to play more golf, and Magic wanted to do something else after certain members of the league didn't want him to play any more. Using the platitude, "I want to spend more time with my family," was disingenuous. Their fans deserved better than that from these two icons.

Close on the heels of his first announcement, Magic Johnson announced his return to basketball, saying he was coming back because he wanted his son to see him play. He had been working out, he said, and was confident that he wouldn't embarrass himself or his son by falling on his face. (Is that the same kid he left the game for, the boy he wanted to spend more quality time with?)

Come on, Magic, did you really come back just because you wanted your son to see you play, did you? You came back because you felt good about yourself, and because basketball is your true love and passion. Your ego kicked in, and you wanted to come back to show people that you could still play at NBA level. You love the spotlight, and basketball gives you the best opportunity to be in it. What better way to indulge yourself than to play in the NBA? Be honest, now. Building movie theaters and developing other businesses is fine, but is there anything quite like having 20,000 fans cheer madly for you as you jog back and forth on a 90-foot hardwood court in your shorts? All you had to say was, "Hey, I wanted to come back, and as long as I feel good, I'm going to play." That would have been enough.

Magic, you are, and will continue to be, an inspiration to all of us. There was no need to use that family thing again. Just by doing what you've done, you've shown all of us that you don't have to give up, just because you have the virus. It is good that people with HIV and AIDS could see you play and realize that they, too, can still accomplish a great deal.

Magic, for sure, does not want to give up his place in the sun. But Magic, whether he wants to or not, will, like everyone else, have to do so sooner or later. The subject of retirement leads to a confusing gray area where answers are hard to come by. Many currently active athletes are far past their prime, and though it might seem obvious that it is time to say good-bye, the salary they are earning makes leaving almost impossible. They are caught up in the old "money vs. doing the right thing" dilemma. Are they doing the wrong thing by taking the money and gaining security for themselves and their families? I am not sure. Even though they run the risk of looking like asses out there, they can smile all the way to the bank.

I think I already know the answer to this one, but maybe you can help me out.

Rodman, undoubtedly the greatest offensive rebounder in the game today, scores few, if any, points. Do you wonder why he doesn't take those offensive rebounds he gets and put them right back into the basket? Well, my guess is that his reason lies in the fact that rebounding is his forte and the basis for his more-than-modest salary. So, very logically, he chooses to throw the ball back for someone else to shoot again, hoping he'll get another rebound. Often, when he is close enough, he throws the ball back to the basket as an attempted shot, rebounds it himself, and then puts it in. That way he gets another rebound *plus* two points. (Darned clever, that Rodman!)

In all honesty, I don't know whether that maneuver is a help for the team or a help for you-know-who. But as long as his ability to control the boards is as complete as it is, I guess he can do whatever he chooses. Eventually, of course, when his control is no longer there, some team is going to ask him, "Hey, what are you doing Rodman? How about putting the ball into the basket? This is a team game, after all, not an individual stat game."

Here is one of the real mysteries of this era in professional sports.

Two or three years ago, a guy named Charlie Ward won the prestigious Heisman trophy (the award given to the year's top collegiate football player) while he was playing at Florida State as a quarterback. He thought for sure he'd be drafted by one of the professional football teams when he got out of college, but as I recall, he wasn't drafted by *any* football team, in any round whatsoever. That's right. He was not picked up in the draft. Since he had played a little college basketball as well as football, he ended up being taken by the New York Knicks, proving what a good athlete he must have been. Now he's sitting on the bench for the Knicks, doing a creditable job when he comes in to play from time to time.

How could a football team not find a place on their roster for an athlete like Ward—a Heisman Trophy winner, no less? I think I may know the answer. It happens that, in addition to being talented, Ward is also a wonderful guy who has his head on straight and does all the right things. Too bad. Seems you're more apt to get picked by a professional team if you're the *wrong* type and do all the *wrong* things.

In contrast to Ward's situation, think for a moment about the guy from Nebraska, Mike Rozier, who was drafted in spite of a history of strange problems involving battery offenses and jail records. Apparently, *this* is the kind of guy they want to make sure of getting.

You'll have to ask the managers and owners about their criteria for making their draft choices and just how far they are willing to go to get a winner. I certainly haven't a clue.

Come on, football organizations; it's time to get a grip!

We all realize that judgements are subjective, and our opinions about the sports or athletes we choose to watch (or whether to watch at all) are our own to make. Certain players can bring smiles to our faces by their actions. And, even though those actions may not contribute much of value to their teams, they may be of value to you, perhaps just as entertainment.

I have tried to give you my idea of the pure essence of the game I love—*as I see it.* What I mean by "pure essence" can perhaps be described as cut-to-the-chase, bottom-line, old-fashioned basketball—forget the show biz crap, razzle-dazzle and hype. Basketball players are not out there to be scored on how they *look* doing their thing. What really counts is what their thing will bring: points!!

In every society, and in every group or endeavor, someone has to play the role of historian. Since tapes, chips, and other modern methods of preserving basketball's